SHAKESPEARE'S FESTIVE COMEDY

A Study of Dramatic Form and its Relation to Social Custom

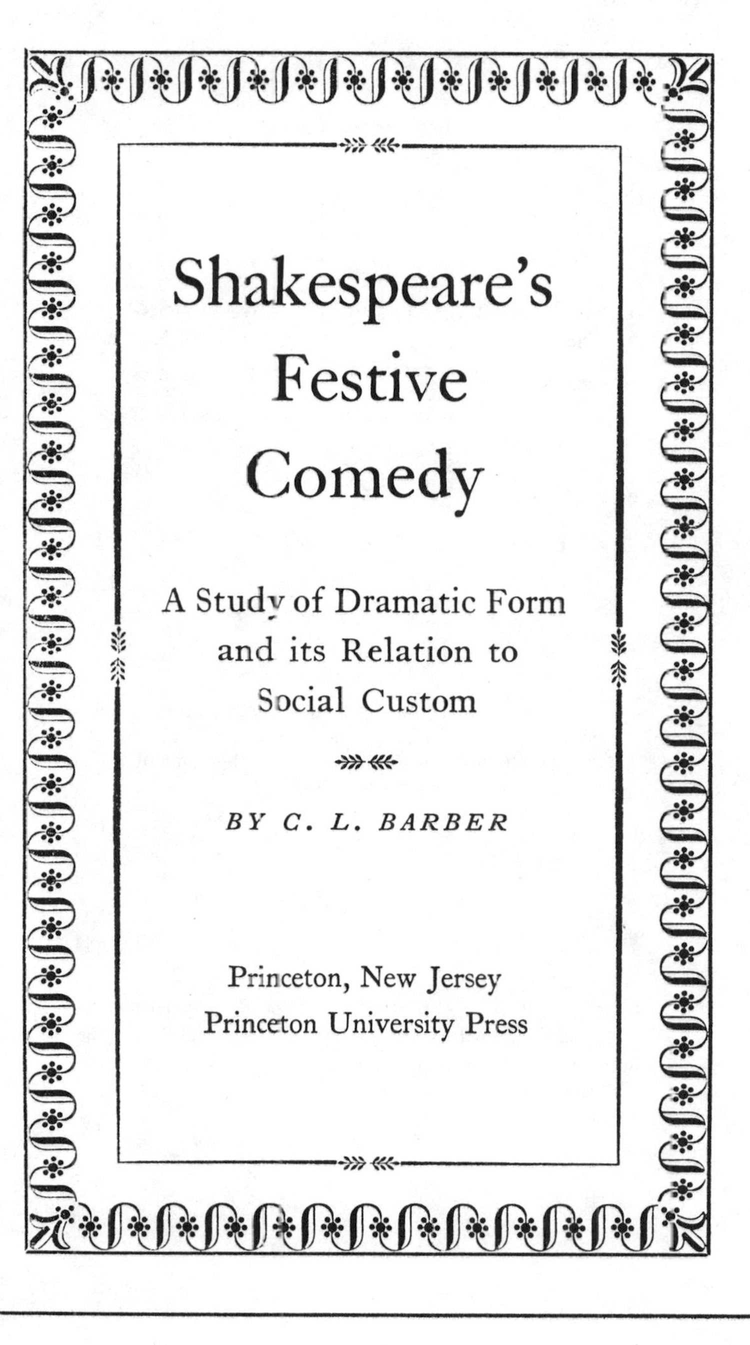

Shakespeare's Festive Comedy

A Study of Dramatic Form and its Relation to Social Custom

BY C. L. BARBER

Princeton, New Jersey
Princeton University Press

The Library of Congress catalog entry for this book
appears at the end of the text

ISBN 0-691-01304-7 (paperback edn.)
ISBN 0-691-06043-6 (hardcover edn.)

◆

First PRINCETON PAPERBACK Edition, 1972

Second Hardcover Printing, 1972
Eighth Paperback Printing, 1990

◆

Publication of this book has been aided by
the Ford Foundation program to support publication,
through university presses, of works in the humanities
and social sciences.

◆

Printed in the United States of America

◆

Princeton University Press books are printed on acid-free paper
and meet the guidelines for permanence and durability of the
Committee on Production Guidelines for Book Longevity of the
Council on Library Resources

16 15 14 13 12 11 10 9

To

ALVIN BARTON BARBER

and

LUCY LOMBARDI BARBER,

my father and mother

and, in 1972

to the memory of my late beloved wife

ELIZABETH PUTNAM BARBER

PREFACE

I HOPE that a reader who is only looking for commentary on one of the comedies will nevertheless take the time to read the first chapter. For the treatment of each major play develops the idea of festive comedy which is sketched there.

An early version of Chapter 9 appeared as "The Use of Comedy in *As You Like It*," in *Philological Quarterly*, Volume XXI (1942). A good deal of the Introduction was printed as "The Saturnalian Pattern in Shakespeare's Comedy," in *The Sewanee Review*, Volume LIX (1951). Part of Chapter 8 was published under the title "From Ritual to Comedy: an Examination of *Henry IV*," in *English Stage Comedy*, edited by W. K. Wimsatt, Jr. (New York, 1955), and profited from Mr. Wimsatt's editorial attention. The same essay was reprinted in *Shakespeare: Modern Essays in Criticism*, edited by Leonard Dean (New York, 1957). Permission to reprint this material is gratefully acknowledged. And I am particularly grateful to the Harvard University Press for permission to reprint in Chapter 3 considerable extracts from the account in Norreys Jephson O'Conor's *Godes Peace and the Queenes* of a "Summer Lord game" in Lincolnshire.

This book was first conceived in the liberty provided by a Junior Fellowship in the Society of Fellows at Harvard University. After the interruption of the war, two Folger Fellowships made it possible to work in the pleasant, efficient, and friendly circumstances of the Folger Shakespeare Library in Washington. A Faculty Fellowship from the Fund for the Advancement of Education and a Travelling Fellowship from Amherst College made possible a full year's sabbatical leave and work at Cambridge in England.

The teacher and friend who contributed most to the book is not here to read it—the late F. O. Matthiessen. Nor is my brother, Alvin Barton Barber, Jr., who saw deeply and clearly into its problems.

Howard Baker first drew my attention to Nashe's *Summer's Last Will and Testament*; his perceptions about the meaning of festivity, and his poetry's expression of contemporary festive experience, contributed greatly to my sense of the subject. So did the thinking of Harry Levin about comedy from the period when we were in the Society of Fellows and starting out to teach. Other friends who contributed criticisms, comments, and most important, conversation about "the supreme theme of art and song" are Beverly and Louise Bowie, George and Mary Dimock, Elizabeth Drew, Richard and Jaquie Goodwin, John and Kristi Hay, Walter and Esther Houghton, Gerta Kennedy, Robert Kennedy, Perry and Betty Miller, Richard Schlatter, Andrews Wanning, Donald Wheeler, and, most important of all, my wife, Bettie Putnam Barber. In the years since the war, my work on my own has been greatly influenced by the cooperative teaching I have done with colleagues at Amherst College, notably Theodore Baird, Reuben Brower, Armour Craig, Walker Gibson, Julian Moynahan and John Moore. Craig Pearson, in the course of writing a thesis with me on comedy, enlarged my understanding of it. I am particularly grateful to George Dimock for generous and valuable criticism of the manuscript.

C. L. B.

Amherst, Massachusetts
September 1, 1958

CONTENTS

SHAKESPEARE'S FESTIVE COMEDY

A Study of Dramatic Form and its Relation to Social Custom

Chapter 1

INTRODUCTION: THE SATURNALIAN PATTERN

Messenger. Your honour's players, hearing your amendment,
Are come to play a pleasant comedy . . .
Beggar. . . . Is not a comonty a Christmas gambold or a tumbling trick?
Lady. No, my good lord; it is more pleasing stuff.
Beggar. What, household stuff?
Lady. It is a kind of history.
Beggar. Well, we'll see it. Come, madam wife, sit by my side and let the world slip. We shall ne'er be younger.

—Induction to *The Taming of the Shrew*

Much comedy is festive—all comedy, if the word festive is pressed far enough. But much of Shakespeare's comedy is festive in a quite special way which distinguishes it from the art of most of his contemporaries and successors. The part of his work which I shall be dealing with in this book, the merry comedy written up to the period of *Hamlet* and the problem plays, is of course enormously rich and wide in range; each new play, each new scene, does something fresh, explores new possibilities. But the whole body of this happy comic art is distinguished by the use it makes of forms for experience which can be termed saturnalian. Once Shakespeare finds his own distinctive style, he is more Aristophanic than any other great English comic dramatist, despite the fact that the accepted educated models and theories when he started to write were Terentian and Plautine. The Old Comedy cast of his work results from his participation in native saturnalian traditions of the popular theater and the popular holidays. Not that he "wanted art"—including Terentian art. But he used the resources of a sophisticated theater to express, in his idyllic comedies and in his clowns' ironic misrule, the experience of moving to humorous understanding through saturnalian release. "Festive" is usually an adjective for an atmosphere, and the word describes the atmosphere of Shakespeare's comedy from *Love's Labour's Lost* and *A Midsummer Night's Dream* through *Henry IV* and *Twelfth Night*. But in exploring this work, "festive" can also be a term for structure. I shall be trying to describe structure to get at the way this comedy organizes experience. The saturnalian pattern appears in many variations, all of which involve inversion, statement and counterstatement, and a basic movement which can be summarized in the formula, through release to clarification.

So much of the action in this comedy is random when looked at as intrigue, so many of the persons are neutral when regarded as character, so much of the wit is inapplicable when assessed as satire, that critics too often have fallen back on mere exclamations about poetry and mood. The criticism of the nineteenth century and after was particularly helpless, concerned as it was chiefly with character and story and moral quality. Recent criticism, concerned in a variety of ways with structure, has had much more to say. No figure in the carpet is the carpet. There is in the pointing out of patterns something that is opposed to life and art, an ungraciousness which artists in particular feel and resent. Readers feel it too, even critics: for every new moment, every new line or touch, is a triumph of opportunism, something snatched in from life beyond expectation and made design beyond design. And yet the fact remains that it is as we see the design that we see design outdone and brought alive.

> O body swayed to music, O brightening glance,
> How can we know the dancer from the dance?

To get at the form and meaning of the plays, which is my first and last interest, I have been led into an exploration of the way the social form of Elizabethan holidays contributed to the dramatic form of festive comedy. To relate this drama to holiday has proved to be the most effective way to describe its character. And this historical interplay between social and artistic form has an interest of its own: we can see here, with more clarity of outline and detail than is usually possible, how art develops underlying configurations in the social life of a culture. The saturnalian pattern came to Shakespeare from many sources, both in social and artistic tradition. It appeared in the theatrical institution of clowning: the clown or Vice, when Shakespeare started to write, was a recognized anarchist who made aberration obvious by carrying release to absurd extremes. The cult of fools and folly, half social and half literary, embodied a similar polarization of experience. One could formulate the saturnalian pattern effectively by referring first to these traditions: Shakespeare's first completely masterful comic scenes were written for the clowns.[1] But the festival occasion provides the clearest paradigm. It can illuminate not only those comedies where Shakespeare drew largely and directly on holiday motifs, like *Love's Labour's Lost, A Midsummer Night's Dream,* and *Twelfth Night,* but also plays where there is relatively little direct use of holiday, notably *As You Like It* and *Henry IV.*

We can get hold of the spirit of Elizabethan holidays because they had form. "Merry England" was merry chiefly by virtue of its community observances of periodic sports and feast days. Mirth took form in morris-dances, sword-dances, wassailings, mock ceremonies of summer kings and queens and of lords of misrule, mummings, disguisings, masques—and a bewildering variety of sports, games, shows, and pageants improvised on traditional models. Such pastimes were a regular part of the celebration of a marriage, of the village wassail or wake, of Candlemas, Shrove Tuesday, Hocktide, May Day, Whitsuntide, Midsummer Eve, Harvest-home, Halloween, and the twelve days of the Christmas season ending with Twelfth Night. Custom prescribed, more or less definitely, some ways of making merry at each occasion. The seasonal feasts were not, as now, rare curiosities to be observed by folklorists in remote villages, but landmarks framing the cycle of the year, observed with varying degrees of sophistication by most

[1] Miss Enid Welsford includes perceptive treatments of Shakespeare's fools in relation to tradition in her fine study, *The Fool: His Social and Literary History* (New York, n.d. [1935]). Professor Willard Farnham characterizes Shakespeare's grotesque or fool comedy in relation to Erasmus and More and the mediaeval feeling for man's natural imperfection in "The Mediaeval Comic Spirit in the English Renaissance," *Joseph Quincy Adams Memorial Studies*, ed. James G. McManaway et al. (Washington, D.C., 1948), pp. 429-439. The use of mediaeval elements for comic counterstatement is described in C. L. Barber, "The Use of Comedy in *As You Like It*," *PQ*, XXI (1942), 353-367, an early version of Ch. 9 below.

elements in the society. Shakespeare's casual references to the holidays always assume that his audience is entirely familiar with them:

> As fit as ten groats is for the hand of an attorney . . . as a pancake for Shrove Tuesday, a morris for May Day, as the nail to his hole . . .[2]

A great many detailed connections between the holidays and the comedies will claim our attention later, but what is most important is the correspondence between the whole festive occasion and the whole comedy. The underlying movement of attitude and awareness is not adequately expressed by any one thing in the day or the play, but is the day, is the play. Here one cannot say how far analogies between social rituals and dramatic forms show an influence, and how far they reflect the fact that the holiday occasion and the comedy are parallel manifestations of the same pattern of culture, of a way that men can cope with their life.

Through Release to Clarification

Release, in the idyllic comedies, is expressed by making the whole experience of the play like that of a revel.

> Come, woo me, woo me! for now I am in a holiday humour, and like enough to consent.
> (*A.Y.L.* IV.i.68-69)

Such holiday humor is often abetted by directly staging pastimes, dances, songs, masques, plays extempore, etc. But the fundamental method is to shape the loose narrative so that "events" put its persons in the position of festive celebrants: if they do not seek holiday it happens to them. A tyrant duke forces Rosalind into disguise; but her mock wooing with Orlando amounts to a Disguising, with carnival freedom from the decorum of her identity and her sex. The misrule of Sir Toby is represented as personal idiosyncrasy, but it follows the pattern of the Twelfth Night occasion; the flyting match of Benedict and Beatrice, while appropriate to their special characters, suggests the customs of Easter Smacks

[2] *All's W.* II.ii.22. Citations of Shakespeare are to *The Complete Works*, ed. George Lyman Kittredge (Boston, 1936). Abbreviations of titles follow the usage recommended by the *Shakespeare Quarterly*.

and Hocktide abuse between the sexes. Much of the poetry and wit, however it may be occasioned by events, works in the economy of the whole play to promote the effect of a merry occasion where Nature reigns.

F. M. Cornford, in *The Origins of Attic Comedy*,[3] suggested that invocation and abuse were the basic gestures of a nature worship behind Aristophanes' union of poetry and railing. The two gestures were still practiced in the "folly" of Elizabethan May-game, harvest-home, or winter revel: invocation, for example, in the manifold spring garlanding customs, "gathering for Robin Hood"; abuse, in the customary license to flout and fleer at what on other days commanded respect. The same double way of achieving release appears in Shakespeare's festive plays. There the poetry about the pleasures of nature and the naturalness of pleasure serves to evoke beneficent natural impulses; and much of the wit, mocking the good housewife Fortune from her wheel, acts to free the spirit as does the ritual abuse of hostile spirits. A saturnalian attitude, assumed by a clear-cut gesture toward liberty, brings mirth, an accession of wanton vitality. In the terms of Freud's analysis of wit, the energy normally occupied in maintaining inhibition is freed for celebration. The holidays in actual observance were built around the enjoyment of the vital pleasure of moments when nature and society are hospitable to life. In the summer, there was love in out-of-door idleness; in the winter, within-door warmth and food and drink. But the celebrants also got something for nothing from festive liberty—the vitality normally locked up in awe and respect. E. K. Chambers found among the visitation articles of Archbishop Grindal for the year 1576 instructions that the bishops determine

> whether the ministers and churchwardens have suffered any lord of misrule or summer lords and ladies, or any disguised persons, or others, in Christmas or at May games, or any morris-dancers, or at any other times, to come unreverently into the church or churchyard, and there to dance, or play any unseemly parts, with scoffs, jests, wanton gestures, or ribald talk. . . .[4]

Shakespeare's gay comedy is like Aristophanes' because its expres-

[3] London, 1914.

[4] *The Mediaeval Stage* (Oxford, 1903), I, 181, n. 1.

sion of life is shaped by the form of feeling of such saturnalian occasions as these. The traditional Christian culture within which such holidays were celebrated in the Renaissance of course gave a very different emphasis and perspective to Shakespeare's art. But Dicaeopolis, worsting pompous Lamachus in *The Acharnians* by invoking the tangible benefits of Bacchus and Aphrodite, acts the same festive part as Sir Toby baffling Malvolio's visitation by an appeal to cakes and ale.

The *clarification* achieved by the festive comedies is concomitant to the release they dramatize: a heightened awareness of the relation between man and "nature"—the nature celebrated on holiday. The process of translating festive experience into drama involved extending the sort of awareness traditionally associated with holiday, and also becoming conscious of holiday itself in a new way. The plays present a mockery of what is unnatural which gives scope and point to the sort of scoffs and jests shouted by dancers in the churchyard or in "the quaint mazes in the wanton green." And they include another, complementary mockery of what is merely natural, a humor which puts holiday in perspective with life as a whole.

The butts in the festive plays consistently exhibit their unnaturalness by being kill-joys. On an occasion "full of warm blood, of mirth," they are too preoccupied with perverse satisfactions like pride or greed to "let the world slip" and join the dance. Satirical comedy tends to deal with relations between social classes and aberrations in movements between them. Saturnalian comedy is satiric only incidentally; its clarification comes with movement between poles of restraint and release in everybody's experience. Figures like Malvolio and Shylock embody the sort of kill-joy qualities which the "disguised persons" would find in any of Grindal's curates who would not suffer them to enter the churchyard. Craven or inadequate people appear, by virtue of the festive orientation, as would-be revellers, comically inadequate to hear the chimes at midnight. Pleasure thus becomes the touchstone for judgment of what bars it or is incapable of it. And though in Shakespeare the judgment is usually responsible—valid we feel for everyday as well as holiday—it is the whirligig of impulse that tries the characters. Behind the laughter at the butts there is always a sense of solidarity about pleasure, a communion embracing the merrymakers in the play and the audience, who have gone on holiday in going to a comedy.

While perverse hostility to pleasure is a subject for aggressive festive abuse, highflown idealism is mocked too, by a benevolent ridicule which sees it as a not unnatural attempt to be more than natural. It is unfortunate that Shakespeare's gay plays have come to be known as "the romantic comedies," for they almost always establish a humorous perspective about the vein of hyperbole they borrow from Renaissance romances. Wishful absolutes about love's finality, cultivated without reserve in conventional Arcadia, are made fun of by suggesting that love is not a matter of life and death, but of springtime, the only pretty ring time. The lover's conviction that he will love "for ever and a day" is seen as an illusion born of heady feeling, a symptom of the festive moment:

> Say 'a day' without the 'ever.' No, no, Orlando! Men are April when they woo, December when they wed. Maids are May when they are maids, but the sky changes when they are wives.
>
> (*A.Y.L.* IV.i.146-150)

This sort of clarification about love, a recognition of the seasons', of nature's part in man, need not qualify the intensity of feeling in the festive comedies: Rosalind when she says these lines is riding the full tide of her passionate gaiety. Where the conventional romances tried to express intensity by elaborating hyperbole according to a pretty, pseudo-theological system, the comedies express the power of love as a compelling rhythm in man and nature. So the term "romantic comedies" is misleading. Shakespeare, to be sure, does not always transform his romantic plot materials. In the Claudio-Hero business in *Much Ado*, for example, the borrowed plot involved negative behavior on the basis of romantic absolutes which was not changed to carry festive feeling. Normally, however, as in *Twelfth Night*, he radically alters the emphasis when he employs romantic materials. Events which in his source control the mood, and are drawn out to exhibit extremity of devotion, producing now pathos, now anxiety, now sentiment, are felt on his stage, in the rhythm of stage time, as incidents controlled by a prevailing mood of revel. What was sentimental extremity becomes impulsive extravagance. And judgment, not committed to systematic wishful distortion, can observe with Touchstone how

> We that are true lovers run into strange capers; but as all is mortal in nature, so is all nature in love mortal in folly.
>
> (*A.Y.L.* II.iv.53-56)

To turn on passionate experience and identify it with the holiday moment, as Rosalind does in insisting that the sky will change, puts the moment in perspective with life as a whole. Holiday, for the Elizabethan sensibility, implied a contrast with "everyday," when "brightness falls from the air." Occasions like May day and the Winter Revels, with their cult of natural vitality, were maintained within a civilization whose daily view of life focused on the mortality implicit in vitality. The tolerant disillusion of Anglican or Catholic culture allowed nature to have its day. But the release of that one day was understood to be a temporary license, a "misrule" which implied rule, so that the acceptance of nature was qualified. Holiday affirmations in praise of folly were limited by the underlying assumption that the natural in man is only one part of him, the part that will fade.

"How that a life was but a flower" (*A.Y.L.* V.iii.29) was a two-sided theme: it was usually a gesture preceding "And therefore take the present time"; but it could also lead to the recognition that

> so, from hour to hour, we ripe and ripe,
> And then, from hour to hour, we rot and rot.
>
> (*A.Y.L.* II.vii.26-27)

The second emphasis was implicit in the first; which attitude toward nature predominated depended, not on alternative "philosophies," but on where you were within a rhythm. And because the rhythm is recognized in the comedies, sentimental falsification is not necessary in expressing the ripening moment. It is indeed the present mirth and laughter of the festive plays—the immediate experience they give of nature's beneficence—which reconciles feeling, without recourse to sentimentality or cynicism, to the clarification conveyed about nature's limitations.

Shakespeare's Route to Festive Comedy

In drawing parallels between holiday and Shakespeare's comedy, it has been hard to avoid talking as though Shakespeare were a primitive who began with nothing but festival custom and invented a comedy to express it. Actually, of course, he started work with theatrical and literary resources already highly developed. This tradition was complex, and included folk themes and conventions along with the practice of classically trained innovators like Lyly, Kyd, and Marlowe. Shakespeare, though perfectly aware of unsophisticated forms like the morality and the jig, from the outset wrote plays which presented a narrative in three dimensions. In comedy, he began with cultivated models—Plautus for *The Comedy of Errors* and literary romance for *Two Gentlemen of Verona*; he worked out a consistently festive pattern for his comedy only after these preliminary experiments.

In his third early comedy, *Love's Labour's Lost*, instead of dramatizing a borrowed plot, he built his slight story around an elegant aristocratic entertainment. In doing so he worked out the holiday sequence of release and clarification which comes into its own in *A Midsummer Night's Dream*. This more serious play, his first comic masterpiece, has a crucial place in his development. To make a dramatic epithalamium, he expressed with full imaginative resonance the experience of the traditional summer holidays. He thus found his way back to a native festival tradition remarkably similar to that behind Aristophanes at the start of the literary tradition of comedy.[5] And in expressing the native holiday, he was in a position to use all the resources of a sophisticated dramatic art. So perfect an expression and understanding of folk cult was only possible in the moment when it was still in the blood but no longer in the brain.

Shakespeare never made another play from pastimes in the same direct fashion. But the pattern for feeling and awareness which he derived from the holiday occasion in *A Midsummer Night's Dream* becomes the dominant mode of organization in subsequent

[5] Mr. Northrop Frye has formulated a similar view of Shakespeare's development in a brilliant, compressed summary of the whole tradition of literary comedy and Shakespeare's relation to it, "The Argument of Comedy," *English Institute Essays, 1948*, ed. D. A. Robertson, Jr. (New York, 1949).

comedies until the period of the problem plays. The relation between his festive comedy and naive folk games is amusingly reflected in the passage from *The Taming of The Shrew* which I have used as an epigraph. When the bemused tinker Sly is asked with mock ceremony whether he will hear a comedy to "frame your mind to mirth and merriment," his response reflects his ignorant notion that a comedy is some sort of holiday game—"a Christmas gambold or a tumbling trick." He is corrected with: "it is more pleasing stuff . . . a kind of history." Shakespeare is neither primitive nor primitivist; he enjoys making game of the inadequacy of Sly's folk notions of entertainment. But folk attitudes and motifs are still present, as a matter of course, in the dramatist's cultivated work, so that even Sly is not entirely off the mark about comedy. Though it is a kind of history, it is the kind that frames the mind to mirth. So it functions like a Christmas gambol. It often includes gambols, and even, in the case of *As You Like It*, a tumbling trick. Though Sly has never seen a comedy, his holiday mottoes show that he knows in what spirit to take it: "let the world slip"; "we shall ne'er be younger." Prince Hal, in his festive youth, "daff'd the world aside / And bid it pass" (*1 H.IV* V.i.96). Feste sings that "Youth's a stuff will not endure" (*Twel.* II.iii.53).

The part of Shakespeare's earliest work where his mature patterns of comedy first appear clearly is, as I have suggested, the clowning. Although he did not find an entirely satisfactory comic form for the whole play until *A Midsummer Night's Dream*, the clown's part is satisfactory from the outset. Here the theatrical conventions with which he started writing already provided a congenial saturnalian organization of experience, and Shakespeare at once began working out its larger implications. It was of course a practice, going back beyond *The Second Shepherds' Play*, for the clowns to present a burlesque version of actions performed seriously by their betters. Wagner's conjuring in *Dr. Faustus* is an obvious example. In the drama just before Shakespeare began writing, there are a great many parallels of this sort between the low comedy and the main action.[6] One suspects that they often re-

[6] William Empson discusses the effects achieved by such double plots in *English Pastoral Poetry* (New York, 1938; originally printed with the better title, *Some Versions of Pastoral*, London, 1935), pp. 27-86. I am much indebted to Mr. Empson's work: festive comedy, as I discuss it here, is a "version of pastoral."

sulted from the initiative of the clown performer; he was, as Sidney said, thrust in "by head and shoulders to play a part in majestical matters"—and the handiest part to play was a low take-off of what the high people were doing. Though Sidney objected that the performances had "neither decency nor discretion," such burlesque, when properly controlled, had an artistic logic which Shakespeare was quick to develop.

At the simplest level, the clowns were foils, as one of the aristocrats remarks about the clown's show in *Love's Labour's Lost*:

> 'tis some policy
> To have one show worse than the King's and his company.
> (*L.L.L.* V.ii.513-514)

But burlesque could also have a positive effect, as a vehicle for expressing aberrant impulse and thought. When the aberration was made relevant to the main action, clowning could provide both release for impulses which run counter to decency and decorum, and the clarification about limits which comes from going beyond the limit. Shakespeare used this movement from release to clarification with masterful control in clown episodes as early as *2 Henry VI*. The scenes of the Jack Cade rebellion in that history are an astonishingly consistent expression of anarchy by clowning: the popular rising is presented throughout as a saturnalia, ignorantly undertaken in earnest; Cade's motto is: "then are we in order when we are most out of order" (IV.iii.199). In the early plays, the clown is usually represented as oblivious of what his burlesque implies. When he becomes the court fool, however, he can use his folly as a stalking horse, and his wit can express directly the function of his role as a dramatized commentary on the rest of the action.

In creating Falstaff, Shakespeare fused the clown's part with that of a festive celebrant, a Lord of Misrule, and worked out the saturnalian implications of both traditions more drastically and more complexly than anywhere else. If in the idyllic plays the humorous perspective can be described as looking past the reigning festive moment to the work-a-day world beyond, in *1 Henry IV*, the relation of comic and serious action can be described by saying that holiday is balanced against everyday and the doomsday of battle. The comedy expresses impulses and awareness inhibited by the urgency and decorum of political life, so that the comic and serious strains are contrapuntal, each conveying the ironies limiting the other. Then in *2 Henry IV* Shakespeare confronts the anarchic potentialities of misrule when it seeks to become not a holiday extravagance but an everyday racket.

It might be logical to start where Shakespeare started, by considering first the festive elements present in the imitative comedies and the early clowns and in the literary and theatrical traditions of comedy into which he entered as an apprentice. Instead, because Shakespeare's development followed the route I have sketched, I start with three chapters dealing with the Elizabethan tradition of holiday and with two examples of holiday shows, then enter Shakespeare's work at *Love's Labour's Lost*, where he first makes use of festivity in a large way. To begin with the apprenticeship would involve saying over again a great deal that has been said before in order to separate out the festive elements with which I am properly concerned. It is important to recognize, however, here at the outset, that the order of my discussion brings out the social origins of the festive mode of comedy at the expense of literary and theatrical origins. It would be possible to start with festive affinities of the comic plots Shakespeare found at hand. One could go on to notice how Shakespeare tends to bring out this potential in the way he shapes his early comedies. And one could say a great deal about the way he uses his early clowns to extrapolate the follies of their masters, notably about Launce's romance with his dog Crab as a burlesque of the extravagant romantic postures of the two gentlemen of Verona. Much of this "apprentice" work is wonderful. And it is wonderful what powers are in the comic machine itself, in the literary-theatrical resource for organizing experience which was there for the young Shakespeare to appropriate. But by looking first at the social resource of holiday customs, and then at the early masterpieces where he first fully uses this resource on the stage, we shall be able to bring into focus an influence from the life of his time which shaped his comic art profoundly.

The sort of interpretation I have proposed in outline here does not center on the way the comedies imitate characteristics of actual men and manners; but this neglect of the social observation in the plays does not imply that the way they handle social materials is unimportant. Comedy is not, obviously enough, the same thing as ritual; if it were, it would not perform its function. To express the underlying rhythm his comedy had in common with holiday, Shakespeare did not simply stage mummings; he found in the social life of his time the stuff for "a kind of history." We can see in the Saint George plays how cryptic and arbitrary action derived from ritual becomes when it is merely a fossil remnant. In a self-conscious culture, the heritage of cult is kept alive by art which makes it relevant as a mode of perception and expression. The artist gives the ritual pattern aesthetic actuality by discovering expressions of it in the fragmentary and incomplete gestures of daily life. He fulfills these gestures by making them moments in the complete action which is the art form. The form finds meaning in life.

This process of translation from social into artistic form has great historical as well as literary interest. Shakespeare's theater was taking over on a professional and everyday basis functions which until his time had largely been performed by amateurs on holiday. And he wrote at a moment when the educated part of society was modifying a ceremonial, ritualistic conception of human life to create a historical, psychological conception. His drama, indeed, was an important agency in this transformation: it provided a "theater" where the failures of ceremony could be looked at in a place apart and understood as history; it provided new ways of representing relations between language and action so as to express personality. In making drama out of rituals of state, Shakespeare makes clear their meaning as social and psychological conflict, as history. So too with the rituals of pleasure, of misrule, as against rule: his comedy presents holiday magic as imagination, games as expressive gestures. At high moments it brings into focus, as part of the play, the significance of the saturnalian form itself as a paradoxical human need, problem and resource.

Chapter 2

HOLIDAY CUSTOM AND ENTERTAINMENT

I came once myself to a place, riding on a journey homeward from London, and I sent word overnight into the town that I would preach there in the morning because it was a holy day, and me thought it was an holy day's work. The church stood in my way, and I took my horse, and my company, and went thither. I thought I should have found a great company in the church, and when I came there, the church door was fast locked.

I tarried there half an hour and more, at last the key was found and one of the parish comes to me and says: "Sir this is a busy day with us, we cannot hear you, it is Robin Hood's day. The parish are gone abroad to gather for Robin Hood. I pray you let them not."

—Bishop Hugh Latimer, Sixth Sermon before Edward VI

During Shakespeare's lifetime, England became conscious of holiday custom as it had not been before, in the very period when in many areas the keeping of holidays was on the decline. Festivals which worked within the rhythm of an agricultural calendar, in village or market town, did not fit the way of living of the urban groups whose energies were beginning to find expression through what Tawney has called the Puritan ethic. The Puritan spokesmen who attacked the holidays looked at them from the outside as people had not had occasion to do before. The effect of the Reformation throughout the Elizabethan church was to discourage festive ceremonials along with ceremonies generally. The traditional saturnalian customs were kept up in the unselfconscious regions of the countryside. But attitudes that meant one thing in the static, monolithic world of village and manor meant other things, more complex and challenging, when continued in the many-minded world of city and court. Under Elizabeth, the court circle kept high days without making an issue of them and enjoyed the elaboration of native customs in all sorts of neo-classical guises. Under James, courtiers and their literary spokesmen began to be militant in defending holiday, the king himself intervening to protect the popular pastimes from Puritan repression. In the Jacobean period the defense of holiday pleasures by a group whose everyday business was pleasure often became trivial and insincere. Shakespeare, coming up to London from a rich market town, growing up in the relatively unselfconscious 1570's and 80's and writing his festive plays in the decade of the 90's, when most of the major elements in English society enjoyed a moment of reconcilement, was perfectly situated to express both a countryman's participation in holiday and a city man's consciousness of it.

The evidence about the Elizabethan holidays has been thoroughly gathered and marshalled by responsible modern scholars. Renaissance accounts tend to be either cryptic or highly colored: those who take the customs for granted do not spell them out, while the fuller descriptions come from moralizing Puritans or pastoralizing poets. Some quotations, several of them very familiar, can convey what the popular holiday was like; then I shall indicate briefly how aristocratic entertainments elaborated and supplemented the customary pastimes. C. R. Baskervill has two paragraphs which provide a useful modern survey of the range of festive custom:

> During the Middle Ages and Renaissance a great variety of sports and pastimes were popular with all classes. The occasion might be a simple gathering on the village green of a summer afternoon or in the hall on a winter night. It might be a marriage feast, a harvest supper, or a local wake or fair. More likely it was one of the great festivals celebrated pretty generally throughout Western Europe, as those of Easter, May, Whitsuntide, Midsummer, or the Christmas season. The nature of the festivities depended partly on the occasion celebrated, so that the same group varied its pastimes at Christmas, May Day, Midsummer, or Harvest. Often the chief feature was some modification of ancient pagan ritual, but even here the different parishes had their special customs. . . .

Of course such revelry was often of the most informal sort; but the general tendency, especially on the great festival occasions, was to organize it under leaders, usually a lord and a lady or a king and a queen, with attendants who paralleled the functionaries of a castle or a royal court. The leaders presided over the pastimes and often played a prominent part in them. No doubt the celebrants generally engaged in social dancing, in the pastimes that have survived as singing games of children, and in sports and contests of various sorts, the festival king or queen awarding prizes in contests or dispensing punishments in forfeit games. But there was a special group of entertainers representing the talent of the community. Some of these prepared a group dance like the morris, or a mummers' play, or perhaps even a dramatic performance of some sort drawn from a more sophisticated source. Much of the entertainment, however, seems to have been of a simpler type, consisting of comic speeches or of special dances and songs by one or two characters. At least one disard in the role of fool or daemon commonly took a conspicuous part in the procedure, at times as leader. After the local celebration the whole organization was often carried to the neighboring villages, and groups from villages in the same general region exchanged visits. Groups of performers also frequently went on rounds of visits to the castles of neighboring lords and to the more important towns during their holidays, becoming for the time bodies of strolling players. To the whole procedure of the organized group various names were applied, like revels, disguising, interlude, or game.[1]

The May Game

For our purposes, it will be enough to consider two principal forms of festivity, the May games and the Lord of Misrule, noticing particularly how what is done by the group of celebrants involves the composition of experience in ways which literature and drama could take over. When the parish went abroad "to gather for Robin Hood" they did not need to put into words what they were gathering, since they had it in their hands in hawthorn

[1] *The Elizabethan Jig* (Chicago, 1929), pp. 6-8.

branches: one name for hawthorn is "may." The bringing home of May acted out an experience of the relationship between vitality in people and nature. The poets have merely to describe May Day to develop a metaphor relating man and nature. In Herrick's *Corinna's Going a Maying*, where the tradition has become elegantly conscious art, the gesture towards nature is conveyed by witty identifications: he speaks of "a budding Boy or Girl . . ." and says deliberately impossible things like

> Rise, and put on your foliage, and be seen
> To come forth like the Springtime, fresh and green,
> And sweet as Flora.

In Spenser's more straightforward account in *The Shepherd's Calendar*, written early in the period, the same metaphorical action is scarcely detached from direct description of behavior:

> *Palinode.* Is not thilke the mery moneth of May,
> When loue lads masken in fresh aray?
> How falles it then, we no merrier bene,
> Ylike as others, girt in gawdy greene?
> Our blouncket liueryes bene all to sadde,
> For thilke same season, when all is ycladd
> With pleasaunce: the grownd with grasse, the Woods
> With greene leaues, the bushes with bloosming Buds.
> Yougthes folke now flocken in euery where,
> To gather may buskets and smelling brere:
> And home they hasten the postes to dight,
> And all the Kirke pillours eare day light,
> With Hawthorne buds, and swete Eglantine,
> And girlonds of roses and Sopps in wine.
> Such merimake holy Saints doth queme,
> But we here sytten as drownd in a dreme.
> *Piers.* For Younkers Palinode such follies fitte,
> But we tway bene men of elder witt.
> *Palinode.* Sicker this morrowe, ne lenger agoe,
> I sawe a shole of shepeheardes outgoe,
> With singing, and shouting, and iolly chere:
> Before them yode a lusty Tabrere,

That to the many a Horne pype playd,
Whereto they dauncen eche one with his mayd.
To see those folkes make such iouysaunce,
Made my heart after the pype to daunce.
Tho to the greene Wood they speeden hem all,
To fetchen home May with their musicall:
And home they bringen in a royall throne,
Crowned as king: and his Queene attone
Was Lady Flora, on whom did attend
A fayre flocke of Faeries, and a fresh bend
Of louely Nymphs. (O that I were there,
To helpen the Ladyes their Maybush beare)
Ah Piers, bene not thy teeth on edge, to thinke,
How great sport they gaynen with little swinck?[2]

Palinode sets the people-vegetation metaphor in motion merely by saying "We clerics are dressed in the wrong liveries. Look at the others, all dressed in gaudy green, and the grass, and the trees." In such festive poetry, even though it had a long literary history, the activity of the holiday shapes the meaning seen and felt in nature—a different meaning from that arrived at when people "outgo" in a different fashion, for example by taking Wordsworth's kind of contemplative walk. Nature is "May"—what they dance out to, and fetch home for decorating house and church. At the same time "May" is a lord, so they can express a relation to the season by doing honor to him and his lady Flora.

A feeling for the spring stemming from actual holiday celebration appears in the earliest surviving English love poems:

Lenten is come with love to toune
With blosmen and with briddés roune,
That all this blissé bryngeth . . .

In the manner of "Sumer is icumen in," this fourteenth-century lyric goes on to describe how all living things are stirring together. The leaves "waxen al with wille," wild creatures make merry,

[2] *The Poetical Works of Edmund Spenser*, ed. J. C. Smith and E. De Selincourt (London, 1926), p. 436.

Wormés woweth under cloude,
Wymmen waxeth wounder proud.[3]

The worms below and the women above are connected by the holiday institution, which is prior to metaphor. The composition of the poetry follows relations made by the composition of the holiday. We shall consider later the way many of Shakespeare's songs are similarly organized by implicit or explicit reference to a festive occasion.[4]

Some of the most circumstantial accounts of the games were produced by the Puritan Phillip Stubbes in his popular *Anatomie of Abuses . . . in the Country of Ailgna.* The transparent fiction of describing a foreign country was not altogether inappropriate, for Merry England was becoming foreign to the pious tradesman's London for which Stubbes was spokesman. His assumptions in describing the games can serve to bring out, by contrast, several of the fundamental social conditions on which the holiday customs depended:

> Against May, Whitsunday, or other time all the young men and maids, old men and wives, run gadding over night to the woods, groves, hills, and mountains, where they spend all the night in pleasant pastimes. . . . And no marvel, for there is a great Lord present amongst them, as superintendent and Lord over their pastimes and sports, namely, Satan, prince of hell.

Stubbes equates the traditional summer lord with Satan!

> But the chiefest jewel they bring from thence is their Maypole, which they bring home with great veneration, as thus: They have twenty or forty yoke of oxen, every oxe having a sweet nose-gay of flowers placed on the tip of his horns, and these oxen draw home this Maypole (this stinking idol, rather) which is covered all over with flowers and herbs, bound round about with strings, from the top to the bottom, and sometime painted with variable colours, with two or three hundred men, women and children following it with great devotion. And thus being reared up with handkerchiefs and flags hovering on the top, they

[3] *Early English Lyrics*, ed. E. K. Chambers and F. Sidgwick (London, 1947), no. V.

[4] See below, pp. 113 ff.

> strew the ground round about, bind green boughs about it, set up summer halls, bowers and arbors hard by it. And then fall they to dance about it, like as the heathen people did at the dedication of the Idols, whereof this is a perfect pattern, or rather the thing itself. I have heard it credibly reported (and that *viva voce*) by men of great gravity and reputation, that of forty, three-score, or a hundred maids going to the wood over night, there have scarcely the third part of them returned home again undefiled. These be the fruits which these cursed pastimes bring forth.[5]

It is remarkable how pleasantly the holiday comes through in spite of Stubbes' railing on the sidelines. Partly this appeal comes from shrewd journalism: he is writing "a pleasant invective," to use a phrase from the title of Stephen Gosson's similar *School of Abuse*. Partly it is the result of the fact that despite his drastic attitude he writes in the language of Merry England and so is betrayed into phrases like "sweet nosegays." And his Elizabethan eye is too much on the object to leave out tangible details, so that, astonishingly, he describes "this stinking idol" as "covered all over with flowers and herbs." By way of emphasizing the enormity of the evil, Stubbes insists that it is not confined to young men and maids, that "old men and wives" also "run gadding to the woods," that "men, women and children" follow the Maypole home. The consequence of this emphasis, for a modern reader, is to bring out how completely all groups who lived together within the agricultural calendar shared in the response to the season.

Elsewhere Stubbes explicitly objects to people all keeping holiday together. In objecting to wakes, he acknowledges that it is proper for "one friend to visit another" and "congratulate their coming with some good cheer." "But," he says, "why at one determinate day more than at another (except business urged it)?"

> I think it convenient for one friend to visit another (at sometimes) as opportunity and occasion shall offer itself; but wherefor should the whole town, parish, village, and country keep

[5] *The Anatomie of Abuses . . . in Ailgna* (1583), ed. F. V. Furnival (London, 1877-82), p. 149. Here, and elsewhere in all quotations except those from Spenser, I have modernized the spelling and punctuation.

> one and the same day, and make such gluttonous feasts as they do?

Clearly Stubbes assumes a world of isolated, busy individuals, each prudently deciding how to make the best use of his time. Another of his objections is that "the poor men that bear the charges of these feasts and wakes, are the poorer, and keep the worser houses a long time after."[6] Here again he assumes that what matters is the maintenance of individual households at as respectable a level as thrift can contrive. The Puritan ethic contrasts all along the line with the sort of "housekeeping" which went with festive liberty. The excesses Stubbes deplores did not threaten people whose places in a traditional arrangement of life one gaudy night or day could not disturb. Since everyone was out together, and the high day came only at an established time, no one need be anxious. Where morality was necessary for the city merchant, and discretion for the city gentleman of leisure, to avoid bankruptcy or a rake's progress, the merrimakers could rely on a communal rhythm to bring them, all together still, back on an even keel.

No doubt there were consequences, sometimes unpleasant, for some of those maids about whom the men of great gravity put their heads together. As Ophelia sings about Saint Valentine's Day:

> Young men will do't if they come to't . . .

Nashe, in presenting the delights of Spring in *Summer's Last Will and Testament*, has a song sung by "three clowns and three maids" which enjoys the same fact Stubbes deplores:

> From the town to the grove
> Two and two let us rove
> A Maying, a playing:
> Love hath no gainsaying: . . .[7]

When this side of the holiday is isolated, the relishing of it can become merely prurient. But usually there is a recognition, coming through the bawdry, of a larger force at work, whether the tone be harsh or genial. Nashe has another song, earlier in his Spring scene, which has this wider focus:

[6] *Ibid.*, p. 153.
[7] *The Works of Thomas Nashe*, ed. R. B. McKerrow (London, 1910), III, 240.

The fields breathe sweet, the daisies kiss our feet,
Young lovers meet, old wives a sunning sit;
In every street, these tunes our ears do greet,
Cuckoo, jug, jug, pu we, to witta woo.
Spring, the sweet spring.[8]

Nashe's pageant dramatizes Spring as a prodigal gallant who flaunts unrepentant extravagance:

> what I had, I have spent on good fellows. In these sports you have seen, which are proper to the Spring, and others of like sort (as giving wenches green gowns, making garlands for fencers, and tricking up children gay) have I bestowed all my flowery treasure, and flower of my youth.[9]

Here again the children are in it too—as well as those old wives who sit a sunning. And it is in the grove that love hath no gainsaying. The gathering of foliage in the woods, the setting up of summer halls, the straining towards identification in wearing garlands, even dressing entirely in foliage as "jacks o'th'green"—all such custom relates the emotions of love to its fructifying functions. Separation of feeling from function is at the root of perversity and lust. May-game wantonness has a reverence about it because it is a realization of a power of life larger than the individual, crescent both in men and in their green surroundings.

The Lord of Misrule

In the customs which center on a Lord of Misrule, the rougher pleasures of defiance and mockery are uppermost, in contrast to the lyric gathering-in of the May games; Abuse predominates over Invocation, though both gestures are usually present, in varying degree, when a holiday group asserts its liberty and promotes its solidarity. The formal Lord of Misrule presided over the eating and drinking within-doors in the cold season. But the title was also applied to the captain of summer Sunday drinking and dancing by the young men of a parish, a leader whose role was not necessarily distinct from the Robin or King of the Maying.

The winter lord of the feast reigns chiefly at night: the Duchess

[8] *Ibid.*, p. 239.

[9] *Ibid.*, p. 240.

of Malfi, rallying her husband Antonio when he insists on staying with her overnight, says "you are a Lord of Misrule," and he answers with a wry reference to his clandestine role, "True, for my reign is only in the night."[10] On Twelfth Night the Lord was often the King of the Bean, having found the bean in his portion of cake. Although identified especially with the twelve days of feasting at Christmas, the custom was naturally used at feasts in other seasons, notably at Shrovetide, and at harvest: Carew, in his *Survey of Cornwall* (1602), speaks of "next neighbors and kindred" consuming "a great part of the night in Christmas rule" at the harvest dinners customarily given "by every wealthy man, or, as we term it, every good liver."[11] It was in the households of such men, or in the still larger establishments of institutions or of the nobility, that the more formal lords were set up at feasts. Holinshed observes that at Christmas

> of old ordinary course, there is always one appointed to make sport in the court, called commonly lord of misrule: whose office is not unknown to such as have been brought up in noblemen's houses, and among great housekeepers which use liberal feasting in that season.[12]

One can see why formal misrule would be most used in formal households, where people regularly ate, more or less in awe, under the countenance of My Lord. My Lord of Misrule, burlesquing majesty by promoting license under the forms of order, would be useful to countenance the revelry of such a group.

And by giving way to a substitute, the master's own authority was kept clear of compromise. The custom seems to have been a secularized version of the Feast of Fools, when the solemn decorum of cathedral services would be suddenly turned upside down as the inferior clergy heard the glad tidings that "He hath put down the mighty from their seats, and exalted them of low degree" (*Deposuit potentes de sede: et exaltavit humiles*).[13] In the secular

[10] John Webster, *The Duchess of Malfi*, in *The Best Plays of Webster and Tourneur*, ed. John Aldington Symonds (London, 1948), p. 175 (III.ii.9).

[11] *Popular Antiquities of Great Britain . . . from the Materials Collected by John Brand*, ed. W. Carew Hazlitt (London, 1870), I, 307.

[12] Quoted by Chambers, *Mediaeval Stage*, I, 403, n. 3.

[13] *Ibid.*, pp. 278 ff. and 403 ff.; and Welsford, *Fool*, pp. 211 ff.

life of the Renaissance period, as awe of man for master diminished, so would the fun of such a custom. A decline is apparent in the discontinuance of the Lord of Misrule at court under Mary and Elizabeth—after most elaborate ceremonies at court and in the city under Edward VI and occasionally under Henry VIII. There was also a decline of Christmas rule in most of the University colleges and in the Inns of Court. But the custom was perfectly familiar in such institutions, as is clear from Chambers' summary of the quite numerous occasions for which evidence survives of collegiate misrule during Elizabeth's reign.[14] The few circumstantial accounts show farced protocol and titles worked out with the completeness that young lawyers and scholars would relish, while the whole occasion is for the most part rather decorously formal. But though it was usually misrule by the book, taking no chance, there are glimpses of moments when the mummery came alive, and occasionally something headlong would boil up. Hazlitt's edition of Brand's *Antiquities* quotes Sir Thomas Urquhart:

> They may be said to use their King as about Christmas we used to do the King of Misrule, whom we invest with that title to no other end, but to countenance the Bacchanalian riots and preposterous disorders of the family where he is installed.[15]

Herrick's treatment of the custom is rather insipid, concluding with

> Give then to the King
> And Queen wassailing;
> And though with ale ye be whet here;
> Yet part ye from hence,
> As free from offence,
> As when ye innocent met here.[16]

Selden takes the custom for granted in noting its relation to its Roman prototype:

> Christmas succeeds the Saturnalia, the same time, the same num-

[14] *Ibid.*, pp. 407-419.
[15] Hazlitt, *Antiquities*, II, 370.
[16] "Twelfth Night, or King and Queen," *The Poetical Works of Robert Herrick*, ed. F. W. Moorman (New York, 1947), p. 310.

ber of holidays; then the master waited upon the servant, like the Lord of Misrule.[17]

The basic pattern of a mock king or lord was adaptable to a variety of occasions less formal than seasonal feasts: the Ale-cunner, for example, had this sort of role in presiding over village wake or church ale. Mock-majesty was often improvised in taverns, as we shall see in considering how Nashe presents Bacchus as a prince of tavern mates.

In the Sunday pastimes of villages during the summer, a Lord of Misrule would be set up by "all the wildheads of the parish," as Stubbes calls them in a pleasant and indignant description of the mock-king and his morris-dancing retinue. This could be a very different sort of role from that of the Lord of a gentlemen's feast. Stubbes recognizes explicitly a connection of such games with drama; he speaks of them just after denouncing the theaters, and calls them "the other kind of plays, which you call Lords of Misrule." We shall consider in detail in the next chapter an instance in Lincolnshire of the kind of thing he describes in general terms:

> First, all the wildheads of the parish, conventing together, choose them a grand captain (of all mischief) whom they ennoble with the title of "my Lord of Misrule," and him they crown with great solemnity, and adopt for their king. This king anointed chooseth forth twenty, forty, threescore or a hundred lusty guts, like to himself, to wait upon his lordly majesty and to guard his noble person. Then every one of these his men, he investeth with his liveries of green, yellow, or some other light wanton colour. And as though that were not (bawdy) gaudy enough, I should say, they bedeck themselves with scarves, ribbons and laces hanged all over with gold rings, precious stones, and other jewels. This done, they tie about either leg twenty or forty bells, with rich handkerchiefs in their hands, and sometimes laid across over their shoulders and necks, borrowed for the most part of their pretty Mopsies and loving Besses, for bussing them in the dark.
>
> Thus all things set in order, then have they their hobby-horses,

[17] *Table Talk*, ed. Frederick Pollock (London, 1927), p. 28.

dragons and other antiques [i.e. antics?] together with their bawdy pipers and thundering drummers to strike up the devil's dance withal. Then march these heathen company towards the church and churchyard, their pipers piping, their drummers thundering, their stumps dancing, their bells jingling, their handkerchiefs swinging about their heads like madmen, their hobbyhorses and other monsters skirmishing amongst the rout. And in this sort they go to the church (I say) and into the church (though the minister be at prayer or preaching) dancing and swinging their handkerchiefs over their heads in the church, like devils incarnate, with such a confused noise, that no man can hear his own voice. Then the foolish people they look, they stare, they laugh, they fleer, and mount upon forms and pews to see these goodly pageants solemnized in this sort.

Then, after this, about the church they go again and again, and so forth into the churchyard, where they have commonly their summer halls, their bowers, arbors and banqueting houses set up, wherein they feast, banquet and dance all that day and (peradventure) all the night too. And thus these terrestrial furies spend the sabbath day.

They have also certain papers, wherein is painted some babblery or other of imagery work, and these they call "my Lord of Misrule's badges." These they give to everyone that will give money for them to maintain them in their heathenry, devilry, whoredom, drunkenness, pride and what not. And who will not be buxom to them and give them money for these their devilish cognizances, they are mocked and flouted at not a little. And so assotted are some, that they not only give them money to maintain their abomination withal, but also wear their badges and cognizances in their hats or caps openly.[18]

The morris-dance Stubbes here describes was thoroughly traditional: the dance typically included the skirmishing, curvetting hobbyhorse, the Besse or Maid Marian who dressed himself up in women's clothes, and the fool, usually the leading dancer, often in regalia which carried bawdy suggestions. Hazlitt quotes a description from 1614:

[18] Stubbes, *Anatomie*, pp. 147-148. Chambers cites several instances of lords of misrule in the summer in *Mediaeval Stage*, I, 173, n. 7.

It was my hap of late, by chance
To meet a country morris dance,
When, chiefest of them all, the fool
Played with a ladle and a tool;
When every younger shak'd his bells[19]

Part of the by-play was the fool's courting of the Maid Marian by dancing about her. But group dancing was the chief thing. The jerking about of handkerchiefs and the stiff-kneed step of the morris conveyed a super-abundance of vitality. Each foot was brought "forward alternately with a sharp swing (almost a jerk)"; frequently every alternate or every fourth step was a hop; a dancer made capers by exaggerating the regular step with a vigorous jump by the supporting foot; he made jumps by springing as high as possible with both legs straight.[20] The virile self-assertion of such dancing is caught effectively in lines of the Duke of York in *2 Henry VI* when he is plotting to incite Jack Cade to lead a rebellion and describes Cade's hardihood in the Irish wars:

his thighs with darts
Were almost like a sharp-quill'd porpentine;
And in the end being rescued, I have seen
Him caper upright like a wild Morisco,
Shaking the bloody darts as he his bells.
(*2 H.VI* III.i.362-366)

Such an upstarting, indomitable gesture is perfect for the leader of a rising which is presented as a sort of saturnalia. The village saturnalia of the Lord of Misrule's men was in its way a sort of rising; setting up a mock lord and demanding homage for him are playfully rebellious gestures, into which Dionysian feeling can flow. Stubbes is clearly exaggerating when he talks as though such groups regularly interrupted divine service inside the church. But the churchyard was certainly a center for merrymaking, partly because the church had taken the place of the pagan fane which dances once honoured, partly because the churchyard was in any

[19] From Rablet's *Cobbes Prophesies* (1614), quoted in Hazlitt, *Antiquities*, II, 423.

[20] Baskervill, *Jig*, pp. 353 f. His account is based on Cecil Sharp, who studied still-continuing traditions of dancing which fit with illustrations and descriptions from the Renaissance.

case the parish meeting place, partly perhaps because to go there was excitingly impudent. The wanton mood would be abetted by encountering someone who, refusing to give homage to My Lord in return for one of his badges, declared himself a craven or a kill-joy, was "mocked and flouted not a little," and so, as we shall see, might provide an occasion for the birth of satire from festive abuse.

Aristocratic Entertainments

Chambers observes that

> Tudor kings and queens came and went about their public affairs in a constant atmosphere of make-believe, with a sibyl lurking in every court-yard and gateway, and a satyr in the boscage of every park, to turn the ceremonies of welcome and farewell, without which sovereigns must not move, by the arts of song and dance and mimetic dialogue, to favour and to prettiness. The fullest scope for such entertainments was afforded by the custom of the progress, which led the Court summer by summer, to remove from London and the great palaces on the Thames and renew the migratory life of earlier dynasties, wandering for a month or more over the fair face of the land, and housing itself in the outlying castles and royal manors, or claiming the ready hospitality of the territorial gentry and the provincial cities. This was a holiday, in which the sovereign sought change of air and the recreation of hunting and such other pastimes as the country yields.[21]

Obviously the pastimes of the court were occasions of a very different character from the free-and-easy festivities of a parish or the convivialities of a group of next neighbors and kindred at a manor. Yet the courtly entertainments tendered Elizabeth reflected the popular tradition of seasonal holidays and greatly influenced its translation into comedy. The Queen's presence inevitably made for constraint: though she herself could be wonderfully downright and spontaneous, she was not one to suspend her majesty—misrule had to keep well clear of that. And at court play and business were not distinct: much of the art of the courtier lay

[21] *The Elizabethan Stage* (Oxford, 1923), I, 107.

in deftly working through pleasure to profit. Anxiety and ambition were apt to be involved in the exceedingly expensive entertainments provided by noble families. One is repeatedly surprised at how much good fun the noble company could have under the conditions of court life. Because they were habituated to decorum, they could be relatively free within its limits. A fountain in Leicester's garden at Kenilworth, during the famous entertainment of 1575, was fitted with a hidden spout, so that when unwary guests lingered to look closely at its ornate carvings, "with the wreast of a cock," water spouted upward and drenched them "from top to toe; the he's to some laughing, but the shee's to more sport. This some time was occupied to very good pastime."[22] The highest class shared in the feeling for holiday freedom. But the conditions of court life made its expression complex, and put a premium on detached artistic realization. Of course the pastimes presented were often not even indirectly expressive of festive attitudes or themes. There was much solemn flattery of Elizabeth; there were presentations of local or family history or heroes; allegorical shows of virtues and vices; romantic narratives tied to the appearance of local nymphs whom only Elizabeth could release from vile enchantments. Literary pastoral and mythology were the most common idiom, frequently handled in a merely literary way. But mythological and pastoral materials often drew life from native traditions. Music, song, and dance could have the same functions as at simpler merrymakings. And the traditional popular pastimes themselves were often an element in the entertainment, either as a spectacle performed by "the country people" and watched with complacency and amusement by the court circle, or as a holiday exercise in which the courtiers themselves participated, as they participated in the disguisings of the masque.

The commonest style of pageantry in tribute to the queen is pleasantly epitomized in a madrigal contributed by George Kirbye to *The Triumphes of Oriana* (1601):

> Bright Phoebus greets most clearly
> With radiant beams fair Oriana sitting.

[22] From Robert Laneham's account of the entertainment, reprinted in John Nichols, *The Progresses, Processions, etc. of Queen Elizabeth* (London, 1823), I, 476 ff.

Her apple Venus yields as best befitting
  A queen beloved most dearly.
  Rich Pluto leaves his treasures.
And Proserpina glad runs in her best array.
  Nymphs deck her crown with bay
  (At) her feet are lions kissing.
  No joy can there be missing.
Now Thetis leaves the mermaids' tunes admired,
And swells with pride to see this Queen desired.
  Then sang the shepherds and nymphs of Diana:
    Long live fair Oriana.[23]

Poetic fictions such as these were acted out repeatedly at country houses. Thetis would leave "the mermaids' tunes admired" at the climax of a show where music crept by upon the waters of a garden lake. To make the most of elaborating fact with fiction, the presentation of a gift was often tied into a story, as in Peele's *Arraignment of Paris* (1584), where the gift of the apple to the queen resolves the jealous conflict previously depicted between the rival goddesses.[24]

The whole conception of gathering in the powers reigning in the countryside to yield them to Elizabeth, and of Elizabeth vivifying the countryside by her magic presence, has affinities with the traditional lustral visit of mummery lord and lady, when they made their *quête* to bring the luck of the season to the village and the house. On many occasions the queen herself is put in the role of a supreme summer lady, to whom the others come to do homage. Thus at Elvetham in 1591, although she comes late in September she is greeted with verses describing a spring renewal from her influence:

The crooked-winding kid trips o'er the lawns,
The milk-white heifer wantons with the bull;
The trees show pleasure with their quivering leaves,
The meadow with new grass . . .

[23] F. H. Fellowes, *English Madrigal Verse* (Oxford, 1920), p. 150. Chambers conjectures (*Elizabethan Stage*, I, 123, n. 3) that *The Triumphes of Oriana* "may have been written as a whole for a royal birthday or wedding."

[24] *Works*, ed. A. H. Bullen (London, 1888), I, 66-72.

When the time comes for her departure,

> Leaves fall, grass dies, beasts of the wood hang head,
> Birds cease to sing, and every creature wails
> To see the season alter with this change:
> For how can Summer stay, when Sun departs?[25]

The outdoor country gods drawn from classical paganism find a natural place as patrons of native festive observances; they themselves are not distinct from native figures. Laneham, fancifully summarizing what each god contributed to the Kenilworth entertainment of 1575, observes that Pan sent "his merry morris, with their pipe and taber." This morris was part of a mimic bridal procession staged by the local people: Pan has clearly stolen here from Robin. So too, Bacchus is naturally taken as Lord of Misrule; Ceres is a harvest queen and rides on a hockcart.[26] The grotesque Sylvanus who at Elvetham frightened the country people, "and thereby moved great laughter," is at least a first cousin of the Savage Man or Woodwose, a folk wood spirit, who at Kenilworth held a dialogue with the classical Echo.[27] At Kenilworth, certain good-hearted men of Coventry brought their town's "old storial show": it was a Hocktide sword dance and free-for-all fight between Danes and English, the Danes in the end "led captive for triumph by our English women." The same mock-martial spirit animated a battle at Elvetham between Sylvanus with his forest men and Neptune with his Tritons, the latter using "great squirts."[28] The Coventry show seems to have been a rationalized version of a battle of summer and winter. Its conclusion probably reflects the Hocktide custom by which men and women capture each other.

The practice of superimposing classical motifs on the holiday games, as perhaps in an earlier epoch a battle of the seasons at Coventry had been rationalized as a conflict of Danes and English, appears in a passage from *The Two Gentlemen of Verona*. Forsaken Julia, in her page's disguise, tells Silvia that

[25] Nichols, *Progresses of Elizabeth*, III, 107 and 120.

[26] *Ibid.*, III, 135.

[27] *Ibid.*, III, 113-115 and I, 436 and 494-498. At Bisham (1592), the "Wilde Man" is one of Sylvanus' satyrs (*Ibid.*, III, 131). Chambers effectively summarizes the fusion and medley of literary and folk elements at noble entertainments in *Elizabethan Stage*, I, 124.

[28] Nichols, I, 446-456 and III, 115.

at Pentecost
When all our pageants of delight were play'd,
Our youth got me to play the woman's part,
And I was trimmed in Madam Julia's gown.
(*T.G.V.* IV.iv.163-165)

Chambers, in *The Mediaeval Stage*, assumes that "the pageants of delight" were May games, and "the woman's part" Maid Marian's.[29] He happened to neglect what Julia goes on to say: that the part was

Ariadne passioning
For Theseus' perjury and unjust flight.
(*T.G.V.* IV.iv.173-174)

And yet the pageants undoubtedly were to be understood as May games, and Ariadne is conceived as taking over the May Lady's part by an entirely familiar sort of Ovidian elaboration on native ground-work. Many pagan goddesses, as well as nymphs, could play "the woman's part": Proserpina glad, running in her best array, might with no change of costume be the Flora who gayly leads a morris described in one of Morley's madrigals.[30] On other occasions there is an English name for the goddess, the Fairy Queen; she may come with her maids to dance and sing in the garden, or may be "drawen with six children in a waggon of state."[31]

In the written accounts of entertainments, the formal part is obviously more adequately recorded than the impromptu or traditional humor, since a principal motive for publication was to give to the world at large verses written for the occasion. Clearly, therefore, Nichols' collection of documents does not do justice to the informal traditional games and shows used at entertainments. Gascoigne's account of the great Kenilworth festivities gives in full the verse he contributed, including a masque which was not finally

[29] I, 173, n. 1.

[30] Fellowes, *Madrigals*, p. 129.

[31] Nichols, III, 119; and Chambers, *Elizabethan Stage*, III, 401. At Elvetham in 1591 her name is Aureola; she speaks of her consort as "Auberon, the Fairy King." One of Campion's madrigals (1591) is addressed to "the fairy queen Proserpina" (Fellowes, p. 593). The relation of the Elvetham occasion to *Dream*, much handled by speculators about court intrigue, is effectively treated by Alice S. Venezky in *Pageantry on the Shakespearean Stage* (New York, 1951), pp. 139 ff. See below, pp. 121-22.

used; he merely mentions the comical shows presented by the common people. Laneham, the lively little hanger-on whose unusual pamphlet Scott used for *Kenilworth*, had no literary equity to salvage; it is from him that we learn of the folk bride-ale and Battle of Danes and English, "whereat her Majesty laughed well." The Bride-ale seems to have been presented very solemnly by "his lordship's simple neighbors," yet for his lordship's guests it was burlesque. Laneham has art enough to make it funny in the telling. The "bride," by someone's contrivance, was "a maid of thirty-five years"; and the "bridegroom" had "this special grace by the way, that ever as he would have formed him the better countenance, with the worse face he looked."[32] When holiday was translated to the stage, such shows were a natural for the clowns; and the comments of Shakespeare's aristocrats on their performance are in the same vein as Laneham's.

Another source of fun at entertainments, which is merely glanced at in the accounts of them, must have been the incongruity between fact and fiction, and the fun of quick transitions between the two. When one reads the texts of welcomes, of presentation ceremonies, where nymphs appear when trees rive, etc., they often seem almost tediously solemn. But they were witty, or "conceited," when they were performed, by virtue of the deftness with which they extended actuality into make-believe. Because this dramatic dimension was furnished by the occasion, it did not need to be expressed in the language of occasional verses. When Shakespeare puts pageantry on the stage, he makes comedy out of incongruity between make-believe and reality. He contrives dramatic situations which will give the lie to fiction; and he makes the language of the pageant figures themselves betray their dubious status.

But before we look at the way Shakespeare made holiday pastimes into comedy for the theater's everyday use, we must look at dramatic games and shows produced on holiday for holiday use.

[32] Nichols, I, 443.

Chapter 3

MISRULE AS COMEDY; COMEDY AS MISRULE

". . . is it fit infirmities of holy men should be acted upon a stage . . . ? . . . no passion wherewith the king was possessed, but is amplified, and openly sported with, and made a May game to all the beholders."

—Henry Crosse, *Virtues Common-wealth*, 1603[1]

DISTINCTIONS between life and art, the stage and the world, which are obvious for our epoch were not altogether settled for Elizabethans. Such distinctions are not settled for us either in areas where new circumstances are leading to the development of new artistic forms, notably in the case of television. This chapter will consider the tendency for Elizabethan comedy to *be* a saturnalia, rather than to *represent* saturnalian experience. Renaissance critics discussed this difference in distinguishing between Old Comedy and New and by regularly explaining how Old Comedy was banned for its scurrility in abusing actual individuals. We can make out, as they did not, rudimentary English versions of Old Comedy, produced on holiday where festive abuse turned into *ad hominem* satire, and in the newly established professional theater when players borrowed forms of festive abuse from holiday. In 1601, the "Summer Lord Game" of the village of South Kyme in Lincolnshire developed into such satire under the leadership of one Talboys Dymoke, the younger brother of Sir Edward Dymoke, whose house had a bitter and long standing antagonism to the Dymoke's uncle, the avaricious Earl of Lincoln. In dramatizing what he called "The Death of the Lord of Kyme" on the "Maypole green" before Sir Edward's house, Talboys Dymoke and his yeomen friends seem to have alluded to the Earl, and taken off his mannerisms, in a fashion which he regarded as lese majesty.

[1] Printed by Chambers, *Elizabethan Stage*, IV, 247.

Although we have no text of the performance, only descriptions of it in Star Chamber testimony, its similarity to *vetus comoedia* is clear. It was composed for performance with the license of a festival; it used traditional roles and stock scenes instead of a fully developed narrative plot; the zest of it came from abuse directed at an actual spoil-sport *alazon*. But of course, although the occasion and form were broadly Aristophanic, Dymoke's *art* was rudimentary. A direct development of comedy out of festivity, such as may have happened in Greece, was prevented in Elizabethan England by the existence of an already developed dramatic literature—and by the whole moral superstructure of Elizabethan society. When the issue was put to the test, license for festive abuse was never granted by Elizabethan officials. The performers of the South Kyme play learned this to their cost; so did the professional players when they tried to step into the Marprelate controversy. Yet the tendency which we shall be examining in this chapter has significance beyond its abortive fruits, because it witnesses to the saturnalian impulse which did find expression in dramatic fiction. Saturnalia could come into its own in the theater by virtue of the distinction between the stage and the world which Puritans were unwilling to make in London but which fortunately prevailed across the river on the Bankside.

License and Lese Majesty in Lincolnshire

When we write about holiday license as custom, our detached position is apt to result in a misleading impression that no tensions or chances are involved. For those participating, however, license is not simply a phase in a complacent evolution to foreknown conclusions: it means, at some level, disruption. When majesty in lords is dangerous to meddle with, to act "My Lord of Misrule" or be created one of his retainers says "We are as good as Lords" and at the same time, "Lords are no better than we." The man who acts as a mock lord enjoys building up his dignity, and also exploding it by exaggeration, while his followers both relish his bombast as a fleer at proper authority and also enjoy turning on him and insulting his majesty. Huff-snuff bombast asks for cat-calls. The instability of an interregnum is built into the dynamics of misrule: the game at once appropriates and annihilates the mana of authority. In the process, the fear which normally maintains inhibition is temporarily overcome, and the revellers become wanton, swept along on the freed energy normally occupied in holding themselves in check.

To reach this fear and so defy it with intoxicating impunity, misrule has to take a chance. Give it an inch and it must take an ell—or at least more than the allowed inch. One way to get beyond bounds was to move from flouting in general to flouting particular people, from *symbolic* action toward symbolic *action*, to use a distinction of Mr. Kenneth Burke's. This impulse is amusingly graphic in a satirical description, written by John Taylor the water-poet, of London apprentices rioting on Shrove Tuesday:

> Then Tim Tatters, a most valiant villain, with an ensign made of a piece of a baker's mawkin fixed upon a broom staff, he displays his dreadful colors, and calling the ragged regiment together, makes an illiterate oration, stuffed with most plentiful want of discretion, the conclusion whereof is, that somewhat they will do, but what they know not. Until at last comes marching up another troop of tatterdemalions, proclaiming wars against no matter who, so they may be doing. Then these youths . . . put play houses to the sack, and bawdy houses to the spoil, in the quarrel breaking a thousand quarrels (of glass I mean) . . . tumbling from the tops of lofty chimneys, terribly untilling houses, ripping up the bowels of feather beds.[2]

The custom of misrule obviously provided a whirligig that could catch up simmering antagonisms and swing them into the open. In the Dymoke case, it was the animus of a county family and their retainers against a tyrannical nobleman. The Earl of Lincoln's almost insane avarice and inhumanity were repeatedly a problem to the Privy Council and a plague to his neighborhood.

[2] *Jack a Lent His Beginning and Entertainment: With the mad prankes of his Gentleman-Usher Shrove-Tuesday that goes before him, and his Footman hunger attending*. By John Taylor (London, 1630), p. 12, in *The Old Book Collector's Miscellany*, ed. Charles Hindley (London, 1872), Vol. II. There seems to have been a positive tradition of sacking bawdy houses on Shrove Tuesday—a festive way to give them up for Lent! One is reminded of Doll Tearsheet's indignant scorn of Pistol (2 *H.IV* II.iv.155): "You a captain? You slave, for what? For tearing a poor whore's ruff in a bawdy house?" See *Brand's Popular Antiquities*, ed. J. O. Halliwell (London, 1848), I, 89-90.

The case will be worth following in the full human dimensions which have been skillfully presented through excerpts from the Star Chamber Records and the Duke of Northumberland's papers, in Mr. Norreys Jephson O'Conor's study of the Norreys family and their conflict with the Earl, *Godes Peace and the Queenes*.[3] Since the customs involved are clearly of long standing, the fact that the episode took place in 1601 does not diminish its significance in relation to festive comedy written in the previous decade.

The repugnance which the Earl of Lincoln could inspire can be suggested by the remarks of his son-in-law, Sir Arthur Georges, in a letter written to Sir Robert Cecil in 1600 when Lincoln was attempting to deprive his own daughter and Sir Arthur of an estate:

> None can testify my careful zeal towards this ungrateful miser (better) than you, whom I have so often solicited with excusing his vices. The love I bore his daughter made me do so, and his cankered disposition requites me accordingly. . . . He has already brought my poor wife to her grave, as I fear, with his late most odious and unnatural despites that he has used towards her, the most obedient child of the world. His wickedness, misery, craft, repugnance to all humanity, and perfidious mind is not among the heathens to be matched. God bless me from him. To have his lands after his death, I would not be tied to observe him in his life. (pp. 98-99)

The council repeatedly intervened in attempts to persuade the Earl to do justice to his wife, his children, old retainers, and neighbors; at one point he had to be put in the Tower to compel the payment of a judgment against him. Sir Edward Dymoke and his Lady lived near the Earl's castle at Tattershall in Lincoln. That there was very bad blood between them appears from the fact that in 1595 Sir Edward complained to Cecil that he had at one point been "forced by his Lordship's molestations to break up my house and disperse my servants." Sir Edward's younger brother Talboys, who lived in the Dymoke household, was just the sort

[3] Cambridge, 1934. I am grateful to Harvard University Press for permission to use the very substantial excerpts which follow. I have modernized the spelling and punctuation of Mr. O'Conor's quotations from the records. In the rest of this chapter, references to his text are given by page numbers in parentheses after quotations. My few interpolations, as well as Mr. O'Conor's, are enclosed in parentheses.

of free-wheeling wildhead to come into collision with the Earl. We catch a glimpse of him, through the Star Chamber testimony, stopping at the door of an alehouse kept by one William Hollingshead in Tattershall: "and at that time Anne (Hollingshead) brought forth drink to him and his company as they sat on horseback." "At which time with a loud voice," according to Hollingshead, he said "Commend me, sweetheart, to My Lord of Lincoln . . . and tell him that he is an ass and a fool. . . . Is he my uncle and hath no more wit?" Dymoke contended that he had spoken only "about a fortification which the Earl had made about his castle," saying only "What a foolish fortification is this! My Lord sayeth that I am a fool, but I would to God he had a little of my wit in the making of it, for this is the most foolish thing that ever I saw" (pp. 109-110). By either version, Dymoke was a man who called his soul his own, aptly named Talboys.

In the summer of 1601, Talboys' summer games gave the Earl a chance to attack the Dymoke family by a bill of complaint to the Star Chamber. The bill emphasized the offense of lese majesty done to the Earl:

> Whereas your Royal Majesty in the whole course of your happy and flourishing reign . . . have ever had a gracious regard of the honour and estate of the nobility and peers of this your highness' realm, and men of more inferior condition to them have carried such respective and due observance to the nobles of this kingdom, as they have not once presumed to scandalize or deprave their persons and place by public frowns and reproaches, yet how so it is . . . one Talboys Dymoke, a common contriver and publisher of infamous pamphlets and libels, Roger Bayard of Kyme, in your highness' county of Lincoln, yeoman, Marmaduke Dickinson, John Cradock, the elder, and John Cradock, the younger, of Kyme . . . yeomen, and other their accomplices, intending as much as in them consisted to scandalize and dishonour your . . . subject (i.e. Lincoln) and to bring him into the frown and contempt of the vulgar people of his country, have of late, and since your majesty's last free and general pardon, by the direction, consent, or allowance of Sir Edward Dymoke of Kyme, . . . Knight, contrived, published, used, and

> acted, these disgraceful, false, and intolerable slanders, reproaches, scandalous words, libels, and irreligious profanations ensuing. (pp. 108-109)

The principal basis for the charges lay in two episodes of the summer games. The Earl first ran foul of Talboys Dymoke in the course of Sunday misrule of the kind that Stubbes described. Mr. O'Conor has presented the encounter by quoting from testimony of both sides before the Star Chamber:

> The May day games at South Kyme, where some of the Dymoke family seem then to have been living, were carried on through most of the summer, and, on Sunday, July 25th or 26th, 1601, twelve or thirteen of those who had been taking part in the games went to the neighbouring village of Coningsby "to be merry . . . as Coningsby men had been with them a fortnight before." Among those who rode from South Kyme were: John Cradock, the younger; Richard Morrys, or Morris; Roger Bayard, and Talboys Dymoke; with John, or Henry, Cocke, of Swinstead; John Easton, of Billinghay; and John Patchett, "who were all present at Coningsby . . . and are retainers to Sir Edward Dymoke." Evidently they took with them a few of the theatrical properties used in the games, for "some of the company had reeds tied together like spears, with a painted paper off the tops of them, and one of them had a drum and another a flag." They "did march on horseback two and two together through the streets . . . to one Miles his house, who kept an alehouse" "and there lighting, set up their horses" and "dined."
>
> After dinner the company visited two or three other alehouses; Morris said he did not know how many, adding "he knoweth not certainly whether it were on the Sabbath day . . . but . . . he rather thinketh it was . . . because they were at Evening Prayer." There was indignant denial of their having declared that "they had drunk the town of Coningsby . . . dry"; however, in the afternoon they resumed their parade through the town. Besides the visitors' drum and flag, "Coningsby men had another drum and flag," so that they all must have been able to make a goodly amount of noise, which caused "a great

number of people" to come outdoors for the purpose of "looking upon the company."

While this display was taking place, and "at such time as they were marching homeward," "the Earl of Lincoln . . . had occasion of business to ride through a narrow lane" in Coningsby "through which he was to pass by or near the . . . company," who, according to Thomas Pigott, gentleman, one of his followers, "behaved themselves very rudely, with shoutings, noises . . . that some accompted them to be madmen." To these joyous villagers Pigott was sent "to entreat them to hold still their drums, flags and noise until the . . . Earl might quietly pass by them for scaring of his horse." John Cock, the drummer, said that he "did stay till the Earl was gone, and, after he was passed by, Mr. Talboys Dymoke and one Richard Hunt did call to him to strike up his drum." Edward Miles, the alehouse keeper, saw that "Mr. Pigott was cast down from his horse, but by what means he knoweth not, neither what hurt he had; but he did see him presently afoot again and come to his horse." With this statement the companions of Miles agreed, but Pigott himself declared that when he gave the Earl's message, "Talboys Dymoke, Richard Hunt, and some others . . . answered with great oaths that they had a Lord as good as he, and called the company and drums to them back again, and cried aloud, 'Strike up drums! Strike up drums!' " (pp. 110-112)

"They had a Lord as good as he" clearly refers to their Lord of Misrule. John Cradock, the younger, was "the Summer Lord of Kyme" (p. 117). He wore a piebald coat that went with the other insignia of misrule, for one of the Earl's retainers testified that he "did hear that there was very ill rule at Coningsby . . . and that young Cradock was there in a piebald coat, and that the (Earl) did there call . . . Cradock 'piebald knave' " (p. 116). Thus it appears that the real Lord was foolish enough to undertake to face down a mummery Lord. At any rate, the Earl's henchman Pigott tried to do so, and the fact that he was a "heavy, corpulent man" must have been more grist for the merrymakers' mill. Pigott testified that:

therewithal (Dymoke and Hunt) caused the drummers and

> flag bearers to run at (him) with their drums and flags, and the whole company after and amongst them in such violent sort, that his horse did fling and plunge, and the more he entreated them to be quiet, the more fierce and angry they were upon him and his horse, insomuch as his horse cast him . . . to the ground to his great bruising, hurt and damage, being a heavy corpulent man. And it had like to cost him his life; and he was forced to keep to his bed a good space after, and to take physic for the same . . . When he was helped up by one of his acquaintance that stood by . . . Hunt and some others cried "Strike him down! Knock him down!" (p. 112)

The antagonism which the revellers were expressing was active elsewhere at this same time on a practical plane. At near-by Horncastle, Sir Edward or his men made entry into the parsonage to claim "diverse duties" which according to the Earl belonged by right to him.

Then five weeks later, on the last Sunday in August, Talboys Dymoke "did frame and make a stage play to be played in for sport and merriment at the setting up of a Maypole in South Kyme" (p. 114). Neighbors were invited "to take part at some venison" at the house of John Cradock the elder, "yeoman, servant to" Sir Edward Dymoke, and in the afternoon they saw "an interlude" "hard by a Maypole standing upon the green."

> "Talboys Dymoke, being the then principal actor . . . , did first . . . counterfeit the person of (the Earl) and his speeches and gesture, and then and there termed and named . . . the Earl of Lincoln, his good uncle, in scornful manner, and as actor (he) then took upon him . . . representing (the Earl) fetched away by . . . Roger Bayard, who acted . . . the Devil. And . . . Roger Bayard in another part of the play did . . . represent . . . the part of the Fool, and the part of the Vice . . . and there acting the . . . part did declare his last will and testament and . . . did bequeath his wooden dagger to . . . the Earl of Lincoln, and his cockscomb and bauble unto all those that would not go to Horncastle with . . . Sir Edward Dymoke against him" . . . And in the interlude there was "a dirge sung by Talboys Dymoke . . . and other the . . . actors . . . wherein

> they expressed by name most of the known lewd and licentious women in the cities of London and Lincoln and town of Boston, concluding in their songs after every of their names, *ora pro nobis*." (p. 115)

The defense of the Dymoke party was that the play was traditional, a part of the games, with no allusions to the Earl. Dymoke "of himself termed (it) the Death of the Lord of Kyme, because the same day should make an end of the summer lord game in South Kyme for that year" (p. 114). Dickinson testified that about "a fortnight before the day" Talboys Dymoke left at his house "a certain writing in English, some part whereof was in verse or rhymes, which (Dickinson) doth not now perfectly remember, with request that (he) would learn the same without book." But Dymoke insisted that he and the others were simply playing customary roles, explaining the remark about "his good uncle" as a reference to the summer lord of the next village. The author of the play testified that he

> "did represent and take upon him the title and term of Lord Pleasure . . . and did call the Lord of North Kyme (being another summer lord that year) my Uncle Prince," and he did not do this "in scornful manner." . . . Roger Bayard as the Fool "Did bequeath his wooden dagger to the Lord of North Kyme because he had the day before called the Lord of South Kyme piebald knave." Dickinson declared that Bayard spoke "these words in rhyme: . . .
>
> That Lord shall it have
> Which called the Lord of Kyme piebald knave,
>
> whereunto . . . Talboys answered, that same was his good uncle."

According to their testimony, it was not Dymoke playing the Earl that the Devil carried off, but John Cradock, the younger "(being before the Summer Lord of Kyme) and acting that part in the play," was "feigned to be poisoned and so carried forth" (p. 117).

There is not evidence to determine how commonly this sort of Death of the Summer Lord served as the finale of the season's games. It must have been fairly common, or Dymoke's group could not have relied for their defense on the traditional character of such a play. But the only other case I have run onto is Nashe's far more sophisticated *Summer's Last Will and Testament*. Certainly the particular formulae which Dymoke combined were thoroughly traditional. The Vice or clown was still being carried off the London stage by the Devil in the period when Shakespeare's first plays were appearing; the burlesque testament was also a hardy perennial. The dirge was an equally popular form for satiric burlesque; in the South Kyme performance it was combined with listing actual people by their names in what was sometimes called a "ragman's roll" (with perhaps the implication that the "known lewd women" would be appropriate mourners for the Lord of Kyme, having been close to him during his life).[4] To conclude the career of a mummery lord by a death and dirge, was, moreover, an obvious move for people familiar with accounts of notable deaths in the literature of the *Ars Moriendi*. Winter reigns of Lords of Misrule might end with formal mourning: for example, the "Christmas Lord, or Prince of the Revels" whose rule after a lapse of thirty years was elaborately revived at St. John's, Oxford, in 1607, reigned through the winter until Shrove Tuesday, when "after a show called *Ira seu Tumulus Fortunae*, the Prince was conducted to his private chamber in mourning procession" and there expired.[5] Jack a Lent was another such figure liable to feel Fortune's Wrath. Henry Machyn noted in his diary how on the 17th of March, 1553, in a magnificent London procession which included giants great and small, hobby-horses, "my lo(rd) late being lord of misrule," and the Devil and the Sultan, there came a priest "shreeving Jack of Lent on horseback, and a doctor his physician, and then Jack of Lent's wife brought him his physician and bad save his life, and he should a thousand pounds for his labour. . . ."[6] This was in the brief heyday which the reign of Edward VI granted to old-fashioned pageantry in London; but

[4] Baskervill has a packed discussion of the ragman's roll in *Jig*, pp. 22-23: Udall used the term, which is associated with misrule, to translate *fescennina carmina* in the *Apophthegmes* of Erasmus; a fifteenth-century poem called Ragman Roll is "a series of satiric sketches of women which are represented as drawn by lot at the command of King Ragman Holly, obviously a Christmas festival leader presiding over the medieval game of fortune drawing."

[5] Chambers, *Mediaeval Stage*, I, 410. See the discussion of the death of Carnival, below, pp. 206 and 213.

[6] *The Diary of Henry Machyn*, ed. J. G. Nichols (London, 1948), p. 33.

what the city elaborated on a splendid scale then, were holiday games which continued to be customary in humbler places. Also during Edward's reign, Bishop Gardiner complained that satirists had attacked the discipline of Lent by publishing "Jack of Lent's Testament." Somerset reassured him that "Lent remaineth still . . . although some light and lewd men do bury him in writing."[7] As we shall see in the next section, a satirist also "buried in writing" the Puritan "Jack," Martin Marprelate.

It is unfortunate for us that Dickinson did not repeat more than a scrap of the verses Talboys wrote for him—though no doubt it was wise for Dickinson to forget them. We do get a little of the actual language of a mock funeral sermon which Talboys added to the program. It was "an old idle speech which was made two or three years before," which John Cradock's father, the bailiff, was persuaded to deliver on the spur of the moment, after the play was over. In the heavy language of the Earl's Bill of Complaint,

> John Cradock the elder . . . in frown of religion, and the profession thereof, being attired in a minister's gown and having a corner cap on his head, and a book in his hand opened, did . . . in a pulpit made for that purpose, deliver and utter a profane and irreligious prayer. . . . (p. 118)

The opening of the fustian prayer, which Cradock read out of a "paper book," went

> De profundis pro defunctis. Let us pray for our dear Lord that died this present day,
>
> Now blessed be his body and his bones;
> I hope his legs are hotter than gravestones,
> And to that hope let's all conclude it then,
> Both men and women pray, and say, 'Amen' . . . (p. 119)

Originally the sermon had been delivered "about Christmas," "in the presence of . . . Sir Edward and a number of gentlemen there assembled." This information was furnished by the testimony of a pious neighbor, Robert Hitchcock, who heard it from another neighbor, and who added, "all which manner of counterfeiting

[7] Baskervill, *Jig*, p. 47.

was by many godly ministers held to be very blasphemous" (p. 122). It seems likely that the sermon was originally spoken at the end of the rule of a Christmas prince. Another scrap of the sermon's language also suggests an indoor feast: "The mercy of Mustardseed and the blessing of Bullbeef and the peace of Potluck be with you all. Amen." (p. 120) In an age when everybody had to hear long sermons, the minister's hour-glass must often have been the focus of the congregation's attention; it is easy to see why a crowd would enjoy seeing Sir Edward's bailiff wearing "a counterfeit beard, and, standing in a pulpit fixed to the Maypole on Kyme green, having . . . a pot of ale or beer hanging by him instead of an hourglass, whereof he . . . did drink at the concluding of any point or part of his speech" (p. 120). The speech was organized like a proper sermon, but its divisions were filled with merry morals, tales and local folklore.

> the said person did read a text which he said was taken out of the Heteroclites . . . viz., "Cesar Dando sublevando, ignoscendo gloriam adeptus est, and did English it thus: Bayard's Leap of Ancaster hath the bownder stone in Bollingsbrookes farm. I say the more knaves the honester men." And the . . . parson then divided his text into three parts, viz., the first, a colladacion (collation?) of the ancient plane of Ancaster Heath; the second, an ancient story of Mab as an appendix, and the third, concluding knaves honest men by an ancient story of The Friar and The Boy. (p. 120)

Though it is not possible to get the comic point of all this, it is clear that a main part of the fun for the audience lay in encountering familiar and unpretentious lore in a form where normally the matter would be religious or moral and require constraint. Mr. O'Conor found accounts of Bayard's Leap which described it as a lonely house on an old Roman road, the haunt of a witch, and also the place where four holes in the ground were left by the hooves of the magic horse, Bayard, in taking a prodigious leap. Other testimony in the Star Chamber records makes it clear that the Heteroclites—a surprisingly sophisticated word for "deviations from the standards"—was by another name the Book of Mab. There is of course no need to assume an influence from *Romeo and Juliet* or *A Midsummer Night's Dream*; three witnesses take "the book of Mab" in stride, apparently using the phrase as a general name for the strange and fantastic among stories and beliefs. The ancient story of the Friar and the Boy, on the other hand, was a particular narrative and has survived. It is the sort of merry tale that fits the holiday mood of rebuking niggardliness and, broadly, the proposition that knaves are honest men. The Boy triumphs over his begrudging Stepmother and her ally the Friar, thanks to the magic of a kind stranger with whom he shares his food; by the magic, it happens that whenever the Stepmother glares at the Boy, she involuntarily and thunderously breaks wind; moreover, whenever the Boy plays on a magic pipe, everybody, however malicious, has to dance—the Stepmother, the Judge to whom she appeals, and the Friar, who dances himself into a thorn bush.[8]

Mr. O'Conor points out that one further offense charged by the Earl concerned the posting of a bill of defiance by Talboys Dymoke:

> "At the time that the May-game sports were used in South Kyme" he "did make and write a rhyme" which he "did fix and nail upon the Maypole." These lines, in the allegorical fashion typical of the age, referred to the fact that the Earl "had purchased a messuage, and certain lands, in Kyme . . . of one Ambrose Marshe, Sir Edward Dymoke, and Talboys Dymoke," signifying by the ban dog (a dog chained to guard a house, or else because of his ferocity) the Earl, who had for his crest a white greyhound. According to Talboys Dymoke, the bull was "the cognizance of the town of Kyme . . . And . . . the Lord of the . . . May game John Cradock, the younger, did subscribe to the . . . rhyme with these words, 'Lord Cradock.' " (p. 122)

The elder Cradock's testimony gave "the bull" a more particular meaning as "the only device" of Talboys Dymoke. So the lines which follow, though written presumably by Talboys Dymoke, are addressed, in the running fiction of the game, from the May-

[8] *The Frere and the Boye* ("printed at London in Fleet Street by Wynkyn de Worde, about the year 1512"), ed. Francis Jenkinson (Cambridge, Eng., 1907).

game Lord, Cradock, to his henchman or champion or champion-in-arms, Tom Bull Dymoke:

> The Bandog now, Tom Bull, comes to our town,
> And swears by Ambrose Marshe and much ado,
> To signorize, to seat, and sit him down:
> This marsh must marshall him and his whelps too.
> But let them heed Tom Bull, for, if they stir,
> I'll make it but a kennel for a cur. (p. 123)

Here, as elsewhere, the "summer lord game" permits Dymoke, clearly the moving spirit, to project his feelings towards the Earl into a dramatic fiction in which he and his feelings become only a part of the composition. The Earl's lawyers, concerned to demonstrate damage by individuals to an individual, insisted that the show was directed entirely at Lincoln. Actually, it is clear that the Earl was caught in a wheel of merriment which had been turning before he came along and which kept turning after he had been flung off. The fustian sermon had nothing to do with Lincoln; yet Talboys Dymoke came to Cradock's house after the play was over "and very much begged him to come unto the . . . green and there to deliver an old idle speech"—not to finish off the Earl, but to finish off the occasion, the whirling composition.

When in 1610 the Star Chamber handed down a judgment in Lincoln's favor, the consequences for the Dymoke family and their yeomen friends were drastic. Talboys himself had died by 1603, but the court provided that

> Roger Bayard, John Cradock, and Marmaduke Dickinson, being the chief actors, be committed to the Fleet, led through Westminster Hall with papers, and there to be set on the pillory, and afterwards to be whipped under the pillory; also to be set in the pillory at the assizes in Lincolnshire and acknowledge their offenses and ask God and the Earl forgiveness, and then to be whipped under the pillory, and to pay 300 pounds apiece fine, and be bound to good behavior before enlargement. That Sir Edward Dymoke, who was privy and consenting to the offenses . . . be committed to the Fleet during the King's pleasure and pay 1000 pounds fine. (p. 125)

The Dymoke party had pleaded that all was done "in a merriment at the time of the . . . May games" (p. 124). The humiliations and ruinous fines imposed show how little such a plea availed in the cold, sober, authoritarian atmosphere of the Council sitting as the Star Chamber. It may be, as Mr. O'Conor suggests, that the public tensions about religion which had developed in the interval between 1601 and 1610 worked to the detriment of the Dymokes; the court's judgment stressed the outrage done religion by Cradock's sermon.

But the same sort of discontinuity was present I think throughout the reign of Elizabeth, between what would be tolerated in the festive liberties of settled local groups who did not need to fear mirth, and what would be made of these same liberties if they came to be brought before the highly moral royal council or before a court. The official world, highly conscious of the disruptive potentialities of innovation, assumed that a constant vigilance was needed to cope with things done "in frown of religion" and in contempt of "respective and due observance of the nobles." Incongruities between the official and the informal are always present, of course; but they were made more marked in Elizabethan times by the difference between tradition-directed local communities, which could accommodate holiday licence, and the centers of change and growth, which were anxiously involved in innovating and resisting innovation. Early in Elizabeth's reign an episode is recorded which makes clear how, where innovation is a possibility, saturnalian inversion becomes suspect. In 1564, a group of ardently Protestant Cambridge men, disappointed in their hope of performing a piece before Elizabeth as part of the festivities of her Cambridge visit, followed her to Hinchinbrook, and secured her permission to present their satire after all:

> The actors came in dressed as some of the imprisoned Catholic Bishops. First came the Bishop of London (i.e. Bonner) carrying a lamb in his hands as if he were eating it as he walked along, and then others with different devices, one being in the figure of a dog with the Host in his mouth.[9]

Elizabeth was outraged by this burlesque of the Mass, and abruptly

[9] Baskervill, p. 51; see also Chambers, *Elizabethan Stage*, I, 128.

quitted the chamber, taking the torchbearers with her and leaving the would-be satirists in the dark. They had tried a kind of game which had been tolerated in feasts of fools before the status of the mass became an issue, in the days when a reduction of the ceremony to the physical could only be read as the expression of a saturnalian mood. But in 1564 their burlesque was a taking advantage of holiday to advocate doctrinal revision at issue in everyday controversy. Elizabeth had sanctioned for the first masque of her reign, on Twelfth Night, 1559, a masquerade of crows, asses, and wolves as cardinals, bishops, and abbots.[10] But 1559 was, within limits, a revolutionary moment, and saturnalia, within limits, could serve it. Thereafter, as Elizabeth's response at Hinchinbrook testifies, the precarious religious settlement made religion an area where the authorities were particularly vigilant to exclude temporary, festive revolutions for fear that they might lead on to permanent revolutionary consequences.

The May game of Martin Marprelate

It is beyond my scope here to try to do justice, even in summary, to the way the holiday games contributed to the popular comedy of jig, interlude, clown's recitation, and flyting. As Baskervill's work shows almost poignantly, the evidence of this sort of influence is extraordinarily widespread—and tantalizing cryptic. To look briefly at the use of May-game motifs in the Martin Marprelate controversy, however, can serve to provide a sort of spot sample of the relation of the stage to holiday at the formative period of the drama, the end of the decade of the 1580's. As Dover Wilson has remarked, the gifted Puritan satirist who masqueraded as Martin Marprelate used a humorous style which was "that of the stage monologue . . . , with asides to the audience and a variety of 'patter' in the form of puns, ejaculations and references to current events and persons of popular rumor."[11] Francis Bacon, writing in the year of the controversy, deplored "this immodest and deformed manner of writing lately entertained,

[10] *Elizabethan Stage*, I, 155.

[11] *The Cambridge History of English Literature*, ed. A. W. Ward and A. R. Waller (New York, 1933), III, 436.

whereby matters of religion are handled in the style of the stage."[12] Martin's huff-snuff tone was taken up by his opponents. Like much of the other satire of the period, the Martinist and anti-Martinist pamphlets show a curious mingling of buffoonery and invective, of relish for the opponent with scorn, which goes with the satirist's playing the fool to make a fool of his antagonist. The likeness of this tone to a Lord of Misrule's vaunting and abuse is suggested by several passages alluding to the games. Thus Pasquill of England swaggers on to a title page to challenge Martin Junior like one Summer Lord challenging another:

> A countercuff given to Martin Junior, by the venturous, hardy, and renowned Pasquill of England, Cavaliero. Not of old Martin's making, which newly knighted the Saints in Heaven with rise up Sir Peter and Sir Paul; but lately dubbed for his service at home in the defense of his country, and for the clean breaking of his staff upon Martin's face.[13]

The knighting of boon companions was a tavern game in which "Rise up, Sir Robert Tosspot" was a formula; here Martin is pictured as a Lord of Misrule who presumes to dub the very saints in heaven cavalieros in his retinue. Elsewhere Pasquill asks his friend Marforius to "set up . . . at London stone" a bill, called "Pasquill's Protestation," enlisting aid against Martin: "Let it be done solemnly with drum and trumpet, and look you advance my colors on the top of the steeple right over against it."[14] This is a procedure like Lord Cradock's defiant rhyme on the Maypole at South Kyme. Opponents are sometimes spoken of—or to—as though they were a Vice or clown, or other stock figure of the stage or the games:

> Now Tarleton's dead, the consort lacks a vice:
> For knave and fool thou may'st bear prick and price.[15]

[12] Chambers, *Elizabethan Stage*, IV, 229 and also I, 294.

[13] McKerrow, *Nashe*, I, 57.

[14] "The Returne of the Renowned Cavaliere Pasquil," in *The Complete Works of Thomas Nashe*, ed. Alexander B. Grosart (London, 1883-84), I, 135-136.

[15] Quoted by Chambers, *Elizabethan Stage*, IV, 229, from *A Whip for an Ape: Or Martin Displaied.* Chambers reprints many relevant excerpts in "Documents of Criticism," IV, 229-233; it was in reading this collection that I was first struck with the prominence of holiday motifs in the controversy.

The actors did in fact take the opportunity to put Martin on the stage, probably as the subject for jigs or other brief afterpieces.

> The anatomy lately taken of him, the blood and the humours that were taken from him, by lancing and worming him at London upon the common stage . . . are evident tokens that, being thorough soused with so many showers, he had no other refuge but to run into a hole and die as he lived, belching.[16]

This dramatization of Martin's illness was referred to also in another pamphlet, which observed that Martin "took it very grievously, to be made a May game upon the stage," specifying "The Theater."[17] A satirical excursion, called "A true report of the death and burial of Martin Marprelate," amounts to a description of a playlet in which Martin is put through stages included in Dymoke's "Death of the Lord of Kyme" and Nashe's *Summer's Last Will and Testament.* Martin grows sick, with allegorically appropriate ills; he gives repentant advice to his sons, in a burlesque in the manner of men dying in the *Ars Moriendi* literature; he makes his testament, including the bequest of "all his foolery" to the player Lanam; he dies, is allegorically anatomized, buried in a dunghill, and honoured with a collection of mock epitaphs and a jingling Latin dirge.[18]

The phrase "to make a May game" of somebody implies that one need only bring an antagonist into the field of force of May games to make him ridiculous. A pamphlet promises its readers a "new work" entitled *The May game of Martinism* and gives a preview which is worth quoting in full as an example of the practice of mocking individuals by identifying them with traditional holiday roles. Various prominent Puritans, along with Martin, are put in the game:

> Penry the Welshman is the forgallant of the Morris, with the treble bells, shot through the wit with a Woodcock's bill. I

[16] *Elizabethan Stage,* IV, 231, from *A Countercuffe given to Martin Junior: . . . by Pasquill of England,* in McKerrow, *Nashe,* I, 59.

[17] *Elizabethan Stage,* IV, 230, from *Martins Months Minde* in Grosart, *Nashe,* I, 175.

[18] In *Martins Months Minde* (1589), reprinted in Grosart, *Nashe,* I, 168-205. Bishop Bonner was satirized by a similar burlesque *Commemoration* described by Baskervill (*Jig,* p. 51) as "in the vein of burlesques designed for feasts of misrule."

would not for the fairest hornbeast in all his country, that the Church of England were a cup of Metheglin, and came in his way when he is over-heated! Every bishopric would prove but a draught, when the mazer is at his nose. Martin himself is the Maid Marian, trimly dressed up in a cast gown, and a kercher of Dame Lawson's, his face handsomely muffled with a diaper-napkin to cover his beard, and a great nosegay in his hand, of the principalest flowers I could gather out of all his works. Wiggenton dances round about him in a cotton coat, to court him with a leathern pudding and a wooden ladle. Pagit marshalleth the way, with a couple of great clubs, one in his foot, another in his head; and he cries to the people with a loud voice, "Beware of the man whom God hath marked." I cannot yet find any so fit to come lagging behind, with a budget on his neck, to gather the devotion of the lookers on, as the stock-keeper of the Bridewell-house of Canterbury; he must carry the purse, to defray their charges, and then he may be sure to serve himself.[19]

The vivid description of such business as the wooing of a bearded Maid Marian suggests how, quite apart from any ridicule of persons, the performers would farce their roles just for the fun of it. To make such farce into satire of a sort, or more properly, into festive abuse, Nashe or whoever wrote the pamphlet needed only to add proper names and a few scurrilous allusions like the reference to Pagit's club foot.

It is striking that the May game of Martin is promised as a show rather than a pamphlet, "very deftly set out, with pomps, pageants, motions, masks, scutchions, emblems, impresses, strange tricks, and devices, between the Ape and the Owl, the like was never yet seen in Paris Garden." Stage and holiday were thus close enough together to admit the envisaging of a show, fairly similar in character to the Morris dance and marching of a summer lord game, as an entertainment to rival those of the Bear Garden. Stage satire and holiday abuse are spoken of in one breath by Gabriel Harvey when, taking his cue from the notion of a May game of Martinism, he heaps scorn on the unworthiness of the spokesmen by whom the established church has answered Martin's attacks:

[19] *The Returne of the renouned Cavaliero Pasquil of England* (1589) in McKerrow, *Nashe*, I, 83. Also printed in *Elizabethan Stage*, IV, 231.

> Had I been Martin . . . it should have been one of my May-games, or August triumphs, to have driven Officials, Commissaries, Archdeacons, Deans, Chancellors, Suffragans, Bishops and Archbishops (so Martin would have flourished at the least) to entertain such an odd, light-headed fellow for their defense: a professed jester, a Hickscorner, a scoff-master, a playmonger, an interluder. . . .[20]

Here Martin is set up explicitly as a summer lord; he defies his enemies with a "flourish"; reference to his "August triumphs" suggests Talboys' sort of Sunday marching. Harvey is saying that the bishops have descended to Martin's level, but, significantly, he doesn't put it that way; instead he says that they have entered Martin's May game. They do so by having recourse to a May-game sort of fellow, a professed jester, a scoffmaster, a playmonger. Foolery and comedy are equivalent: "I am threatened with a bauble, and Martin menaced with a comedy," Harvey writes, and goes on to describe ironically a reign of terror by those "that have the stage a commandment, and can furnish-out Vices, and Devils at their pleasure."[21]

The stage satire of Martin is referred to as *Vetus Comoedia* in the same Pasquill pamphlet which describes the May game of Martinism:

> Methought *Vetus Comoedia* began to prick him at London in the right vein, when she brought forth Divinity with a scratched face, holding her heart as if she were sick, because Martin would have forced her, but missing of his purpose, he left the print of his nails upon her cheeks, and poisoned her with a vomit which he ministered unto her, to make her cast up her dignities and promotions. . . .[22]

Vetus Comoedia certainly was an apt term for the theater's way of making a May game of Martin. Such a rough and ready symbolic figure as Divinity is comparable to, say, Aristophanes' Peace; while Martin, when he played opposite to Divinity and tried to force her, must have been a manic sort of clown similar to, say, the

[20] *Elizabethan Stage*, IV, 232, from G. Harvey, *An Advertisement for Papp-Hatchett.*

[21] *Elizabethan Stage*, IV, 233.

[22] *Elizabethan Stage*, IV, 232.

Sausage Seller in the *Knights*. Aristophanes' use of traditional formulae or scenarios, such as the *alazons'* interrupting the feast and being thrown out by the *eiron* hero, is similar to the use of the device of carrying Martin off on the Devil's back. To enact physically a phrase normally used figuratively, like "cast up" dignities, is thoroughly Aristophanic, as is also the connecting of several such fancies into an allegorical plot which is grossly physical in execution. A connection of the Old Comedy sort of mockery with country merriments is suggested near the end of the Anti-Martinist dialogue, when Pasquill asks "But who cometh yonder, Maforius, can you tell me?" and Marforius sees *Vetus Comoedia* coming with a garland, apparently dancing:

> MARFORIUS. By her gait and her garland I know her well, it is *Vetus Comoedia*. She hath been so long in the country, that she is somewhat altered. This is she that called in a council of physicians about Martin, and found by the sharpness of his humour, when they had opened the vein that feeds his head, that he would spit out his lungs within one year. . . .
> PASQUILL. I have a tale to tell her in her ear, of the sly practice that was used in restraining of her.[23]

The remark that "she hath been so long in the country" seems to imply that the sort of drastic *ad hominem* ridicule practiced on Martin had come to be confined to the frank country world, the world of Talboys Dymoke. After a summer of manhandling Martin, the players had been brought up short by the authorities, as Pasquill was going "to tell her in her ear." Lyly in a pamphlet complained that if "these comedies might be allowed to be played that are penned, . . . (Martin) would be deciphered."[24] But instead of welcoming the players' help against the government's Puritan opponent, the Master of the Revels arranged for Burghley to permit the stage's enemy, the Lord Mayor, to prohibit all theatrical exhibitions. And shortly afterwards the Privy Council directed that the Archbishop of Canterbury and the Lord Mayor appoint representatives to work with the Master of the Revels in passing on the books of plays and striking out or correcting "such parts or matters as they shall find unfit and undecent to be handled

[23] *Ibid.*

[24] *Ibid.*

in plays, both for Divinity and State."[25] Here again the Aristophanic impulse, when directly expressed, ran head on into official prohibition. To find expression, saturnalia had to shift from symbolic *action* towards *symbolic* action, from abuse directed from the stage at the world to abuse directed by one stage figure at another.

[25] *Elizabethan Stage*, I, 295. Chambers handles the dramatic part of the Marprelate controversy as an episode in "The Struggles of Court and City." McKerrow's account is in his *Nashe*, IV, 44. Baskervill relates the pamphleteers' descriptions of stage satires to other similar shows in *Jig*, pp. 50-55.

Chapter 4

PROTOTYPES OF FESTIVE COMEDY IN A PAGEANT ENTERTAINMENT: *SUMMER'S LAST WILL AND TESTAMENT*

"Nay, 'tis no play neither, but a show."

"What can be made of Summer's last will and testament?"

NASHE'S *Summer's Last Will and Testament* is worth dwelling on both for what it is and what it is not. " 'Tis no play neither, but a show," says the prologue. Written two or three years before *A Midsummer Night's Dream*, it presents a variety of roles, gestures, and ways of talking which were current in pageantry and game, precisely the traditional materials which Shakespeare used in developing festive comedy. Nashe's piece, because it is a pageant, is not completely detachable from the occasion of its production. Read for a play, it often seems jerky and sprawling, without a controlling movement. It lacks the control provided by plot, by events inside the fiction, because the event it was designed to express was the occasion of its performance. The looseness, to be sure, is partly Nashe's slapdash workmanship; his hasty genius is responsive rather than masterful. But he often shows imaginative power of a very high order indeed. I have let myself quote more extensively than is strictly necessary to establish points about the festive tradition, because his piece is often such good fun, or again, such good poetry, and it is so little read. The high quality of moments in the pageant is, indeed, a persuasive kind of evidence as to the vitality of holiday. Nashe works catch-as-catch-can, and his production shows how much there was to catch that would fit into festive comedy.

As a pageant, produced in 1592 or 1593 for Archbishop Whitgift's household, it expressed for the group the ending of summer at Croydon. An epidemic of plague in London was keeping the Archbishop and his retinue at his country place into the fall.[1] The mocking Induction summarizes the plan of the piece in relation to these circumstances:

> What can be made of Summer's last will and testament? . . . Forsooth, because the plague reigns in most places in this later end of summer, Summer must come in sick; he must call his officers to account, yield his throne to Autumn, make Winter his executor, with tittle tattle Tom boy. (77-85)

The tone implies that the scheme is familiar. Although the piece is not, like Dymoke's, an integral part of a running local fiction, and although it is not so limited as Dymoke's to traditional materials, Nashe builds his pageantry on the basic game of a festive lord and revellers who are his officers and retinue. The satiric device of making a will, which gives the piece its name, amounts only to one speech at the close. The main business is the calling of his officers to account. By this fiction, Nashe brings on stage successively the holiday groups and pageant figures who in the typical progress entertainment for Elizabeth would appear piecemeal, some coming under her majesty's window, others encountering her in the garden, others emerging from the woods. Summer's officers fall roughly into two groups. The most vital are spokesmen for everybody's pastimes: Ver, Harvest, Bacchus. These are accompanied by large trains of followers who dance and sing in the traditional ways. The leaders, acting as apologists for festivity, speak a prose at once fanciful and colloquial, and often behave like the broad comedy figures of the early popular theater. The other group is conceived in the manner of more literary pageantry: Vertumnus, a hermit with a device of hour-glasses expressing moderation; Sol, who is accused of causing a recent drouth by his heat: "Is it pride that is shadowed under this two-legg'd Sun . . .?" (619); "Orion like a hunter, with a horn about his neck, all his men after the same sort, hallowing and blowing their horns" (634). These speak verse,

[1] McKerrow, *Nashe*, IV, 416-418; and B. Nicholson's discussion in Grosart's *Nashe*, VI, xxviii-xxx. References by line numbers to *Summer's Last Will and Testament* in the rest of this chapter refer to McKerrow's edition.

often with a high-riding abusive recklessness. Towards the close of the pageant, by way of variation, the holiday spirit is expressed indirectly, in the comic churlishness of two kill-joy figures, one, "Backwinter," a type of envy, the other a miserly Christmas too stingy to keep the Twelve Days. The rightness of holiday is confirmed in rebuking Christmas:

> I tell thee plain, thou art a snudge, . . .
> It is the honor of nobility
> To keep high days, and solemn festivals.
> (1722-26)

As Summer brings each gay officer to an accounting, seconded by his heirs, Autumn and Winter, the limitations of festive pleasures are brought out by asking the hard question with which Summer's part opens:

> What pleasure always lasts? No joy endures:
> Summer I was, I am not as I was;
> Harvest and age have whitened my green head . . .
> (123-125)

The holiday heroes are floutingly unrepentant. All except Harvest are found wanting and condemned to suffer pains appropriate to their particular kind of excess. The pageant is thus made up of a series of trials of pleasures, reminiscent of mediaeval *debats* and of the encounters between gay vices and sober virtues in the morality plays, but here primarily shaped by a holiday-everyday opposition. It is a kind of serio-comic *Everyman*. Just as *Everyman* begins with the summons from God, so Nashe's pageant begins with a song announcing Summer's approaching death, sung by wood-nymphs and satyrs as Summer enters leaning on Autumn and Winter:

> Fair Summer droops, droop men and beasts therefore;
> So fair a summer look for never more.
> All good things vanish, less than in a day,
> Peace, plenty, pleasure, suddenly decay.
> Go not yet away, bright soul of the sad year;
> The earth is hell when thou leav'st to appear.
> (105-110)

Although most of the pageant is spent in exhibiting pleasures and wittily apologizing for them, we are brought back again and again to the serious view so beautifully and forthrightly stated here. *Ubi Sunt* pathos goes with the late moment in the year at which the pageant was presented, and reflects the darkening prospect of plague and winter towards which the year was turning. One cannot settle whether the piece is "serious" or "comic," because as a pageant, it expresses both aspects of the year's turning as an event happening to its audience. This poised two-sidedness is apparent even in the complaints about perishing: for a small example, Summer's line, "Harvest and age have whitened my green head," links age's sad white hair with the paling out of grain as it ripens, so that death is connected to the consummation of harvest. The playfulness of the wit with which grain is made hair implicitly recognizes that men are more durable than one season's wheaten crown—though they have their season, too. In this two-sidedness Nashe's piece anticipates Shakespeare's way of simultaneously exhibiting revel and framing it with other sorts of experience. But in Nashe merriment is not enfranchised as fully as it is in Shakespeare's gay comedies; Nashe keeps turning on mirth with a jarring abruptness, and his laments for mirth's passing are more convincing than any of his fun. He has far less faith in nature than the young Shakespeare of the festive comedies, even though in this pageant he undertook to celebrate nature's wantonness.

Presenting the Mirth of the Occasion

The fact that, as a pageant, *Summer's Last Will and Testament* served to express the occasion of its performance accounts for the importance of the Presenter or Chorus. The role is fancifully assigned to the Ghost of Will Summers, Henry VIII's famous fool, whose name was a by-word for jesters. There is nothing peculiar to Will Summers in the part; perhaps merely the handy pun suggested the name to Nashe—that is the way he worked. But the figure of the fool is wholly appropriate at once to abet and to qualify the mirth of a holiday show. Will Summers provides an "impromptu" introduction, abuses the author in reading his prologue, and remains "as a Chorus" to "flout the actors and him at the end of every scene" (91). The long and exacting part was played by a professional actor, apparently of some small reputation; his proper name, Toy, is alluded to several times.[2] As a Master of Ceremonies who keeps addressing the audience directly, describing where they are and commenting on what they watch, he mediates between fact and fiction and relates one to the other. Thus, at his first entrance his role serves to express the show as a flurry of excitement in the housekeeping of the Archbishop's official family; he talks about his costume just delivered from the laundry, pretends not to have seen "My Lord" (the Archbishop) on his first coming in, proposes borrowing the chain and fiddle of his "cousin Ned," apparently an idiot or natural fool belonging to the establishment:

Enter Will Summer in his fool's coat but half on, coming out.

Will Summer. Noctem peccatis, et fraudibus obi ice nubem. There is no such fine time to play the knave in as the night.[3] I am a goose, or a ghost at least; for what with turmoil of getting my fool's apparel, and care of being perfect, I am sure I have not yet supp'd tonight. Will Summers' ghost I should be, come to present you with Summer's last will and testament. Be it so, if my cousin Ned will lend me his chain and his fiddle. Other stately-packed Prologues use to attire themselves within; I, that have a toy in my head more than ordinary . . . will here dress me without. Dick Huntley cries, "Begin, begin!" and all the whole house, "For shame, come away!" when I had my things but now brought me out of the laundry. God forgive me, I did not see my Lord before. I'll set a good face on it, as though what I had talked idly all this while were my part.

So it is, *boni viri*, that one fool presents another; and I, a fool

[2] See McKerrow's note on line 1068 in his *Nashe*, IV, 435.

[3] Providing English equivalents for Latin tags is a game Nashe plays in such a way as to amuse those who understood Latin, while providing a crutch for those who might not care to admit their ignorance. Here his equivalent for Horace's "Cast night over your sins and a cloud over your deceits" is "There is no such fine time to play the knave in as the night." Usually his renderings, though downright enough to be funny, are fairly close. Only rarely does he quote Latin without providing some equivalent—as he does at the conclusion of Will Summer's speech on tavern tell-tales, quoted below, p. 64, where he adapts Ovid's "She has not sinned who can deny she has sinned": "*Non pecasse quicunq; potest peccasse negare.*"

> by nature, and by art, do speak to you in the person of the idiot, our playmaker. He, like a fop and an ass, must be making himself a public laughing stock . . . I'll show you what a scurvy prologue he hath made me, in an old vein of similitudes. . . .
>
> (2-27)

In the running commentary which Will keeps up, he is sometimes carried away by the festivities presented, more often he is wryly ironical about them. For example, in watching Ver's morris-dancers, he affects to be caught up like somebody following the dancers along the highwayside, then turns to rallying them:

> Now for the credit of Worcestershire! The finest set of morris dancers that is between this and Stretham: marry, methinks there is one of them danseth like a clothier's horse with a wool-pack on his back. You, friend with the Hobbyhorse, go not too fast, for fear of wearing out My Lord's tilestones with your hobnails.
>
> (201-206)

Nashe overdoes the precaution of forestalling jeering responses in the audience by having Will flout the pageant. But the fool's commentary contributes to our awareness of what the pageant is expressing by describing, in a down-to-earth fashion, the way holiday pleasures can appear without the aura of wit and imagination with which they are invested on the pageant's stage. He provides such perspective, for example, when Bacchus draws him into his drinking bout by compelling the fool to drink and be dubbed knight—to the tune of the Monsieur Mingo song from which Silence sings snatches in *Henry IV*:

> *Bacchus.* This Pupillonian in the fool's coat shall have a cast of martins and a whif. To the health of Captain Rinocerotry; look to it, let him have weight and measure.
>
> *Will Summer.* What an ass is this! I cannot drink so much, though I should burst.
>
> *Bacchus.* Fool, do not refuse your moist sustenance; come, come, dog's head in the pot, do what you are borne to.
>
> *Will Summer.* If you will needs make me a drunkard against my will, so it is; I'll try what burden my belly is of.

Bacchus. Crouch, crouch on your knees, fool, when you pledge god Bacchus.

Here Will Summer drinks, and they sing about him. Bacchus begins.

All. Monsieur Mingo for quaffing did surpass,
In cup, in can, or glass.

Bacchus. Ho, well shot, a toucher, a toucher; for quaffing Toy doth pass, in cup, in can, or glass.

All. God Bacchus do him right,
And dub him Knight.

Here he dubs Will Summer with the black Jack.

Bacchus. Rise up, Sir Robert Tosspot.[4]

(1051-72)

After God Bacchus has been duly rebuked and sent packing by Summer, Will's comment exclaims on the stupidity of tavern drinking bouts, then turns about once more to acknowledge that after all he himself is not above such folly, with a glancing suggestion that the good fellows of the audience are not above it either:

Will Summer. Of all gods, this Bacchus is the ill-favoured'st mis-shapen god that ever I saw. A pox on him, he hath christened me with a new nickname of Sir Robert Tosspot, that will not part from me this twelve-month. Ned Fool's clothes are so perfumed with the beer he poured on me, that there shall not be a Dutchman within 20 miles, but he'll smell out and claim kindred of him. What a beastly thing is it, to bottle up ale in a man's belly, when a man must set his guts on a gallon-pot last, only to purchase the alehouse title of a *boon companion*? "Carouse, pledge me and you dare!" "S'wounds, I'll drink with thee for all that ever thou art worth." It is even as two men should strive who should run furthest into the sea for a wager. . . . I am a sinner as others: I must not say much of this argument. . . . My masters, you that be good fellows, get you into corners and soup off your provender closely; report hath a blister on her tongue; open taverns are tell tales. *Non peccat quicunq; potest peccasse negare.*

(1116-41)

[4] For a comparable game in real life, see Chambers, *Mediaeval Stage*, I, 407. George Ferrers, as Edward VI's Lord of Misrule, knighted the Lord Mayor's Lord of Misrule in the course of a mock-royal procession in 1552.

This sort of irony depends on being able to move easily from inside folly to a vantage outside it. Will Summer's role in relation to the pageant proper is remarkably similar to Touchstone's in relation to the Forest of Arden: Shakespeare's jester also looks with a lack-luster eye at festive enthusiasm—and yet dryly acknowledges his own share in folly. Although Touchstone's range is far greater, and he is officially inside the fiction while Will Summer is officially outside it, Nashe's use of the court fool for ironic mockery and burlesque is the most striking anticipation I have encountered of what Shakespeare did with the type.

A festive solidarity across class differences comes through strongly in the singing of the groups in Nashe's pageant. The performers were probably local people, neighbors and tenants contributing in a customary way to the pastimes of the occasion.[5] After the last song and dance group, "wood nymphs and satyrs," have left the stage, Will Fool asks the "graver sort": "do you think these youths worthy a *plaudite* for praying for the Queen, and singing of the litany? they are poor fellows I must needs say, and have bestowed much labour in sowing leaves, and grass, and straw, and moss upon cast[-off] suits. . . . send them to the tavern with merry hearts" (1886-94). The opening spring episode requires three such groups in succession, a rapid, crowded, gay exhibition. After the first group sing "Spring, the sweet spring, is the year's pleasant king," Will Fool places their song as the sort of thing a holiday troop might

[5] B. Nicholson, in Grosart's *Nashe*, VI, pp. xxx-xxxiii, argues that the performers were some children's company. But the remarks he instances from the pageant, with the one exception of the epilogue, refer rather to youths than to boys whose voices have not changed. And McKerrow plausibly objects that, at a time when, as the pageant repeatedly tells us, the plague was raging, the Archbishop would not have risked entertaining a company of actors from London. McKerrow's conclusion is that "Probably Toy himself was a professional, . . . but it seems to me possible that most of the others were servants of the household" (IV, 419). This does not answer the difficulty, raised by Nicholson, that servants of the household would not be going off to the tavern. But if we assume that the speaking parts were played by members of the household, while those who merely danced and sang were "simple neighbors," this difficulty disappears. Being local people, of course they would go to the tavern, even if first to My Lord's buttery. And local people would bring no London contagion. In commenting on the performance of the revellers, Will Fool repeatedly refers to them as though they were real country folk. The fact that the pageant is a gathering up of items traditional in housekeeping high days makes this hypothesis very natural. Another argument is that the number of supernumeraries required seems unreasonable if all had to travel to Croydon.

use: "this is a pretty thing, if it be but to go a-begging with" (175). The song seems likely to have been written by Nashe; it is a little too detached and descriptive to be an actual game song. But like so many of Shakespeare's adaptations, it implies the dramatic situation of a group going on holiday. So, less richly, does "From the town to the grove," sung a little later by "three clowns and three maids, . . . dancing" (211). The Hobbyhorse and Morris are pastimes brought bodily on stage. And when Harvest and his reapers come on singing of the work they have done, their song is traditional:

Merry, merry, merry, cherry, cherry, cherry,
  Troll the black bowl to me;
  Hey derry, derry, with a poupe and a lerry,
  I'll troll it again to thee.

Hooky, hooky, we have shorn,
  And we have bound,
And we have brought Harvest
  Home to town.
(804-811)

A class difference is assumed between the merrymakers and Summer, Autumn, and Winter, who are like gentry being visited by simple folk in their "guising" (Harvest's men, indeed, call for a largesse). But custom and a common dependence on the seasons, accepted by all without ignoring differences, bring all together. Autumn calls Harvest a "country button'd cap" and rebukes him with: "Thou, Coridon, why answer'st not direct?" (821). But Harvest has the self-respect of a merry bailiff, as well as the licence of "Hooky, hooky," and takes his time before he will answer the gentry's eager question about his crops. Summer acknowledges his right to such behavior: "Plough-swains are blunt, and will taunt bitterly" (919). Even in Will Fool's deliberately flouting commentary on Harvest, there is a backhanded respect:

> Well, go thy ways, thou bundle of straw; I'll give thee this gift, thou shalt be a clown while thou livest. As lusty as they are, they run on the score with George's wife for their posset, and God knows who shall pay goodman Yeomans for his wheat sheaf: they may sing well enough, "Troll the black bowl to

> me, Troll the black bowl to me": for a hundred to one but they will be all drunk, e'er they go to bed: yet, of a slavering fool, that hath no conceit in anything but in carrying a wand in his hand with commendation when he runneth by the highway side, this stripling Harvest hath done reasonably well. O, that somebody had had the wit to set his thatched suit on fire, and so lighted him out. . . .
>
> (941-952)

The joke on two senses of "a clown while thou livest" is the same which Shakespeare uses when Touchstone patronizingly summons Corin as a country fellow, calling arrogantly "Holla, you clown!" —and Rosalind rebukes him with "Peace, fool, he's not thy kinsman" (*A.Y.L.* II.iv.66-67). Here too the jibe cuts both ways, for Will's superior tone is undercut by the fool's coat he is wearing. His mockery of the simple peasant who can express himself only by running with a wand conveys a superiority to the mere folk game, to Sly's sort of inarticulate "gambold." But such antics are in order in their way: "this stripling Harvest hath done reasonably well."

Praise of Folly: Bacchus and Falstaff

To express in talk what the groups present in song and dance, Nashe writes out quite elaborate parts for their leaders. Each praises folly, his own special sort of folly, with the fustian eloquence and equivocation which was customary in maintaining misrule. Nashe is working the same vein as that from which Erasmus produced his *Praise of Folly*; indeed Nashe mentions Erasmus' work, incidentally, in a mock-oration of his own, though there is no reason to regard Erasmus as a source, since the social tradition is common to both writers. It was a tradition with a large dramatic potential, because the statements made in praising folly pointed implicitly to an ironic change back from holiday to everyday. In other words, the praise of folly implied a sort of plot of the grasshopper-ant sort.

This dramatic potential appears clearly in Nashe's handling of Ver, the leader of the spring revels: he is a Prodigal Son flouting his reverend, prudent father:

> *Summer.* Presumptuous Ver, uncivil nurtured boy,
> Think'st I will be derided thus of thee?
> Is this th'account and reckoning that thou mak'st?
>
> *Ver.* Troth, my Lord, to tell you plain, I can give you no other account: *nam quae habui, perdidi*; what I had, I have spent on good fellows. . . . This world is transitory; it was made of nothing, and it must to nothing: wherefore, if we will do the will of our high Creator (whose will it is, that it pass to nothing), we must help to consume it to nothing.
>
> (222-227; 256-259)

In such exchanges, to paraphrase La Rochefoucauld, equivocation is the tribute that Vice pays to Virtue. Ver's equivocating praise of prodigality, a "beggarly oration in the praise of beggary" (347) as Will calls it, is a formal exercise in turning the wrong side out, after the fashion of Craddock's fustian sermon (Will, indeed, says "I thought I had been at a sermon"). Summer exclaims on "wit ill spent!" and sends Ver to meet the prodigal's familiar fate: "lead him the next way to woe and want" (333). A little later Will asks (without avail) that Ver come back, describing him as he would appear at a later stage in the action of plays about a Prodigal Son:

> Actors . . . let the prodigal child come out in his doublet and hose all greasy, his shirt hanging forth, and ne'er a penny in his purse, and talk what a fine thing it is to walk summerly, or sit whistling under a hedge and keep hogs.
>
> (433-439)

This comment shows how conscious Nashe was of the relation between his pageant version of the Spring Lord and the prodigal plots of popular comedy.

Nashe's handling of Bacchus illustrates the pervasive Elizabethan tendency to organize wit around a festival Lord, and so presents a striking prototype of Shakespeare's Falstaff, whether or not there is any direct influence. The stuff of Bacchus' part is the lingo of tavern companions who challenge each other by a chivalric cant:

> What, give me the disgrace? Go to, I say, I am no Pope, to pardon any man. *Ran, ran, tarra*, cold beer makes good blood.

> St. George for England: somewhat is better than nothing. Let me see, hast thou done me justice? Why, so: thou art a king. . . .
> (1042-46)

By re-christening the action of drinking in mock-heroic and mock-moral terms, Bacchus' high words for low matter elude the implications of the downright names for drunkenness, endowing it with decorum; at the same time, serious decorum is mocked by alluding to it verbally even when flouting it in action.

> *Vinum quasi venenum*, wine is poison to a sick body; a sick body is no sound body; Ergo, wine is a pure thing, and is poison to all corruption.
> (1007-09)

Falstaff repeatedly plays the same game, of course with much more deftness. "I see a good amendment of life in thee—from praying to purse-taking."—"Why, Hal, 'tis my vocation, Hal. 'Tis no sin for a man to labour in his vocation" (*1 H.IV* I.ii.114). In one way he is covering up, by using the moral maxim; at the same time he is flouting morality. Earlier he goes out of his way to get Hal to pronounce another proverb which condemns him:

> An old lord of the Council rated me the other day in the street about you, sir, but I mark'd him not; and yet he talk'd very wisely, but I regarded him not; and yet he talk'd wisely, and in the street too.
> (*1 H.IV* I.ii.93-98)

After being so elaborately cued, the prince obliges by recalling the Biblical phrases:

> Thou didst well; for wisdom cries out in the streets, and no man regards it.
> (*1 H.IV* I.ii.99-100)

Hal displaces the emphasis so that a proverb describing the evil of disregarding wisdom can be taken as a direction to disregard wisdom. To enjoy disrespect for wisdom, it is essential that wisdom be present—in equivocating dialogue, "wisdom" is made present by alluding to the sort of statement to which misrule is a counter-statement. Falstaff gives a name to the process when he exclaims with mock-solemnity "O, thou hast damnable iteration."

Wit takes us along with it by preserving a factitious continuity to cover a displacement of the normal emphasis. Although this "wit mechanism," as Freud called it, is most apparent in wordplay, continuities of gesture and manner can likewise serve as a surface to dazzle the critical faculty so that a saturnalian tendency can elude inhibition. To set up the dramatic fiction of a festival Lord, a figure of decorum who is patron of indecorum, makes it possible to *act* as well as talk wittily. As Freud points out, even an isolated verbal witticism of the tendentious sort involves, in the telling, a rudimentary dramatic situation: the teller inveigles his audience into an attitude of licence towards the moral world, which is put outside the circle where they set their heads together.[6] With a Lord of Misrule, the expression of the Lord's dignity and authority develops this situation. So with Bacchus' learned manner in such praise of folly as the following:

> *Summer*. What, Bacchus? still *animus in patinis*, no mind but on the pot?
>
> *Bacchus*. Why, Summer, Summer, how wouldst do, but for rain? What is a fair house without water coming to it? Let me see how a smith can work, if he have not his trough standing by him. What sets an edge on a knife? the grindstone alone? no, the moist element poured upon it, which grinds out all gaps, sets a point upon it, and scours it as bright as the firmament. So, I tell thee, give a soldier wine before he goes to battle, it grinds out all gaps, it makes him forget all scars and wounds, and fight in the thickest of his enemies, as though he were but at foils amongst his fellows. Give a scholar wine, going to his book, or being about to invent, it sets a new point on his wit, it glazeth it, it scours it, it gives him *acumen*. . . . Aristotle saith, *Nulla est magna scientia absque mixtura dementiae*. There is no excellent knowledge without mixture of madness. And what makes a man more mad in the head than wine?
>
> (976-995)

The wit depends in part on deft displacement of the tenor of the discourse behind an apparent, verbal continuity: for example, in Bacchus' unacknowledged shift from liquor to "rain" as though the

[6] Sigmund Freud, *Wit and Its Relation to the Unconscious*, trans. A. A. Brill (New York, 1916), Chap. v, "The Motives of Wit and Wit as a Social Process."

two were the same thing, "the moist element." But the wit consists equally in the tone, the dramatic stance implicit in Bacchus' confident, sweeping manner. He behaves like a triumphant doctor of what he calls "so worshipful an art."

Falstaff, when he describes the twofold operation of a good sherris sack, says the same sort of thing as Bacchus about wine's contribution to valour and wit, with the same sort of burlesque parade of logic and authority (*2 H.IV* IV.iii.92). Falstaff talks of "his first humane principle"; Bacchus quotes Aristotle. The conceits of both are elaborated with consciously specious plausibility, and with obvious mock-heroic touches at the climaxes: Nashe's soldier fights "as though he were but at foils amongst his fellows" in the tavern; Falstaff's microcosm is marshalled by a red nose, "which, as a beacon, gives warning to all the rest of this little kingdom, man, to arm." The large suggestion of fertility in "How would'st do but for rain?" is paralleled by Falstaff's remark about Hal's use of "fertile sherris" to manure and husband "the cold blood he did naturally inherit of his father." In response to Prince John's rebuke, Falstaff talks scornfully of "these demure boys" that never "come to any proof; for thin drink doth so over-cool their blood, and making many fish meals, that they fall into a kind of male greensickness." Bacchus makes similar points in answer to Summer's final condemnation: "I beseech the gods of good fellowship, thou may'st fall into a consumption with drinking small beer. Every day may'st thou eat fish" (1094).

Part of Bacchus' dignity on the stage clearly came from his girth. He is described as "god Bacchus, god fatback . . . god barrell-belly," and dismounts from his ass with difficulty. When he asks rhetorically: "What is flesh and blood without his liquor?" even Autumn cannot resist a little good-humored raillery:

> Thou want'st no liquor, nor no flesh and blood.
> I pray thee may I ask without offence,
> How many tuns of wine hast in thy paunch?
> Methinks that [paunch], built like a round church,
> Should yet have some of Julius Caesar's wine.
>
> (1028-32)

This is the same tone that smaller people adopt towards Falstaff, at once mocking and admiring. "There's a whole merchant's venture of Bordeaux stuff in him," and he follows Pistol "like a church" (*2 H.IV* II.iv.68 and 249). The belly is a sort of insignia of office. Perhaps this emphasis owes something to the mummery figure of Shrove Tuesday. In a burlesque almanack of 1623, called *Vox Graculi, or Jack Dawes Prognostication*, the Shrove Tuesday holiday is introduced with a description that fits Bacchus and Falstaff remarkably:

> ... here must enter that wadling, stradling, bursten-gutted Carnifex of all Christendome, vulgarity enstiled Shrove-Tuesday, but more pertinently, sole Monarch of the Mouth, high Steward of the Stomach, chief Ganimede of the Guts, . . . Protector of the Pan-cakes . . ."[7]

Shakespeare may or may not have seen Nashe's pageant. But it is clear from such a figure as Nashe's Bacchus that in creating figures like Falstaff and Sir Toby, Shakespeare started with an established role and rhetoric. Nashe's figures are types merely, for Nashe is using them to embody only one moment, one gesture of the spirit. This internal simplicity goes with pageantry as against drama. But Shakespeare, in creating characters whom we feel as individuals, does not drop the meaning of the type, or of the festive moment which shapes the type. On the contrary, a measure of his genius, and of the fortunate juncture when he wrote, is that his plot and his circumstantial detail do not obscure the generic moment or type but instead make it more meaningful by finding it a place in social life and subjecting it to the ironies of social and biological vicissitudes. Nashe's Ver, all of a piece, sings a merry note without a groat; Falstaff is perplexed by "this consumption of the purse." Bacchus never has a dead interval in which to exclaim, "Why, my skin hangs about me like an old lady's loose gown. . . . Well, I'll repent, and that suddenly, while I am in some liking" (*1 H.IV*

[7] p. 55. I have used a photostat of a British Museum copy, STC 6386. A quite similar description occurs in *Jack-a-Lent*, by Taylor the Water Poet, cited above p. 38. The almanack passage is quoted in *Brand's Antiquities*, ed. Ellis, I, 65. Shrovetide is called Bacchus' feast in Barnabe Googe's *The Popish Kingdome*, translated from the Latin of Thomas Naogeorgus, 1570 (printed with Stubbes' *Anatomie*, ed. Furnivall, p. 329). "At Eton School it was the custom, on Shrove Monday, for the scholars to write verses either in praise or dispraise of Father Bacchus" (*Brand's Antiquities*, I, 62).

III.iii.3-6). It is as though Shakespeare asked himself: what would it feel like to be a man who played the role of festive celebrant his whole life long? How would the belly of Bacchus or Shrove Tuesday feel from the inside? He moves, so far, in a realistic direction. But the man he creates is not merely a man. He is an incarnation.

Festive Abuse

I have been pointing out that Nashe's mode of expression consists in going to extremes, and that each extreme, whether festive licence or churlish avarice, implies its opposite. When the discourse is argumentative and cast in general terms, the result of this method is lame: the author seems merely to be scurrying from pillar to post and back again. For the opposites of this discourse are polarities, not alternatives: holiday-everyday, summer-winter. We cannot really take one and leave the other, and whenever Nashe proposes doing so, his writing becomes hollow. Consider, for example, Summer's indignant moral condemnation of Ver's equivocation:

> O vanity itself! O wit ill spent!
> So study thousands not to mend their lives,
> But to maintain the sin they most affect,
> To be hell's advocates 'gainst their own souls.
> (322-325)

These high-sounding moral terms are a sort of Sunday-best suit which Nashe wears perforce, here as in his prose "satires," because the moralistic cast of the culture made it the expected thing. He could not speak with the easy, enfranchised voice of the *honnête homme*, so he had no point of rest from which to write a judicious satire. Instead, he combines tiresome moral bombast with delightful praise of folly and festive abuse.

The finest poetry in *Summer's Last Will and Testament*, aside from the songs, is in a triumphantly slanderous diatribe against poets and scholars. It is delivered by Winter in contesting Autumn's right to inherit Summer's treasure. Although the subject of learned humbug is brought into the action on the thinnest of pretexts, and then is treated in a set of speech of some two hundred lines, the speech is poetry of a high order, and dramatic poetry—dramatic, not because it advances an exciting story, but because it must be read as a gesture of the spirit springing from a particular attitude and implying conflict with opposite attitudes. Winter, setting out from the proposition that Autumn is the scholar's favorite season, undertakes to demonstrate, by unmasking scholars, that Autumn is an unworthy heir. He begins with a history of writing, telling how Hermes,

> Weary with graving in blind characters,
> And figures of familiar beasts and plants,
> Invented letters to write lies withall. . . .
> After each nation got these toys in use
> There grew up certain drunken parasites,
> Termed poets, which, for a meal's meat or two,
> Would promise monarchs immortality.
>
> Next them, a company of ragged knaves,
> Sun-bathing beggars, lazy hedge-creepers,
> Sleeping face-upwards in the fields all night,
> Dream'd strange devices of the sun and moon;
> And they, like Gypsies, wandering up and down
> Told fortunes, juggled, nicknam'd all the stars,
> And were of idiots termed philosophers.
> Such was Pythagoras the silencer,
> Prometheus, Thales Milesius,
> Who would all things of water should be made;
> Anaximander, Anaximenes,
> That positively said the air was God. . . .
> The poorer sort of them, that could get nought,
> Profess'd, like beggarly Franciscan Friars,
> And the strict order of the Capuchins,
> A voluntary wretched poverty,
> Contempt of gold, thin fare and lying hard.
> Yet he that was most vehement in these,
> Diogenes, the cynic and the dog,
> Was taken coigning money in his cell.
>
> (1262-65, 1267-70, 1285-96, 1300-08)

A long quotation is necessary because Nashe builds his verse in long breath units which carry across the end-stopped lines—it is poetry written to be spoken, and in a sweeping style. Nashe does not greatly trouble to have every line packed: "wit hath his dregs as well as wine," says his Epilogue, "words their waste, ink his blots, every speech his parenthesis" (1913). He accumulates at leisure as he builds towards a rhetorical rather than a grammatical period; when he is at his best he contrives a single concentrated line for the *détente*: "Invented letters to write lies withal" or "Would promise monarchs immortality." His characteristic fault is to put in too much elaboration, not all of it effective, as he moves through each large unit. But his command of elaborate rhythmical gestures is often very firm. When in quoting I drop out uninspired subordinate or parallel units, I am usually conscious of doing violence to the long speech rhythm.

Nashe is at no pains to make his mockery of learning just; on the contrary, the point is to bring off a triumphant slander. Once letters are invented, the men of art can abandon the involuntary honesty of ignorance, limited to familiar beasts and plants; the sky's the limit now for lying. They undertake to change the world by words: they promise immortality and nickname the stars; Anaxi-this and Anaxi-that say positively, now this, now that (but water is water still, and air is air). The transforming power of mind is a sham: no wonder its products come cheap—"a meal's meat or two."

The Archbishop's household was of course a very learned group: "gods of art and guides unto heaven" (1934) the Epilogue calls them. Such people are precisely the ones to enjoy this sort of slander on learning, just as the gentlemen of Gray's Inn enjoyed farcical writs and trials during the burlesque ceremonies of their Christmas Lord. Nashe draws on the *De Incertitudine et Vanitate Scientiarum* of Cornelius Agrippa for ammunition in working up the proposition that there is no vice which "learning and vile knowledge brought not in," or "in whose praise some learned have not wrote."

> The art of murder Machiavel hath penned:
> Whoredom hath Ovid to uphold her throne; . . .
> That pleasant work *de arte bibendi*,
> A drunken Dutchman spewed out few years since:
> Nor wanteth sloth (although sloth's plague be want)

His paper pillars for to lean upon: . . .
Folly Erasmus sets a flourish on.
For baldness, a bald ass I have forgot
Patched up a pamphletary periwig.
(1395-98, 1406-14)

The wit here moves delightfully through sensuous connections: sloth, too lazy to stand, contrives paper pillars (which will inevitably collapse); the flourish which Erasmus sets on folly (as if topping it with a stroke of the pen could change it!) leads on to the pamphletary periwig set on baldness. A satirist at least pretends to an objective view; he implies that it is his subjects that are distorted, not his mood; however much he may in fact load his language, his attitude is that he is normal, ingenuous, an *honnête homme*. This assumption of a norm goes with speaking for one social group against others, or for "society" against the anti-social. But Nashe's railing or "flyting" sweeps triumphantly to a close with blatant overstatement:

In brief, all books, divinity except,
Are naught but tales of the devil's laws, . . .
Then censure (good my Lord) what bookmen are, . . .
Blest is the commonwealth where no art thrives, . . .
Young men, young boys, beware of schoolmasters,
They will infect you, mar you, blear your eyes: . . .
(1417-18, 1421, 1425, 1450-51)

Will Fool's chorus makes the distortion manifest by chiming in with enthusiastic corroboration:

Out upon it, who would be a scholar? not I, I promise you: my mind always gave me this learning was such a filthy thing, . . . when I should have been at school . . . I was close under a hedge, or under a barn wall, playing at span-counter, or Jack in a box. My master beat me, my father beat me, my mother gave me bread and butter, yet all this would not make me a squitterbook. (1462-70)

The prose here carries Winter's big talk to homely absurdity. Winter's gesture is a festive repudiation of learned discipline like that which Berowne makes for the bookmates at the turning point in *Love's Labour's Lost*. Will Fool demonstrates the ironic consequences when such an attitude is maintained day in and day out.

The dramatic implications of Winter's language are actually more precise and rich than the dramatic situation provided by the relations of persons in the plot of the pageant. Winter, in his railing speech, but not elsewhere, has a very definite implied character which is complementary to the character he imposes on the scholars. The opposition is another variation on the basic antithesis between control and liberty, decorous prudence and impudent recklessness. Thus at the outset he challenges Autumn's worthiness to inherit by setting him up as a bankrupt:

> A weather-beaten bankrout ass it is,
> That scatters and consumeth all he hath:
> Each one do pluck from him without control.
> (1247-49)

As he says this, Winter is a careful purse-proud housekeeper: what one needs is *control*. He has a man of property's scorn of masterless men, "lazy hedge-creepers" skulking to avoid statutes against beggars, creatures without a house over their heads who must sleep in the fields by night. Everybody, he knows, is really all out for money, whatever those who can't get it profess about voluntary poverty: the case of Diogenes proves it—taken coining money in his cell. Winter sees through the "cunning-shrouded rogues":

> Vain boasters, liars, makeshifts they are all,
> Men that, removed from their inkhorn terms,
> Bring forth no action worthy of their bread.
> (1376-78)

Which, then, are we for: the solid man or the coxcomb? Winter's caricature does indeed express real defects of learning, but this awareness implies in turn the defects of his own niggardly attitude. And the learned rogues, even as presented from Winter's standpoint, have at moments a powerful appeal. After all, they have freedom; they are Scholar Gypsies, and they enjoy the contemplative independence Arnold celebrated (along with beggarly humiliations which his proper Oxford muse did not envisage). They "plant a heaven on earth . . . called Contemplation." Winter adds sarcastically: "As much to say as a most pleasant sloth." But nevertheless, in "loitering contemplation," in "walking summerly" like the prodigal, they have brave fantasies:

Sun-bathing beggars, lazy hedge-creepers,
Sleeping face-upwards in the fields all night
Dream'd strange devices of the sun and moon.
(1286-88)

Moon-madness, caught from sleeping face-upwards, leads to strange imaginations. There is a peculiar intensity, a tension between scorn, wonder and pathos, in such lines as these.[8] The delights of cunning and imagination have an appeal which belies the official attitude of the speaker:

Sky-measuring mathematicians,
Gold-breathing alchemists also we have,
Both which are subtle-witted humorists
That get their meals by telling miracles
Which they have seen in travailing the skies.
(1371-75)

The alchemist here suggests Jonson's comedy. Several passages in Nashe's invective amount to descriptions of Jonson's canting knaves—"cunning-shrouded rogues" is perfect for Subtle and Face. The swaggering soldier, brought in by way of comparison with learned cheaters, is presented in a very Jonsonian fashion:

For even as soldiers not employ'd in wars,
But living loosely in a quiet state,
Not having wherewithal to maintain pride,
Nay, scarce to find their bellies any food,
Nought but walk melancholy, and devise
How they may cozen merchants, fleece young heirs,
Creep into favor by betraying men,
Rob churches, beg waste toys, court city dames,

[8] I first encountered these lines in an essay by Mr. Howard Baker in which he quoted them for their similarity to Wallace Stevens' humorous rhetorical effects, "Add This to Rhetoric," in an issue of *The Harvard Advocate* devoted to Stevens (Vol. 127, No. 3, Dec. 1940). Subsequent conversations with Mr. Baker led me to *Summer's Last Will and Testament*; part of the life the pageant has for me came from his comments on it, and from the light thrown on it by a pageant play which Mr. Baker wrote in a mode rather similar to Nashe's but with modern materials and modern tensions between scorn, wonder, and pathos.

Who shall undo their husbands for their sakes;
The baser rabble how to cheat and steal,
And yet be free from penalty of death:
So those word-warriors, lazy star-gazers,
Used to no labour but to louse themselves,
Had their heads fill'd with cozening fantasies.
(1314-28)

It is not only Jonson's subject matter that Nashe anticipates, but his special kind of double attitude mingling scorn and fascination: the beauty in "gold-breathing" undercut by the gold's being merely breath; "meals" balanced against "miracles": the Marlovian reach of "travailing the skies" qualified by the punning suggestion of working a racket. L. C. Knights has observed that the mingled zest and revulsion expressed in Jonson's comic handling of glamorous luxury and cunning license is the response of an old-fashioned, traditionally disciplined sensibility to the new anarchic forces of money-power and irresponsible knowledge.[9] Jonson's poetry, at great moments like Epicure Mammon's rhapsodic description of the delights of wealth, manages to face and express conflict by combining a purgative expression of anarchic appetite with an ironic judgment upon it. A similar reconciliation, momentary but magnificent while it lasts, happens in Nashe's lines about the sun-bathing beggars and the sky-measuring mathematicians. The tension of antithetical attitudes towards liberty is discharged or fulfilled in wit and image and rhythm; conflict becomes a satisfying order of language. Nashe has no proper plot, and so no development of this tension such as we get in Jonson's masterpieces, where it unfolds in the complications of the gulling of fools by knaves. But we can see the potentiality of such development, of such an extrapolation from real life's minglings, in the festive cultivation of extremes of attitude.

"Go not yet away, bright soul of the sad year"

The pervasive seasonal awareness in the pageant, present even in such a casual, proverbial expression as "walk summerly," is

[9] *Drama and Society in the Age of Jonson* (London, 1937), especially Chap. VII, "Jonson and the Anti-acquisitive Attitude."

treated with a remarkable variety of tones and attitudes. For a modern reader, the shifts are often abrupt, even disconcerting and trivializing; he feels the absence of a plot line to carry him from mood to mood. But the original audience could simply sit back in their seats to find "the place," since in one way or another what was being expressed was always where they were. Once a modern reader has the original occasion firmly in mind, he can feel how part of the effectiveness of the most moving moments is that the literal facts are not left behind: "bright soul of the sad year," for example, refers to the plain fact of declining sun and early dark, as well as to more complex, human relations.

Nashe spins out a good deal of argument about the merits and faults of one season as against another, of the sort traditional in debates of Winter and Summer, Owl and Cuckoo. Some of it is tedious; at Oxford in 1605, King James fell asleep watching a pageant called *Vertumnus, sive Annus Recursus*, or *The Year About*; no doubt he had drunk too much at dinner, but parts of Nashe's turning about of the year makes one sympathize with James. Yet the seasonal theme has potential meaning which sometimes, in the middle of forced conceits, suddenly comes through strongly. This happens, for example, when Winter is defending his right to inherit:

> Youth ne're aspires to virtue's perfect growth,
> Till his wild oats be sown: and so the earth,
> Until his weeds be rotted with my frosts,
> Is not for any seed or tillage fit.
> He must be purged that hath surfeited:
> The fields have surfeited with Summer fruits;
> They must be purg'd, made poor, opprest with snow,
> Ere they recover their decayed pride. (1547-54)

A few lines after this suggestion of a sacrificial logic in seasonal change comes the famous song about the inevitability of death. It is characteristic that the two are *not* connected by the action, which is occupied with dispatching Vertumnus to fetch Winter's sons; *as action*, the song seems to be rung in arbitrarily:

Summer. To weary out the time until they come,
Sing me some doleful ditty to the lute,
That may complain my near approaching death.

The Song.

Adieu, farewell earth's bliss,
This world uncertain is,
Fond are life's lustful joys,
Death proves them all but toys,
None from his darts can fly;
I am sick, I must die;
  Lord, have mercy on us.

(1571-80)

But though there is no narrative consequence, there is thematic, imaginative coherence, beneath the casual surface, of the kind that matters most. When the song is read as part of the pageant, it is not incidental, but an imaginative projection of the pageant's whole subject, still another expression of the audience's situation at Croydon. Thus the second stanza mentions the plague which they feared; the refrain, "I am sick, I must die" is primarily the appropriate complaint of dying Summer, but has a poignant urgency because of the plague. The talk of strength stooping to the grave recalls the figures of pride the pageant has presented, Sol and Orion; "Wit in his wantonness" recalls Ver and Bacchus, to whose vain art of equivocation hell's executioners now will not attend. The final stanza's exhortation to "each degree" was addressed directly to the many social levels gathered in the great hall:

Rich men, trust not in wealth,
Gold cannot buy you health;
Physic himself must fade.
All things to end are made,
The plague full swift goes by;
I am sick, I must die;
  Lord, have mercy on us.

Beauty is but a flower,
Which wrinkles will devour,
Brightness falls from the air,
Queens have died young and fair,

Dust hath clos'd Helen's eye.
I am sick, I must die;
  Lord, have mercy on us.

Strength stoops unto the grave,
Worms feed on Hector brave,
Swords may not fight with fate,
Earth still holds ope her gate.
Come, come, the bells do cry.
I am sick, I must die;
  Lord, have mercy on us.

Wit with his wantonness
Tasteth death's bitterness;
Hell's executioner
Hath no ears for to hear
What vain art can reply.
I am sick, I must die;
  Lord, have mercy on us.

Haste therefore each degree,
To welcome destiny:
Heaven is our heritage,
Earth but a players' stage,
Mount we unto the sky.
I am sick, I must die;
  Lord, have mercy on us.

(1581-1615)

The charged line about brightness, which troubled the imagination of Yeats and of Joyce's Stephen Dedalus, is a particularly notable case where the song is resonant to its context. "Brightness falls from the air," goes with "bright soul of the sad year" in the opening song and with lines like "Short days, sharp days, long nights come on apace" in the final song. The line can be referred to the sort of clear autumn evening when light flows down to the edge of the horizon as it drains out of the zenith. A suggestion of "hair" can be present, too, to go with Helen's eye and cheek;[10] other suggestions, beyond enumeration, are present also.

[10] McKerrow commented "It is to be hoped that Nashe meant 'ayre,' but I can-

I have labored the thematic connections between the song and the pageant because they exemplify so clearly the sort of poetic resources available at the inception of the golden age of English literature—that brief moment when, as C. S. Lewis observes, the obvious was entirely satisfying. Nashe does not need to plan it all, indeed he plans too little. The whole complex of metaphors relating man's life to the cycle of days and seasons came to him with his materials, metaphors already just *there* for everybody. This situation permits a remarkable sweetness and humility of tone even at moments of great imaginative intensity, for there is no emphasis on the act of finding or making the metaphors, such as often accompanies more self-conscious writing, no suggestion that the feeling is strong in proportion as the figures are original or fetched from afar.

Another consequence of Nashe's matter-of-course relation to tradition is his freedom to turn and mock—a freedom he is apt to abuse. When the song in farewell to earth's bliss is over, Summer exclaims with a shake of the head, "Beshrew me, but thy song hath moved me!" Will Fool at once chimes in with "Lord have mercy on us, how lamentable 'tis!" The mocking repetition, in a colloquial sense, of the song's moving refrain does not invalidate it, just because the phrase "Lord, have mercy on us" is right out of the Prayer Book. When the forms for serious meaning are inevitable, received from accepted tradition, the comic reapplication of them need not be threatening. People so situated can afford to turn sanctities upside-down, since they will surely come back rightside-up. It is when traditions are in dispute, when individuals or groups are creating new forms and maintaining them against the world, that it becomes necessary for those who "build the lofty rhyme" to be on guard against the "low."

A resource for expressing the situation of a group, similar to the creation of a Summer Lord and his retinue, was the convention of compliment to Elizabeth. We have seen how Elizabeth would be treated as a supreme Summer Lady, under whose influence "the crooked-winding kid trips o'er the lawns." Often the queen, appro-

not help strongly suspecting that the true reading is 'hayre,' which gives a more obvious, but far inferior, sense" (*Nashe*, IV, 440). But when the seasonal theme of the song and the pageant is remembered, it does not seem likely that "ayre" is an accident.

priately (and diplomatically) differs from Summer Lord or similar seasonal genius in that she is presented as transcending natural limitations. So at the outset of Nashe's pageant, Summer explains his being still alive so late in the year with

> And died I had indeed unto the earth
> But that Eliza, England's beauteous queen,
> On whom all seasons prosperously attend,
> Forbad the execution of my fate,
> Until her joyful progress was expir'd.
> (132-136)

Right after Summer has entered attended by his elaborate train, it is delightful and obvious in a golden-age sort of way to envisage Elizabeth's progress as a pageant of pageants, where he and the other seasons are themselves attendants. When, at the close, he makes his will, Summer's charge to Autumn and to Winter charmingly develops the idea of such "prosperous" attendance:

> Autumn, I charge thee, when that I am dead,
> Be pressed and serviceable at her beck,
> Present her with thy goodliest ripened fruits,
> Unclothe no arbors where she ever sat,
> Touch not a tree thou think'st she may pass by.
> And, Winter, with thy writhen frosty face,
> Smooth up thy visage, when thou look'st on her;
> Thou never look'st on such bright majesty.
> A charmed circle draw about her court,
> Wherein warm days may dance, and no cold come. . . .
> (1845-54)

The lines suggest that Elizabeth was present; but there is good evidence that she cannot have been at Croydon in 1592 or 1593, and it does not seem to me likely that, as McKerrow suggested, there was a revival for which these exquisite lines were written in, because they are so much of a piece with the rest.[11] Perhaps the solution to the puzzle about the lines is that Elizabeth's presence was not necessary for Nashe to decide to use one of the stock features of pageantry. A compliment was bread on the waters of

[11] McKerrow, *Nashe*, IV, 418-419.

court favor. And a compliment was an important resource for Nashe's artistic purpose: to envisage Elizabeth as magically exempt from the seasons' change was an effective way of expressing the here and now of the pageant's occasion. The seasonal change which she is to transcend is precisely the change which everyone else must accept—as in *A Midsummer Night's Dream* it is precisely the thralldom to fancy's images, to which everyone else is subject, that the imperial vot'ress escapes in her maiden meditation, fancy-free.

If the "brightness falls" stanza is the highest flight in the pageant, the generous, quiet lines about Elizabeth's pleasures are perhaps the sweetest thing in it—especially the chiming monosyllabic retard of the line

> Wherein warm days may dance, and no cold come.

The pageant's final song has still another kind of perfection, perfect simplicity and directness. It is sung as Summer is carried out—Faustus-like but with a difference—by his Satyrs and Woodnymphs ("Slow marching thus, descend I to the fiends").

> Autumn hath all the Summer's fruitful treasure;
> Gone is our sport, fled is poor Croyden's pleasure;
> Short days, sharp days, long nights come on a pace,
> Ah, who shall hide us from the winter's face?
> Cold doth increase, the sickness will not cease,
> And here we lie, God knows, with little ease;
> From winter, plague, and pestilence, good Lord,
> deliver us.
>
> London doth mourn, Lambeth is quite forlorn,
> Trades cry, Woe worth that ever they were born;
> The want of Term is town and city's harm;
> Close chambers we do want, to keep us warm,
> Long banished must we live from our friends;
> This low-built house will bring us to our ends.
> From winter, plague, and pestilence, good Lord,
> deliver us.
>
> (1872-85)

This brings the group back from the fiction of the Summer Lord game to the bare facts of their situation, to the sleeping on the rushes in the great hall—"Close chambers we do want, to keep us warm"—to the prospect of living on into the winter in a summer residence—"This low built house will bring us to our ends." Such plain statements, by themselves, would be lamely literal. They are so effective because they come as a movement down to the literal after the projection of the same facts into the pageant's fiction. The meaning is brought—quite literally—home. For its original audience, *Summer's Last Will and Testament* not only represented the change of seasons which they were going through, but also helped to control or order the making of this change, in a fugitive but important way, by enabling them to accept it. When the pageant ends, they can say with the songs:

> And here we lie, God knows, with little ease.
> (1187)

And then they can go their several ways "with merry hearts."

Chapter 5

THE FOLLY OF WIT AND MASQUERADE IN *LOVE'S LABOUR'S LOST*

For revels, dances, masques, and merry hours
Forerun fair Love, strewing her way with flowers.

IT seems likely that when in *Love's Labour's Lost* Shakespeare turned to festivity for the materials from which to fashion a comedy, he did so because he had been commissioned to produce something for performance at a noble entertainment. There can be no doubt about this in the case of *A Midsummer Night's Dream*, though just what noble wedding was graced by Shakespeare's dramatic epithalamium no one has been able to determine.[1] But though nothing in *Love's Labour's Lost* points unambiguously out across the dramatic frame to an original occasion, the way the fairy blessing does at the end of the later comedy, the whole character of the piece marks it as something intended for a special group, people who could be expected to enjoy recondite and modish play with language and to be familiar, to the verge of boredom, with the "revels, dances, masques and merry hours" of courtly circles. Part of the character of the piece can be laid to the influence of Lyly. To use fantastic elaboration and artifice like Lyly's would be a natural thing in addressing Lyly's select audience. And whether or not the original occasion was an aristocratic entertainment, Shakespeare made a play out of courtly pleasures. Professor O. J. Campbell, and more recently Professor Alice S. Venezky, have pointed out that the pastimes with which the French Princess's embassy is entertained, the dances, the masque of Muscovites, the show of the Nine Worthies, the pageant of Winter and Summer, are exactly the sort of thing which was a regular part of court life.[2]

[1] See below, pp. 121-22.

[2] O. J. Campbell, "'Love's Labour's Lost' Re-Studied," *Studies in Shakespeare, Milton and Donne*, U. of Michigan Pubs., Language and Literature, Vol. I (New

Although he probably worked initially on commission, Shakespeare's professional interests naturally led him to produce a piece which could be used afterward in the public theater. So instead of simply building make-believe around an audience who were on holiday, as the authors of parts and shows for entertainments were content to do, he needed to express holiday in a way that would work for anybody, any day. Topical reference that might violate the privacy of the original occasion had to be avoided, or taken out by revision—hence, probably, the bafflement of efforts to determine what the original occasion was. And there had to be protagonists whose experience in a plot would define the rhythm of the holiday, making it, so to speak, portable. When one considers the theatrical resources Shakespeare commanded in 1594 or thereabouts, the company's skilled team of actors accustomed to play up to each other, and the dramatist's facility with dialogue and plot, what is striking about *Love's Labour's Lost* is how *little* Shakespeare used exciting action, story, or conflict, how far he went in the direction of making the piece a set exhibition of pastimes and games. The play is a strikingly fresh start, a more complete break with what he had been doing earlier than I can think of anywhere else in his career, unless it be where he starts to write the late romances. The change goes with the fact that there are no theatrical or literary sources, so far as anyone has been able to discover, for what story there is in the play—Shakespeare, here and in *A Midsummer Night's Dream*, and nowhere else, makes up everything himself, because he is making up action on the model of games and pastimes.

"lose our oaths to find ourselves"

The story in *Love's Labour's Lost* is all too obviously designed to provide a resistance which can be triumphantly swept away by festivity. The vow to study and to see no woman is no sooner made than it is mocked. The French Princess is coming; the courteous

York, 1925), pp. 13-20. Venezky, *Pageantry on the Elizabethan Stage*, pp. 70, 139, 158-161, and passim. Professor Venezky presents customary pageantry and the dramatists' use of it in a full, rounded way which brings out what was typical of the age in Shakespeare's practice.

king acknowledges that "She must lie here of mere necessity." And so Berowne can gleefully draw the moral:

> Necessity will make us all forsworn
>   Three thousand times within this three years' space;
> For every man with his affects is born,
>   Not by might mast'red, but by special grace.
> (I.i.150-153)

We know how the conflict will come out before it starts. But story interest is not the point: Shakespeare is presenting a series of wooing games, not a story. Fours and eights are treated as in ballet, the action consisting not so much in what individuals do as in what the group does, its patterned movement. Everything is done in turn: the lords are described in turn before they come on; each comes back in turn to ask a lady's name; each pair in turn exchanges banter. The dancing continues this sort of action; the four lords and four ladies make up what amounts to a set in English country dancing. We think of dancing in sets as necessarily boisterous; but Elizabethan dancing could express all sorts of moods, as one can realize from such a dance as Hunsdon House, at once spirited and stately. The evolutions in *Love's Labour's Lost* express the Elizabethan feeling for the harmony of a group acting in ceremonious consort, a sense of decorum expressed in areas as diverse as official pageantry, madrigal and motet singing, or cosmological speculations about the order of the universe. John Davies' *Orchestra*, which runs the gamut of such analogies, is a poem very much in the spirit of *Love's Labour's Lost.*

A crucial scene, Act IV, Scene iii, dramatizes the folly of release taking over from the folly of resistance. Each lord enters in turn, reads the sonnet love has forced him to compose, and then hides to overhear and mock the next comer. As the last one comes in, Berowne describes their antics as a game of hide and seek:

> All hid, all hid—an old infant play.
> Like a demigod here sit I in the sky
> And wretched fools' secrets heedfully o'er-eye.
> More sacks to the mill. O heavens, I have my wish!
> Dumain transform'd! Four woodcocks in a dish!
> (IV.iii.78-82)

Having wound them into their hiding places one-by-one, Shakespeare unwinds them one-by-one as each in turn rebukes the others. Berowne caps the king's rebuke of Dumain and Longaville with:

> Now step I forth to whip hypocrisy.
> (IV.iii.151)

But he too is betrayed by Costard, so that he too must confess

> That you three fools lack'd me fool to make up the mess.
> He, he, and you—and you, my liege—and I
> Are pickpurses in love, and we deserve to die. . . .
> *Dumain.* Now the number is even.
> *Berowne.* True, true! We are four. . . .
> (IV.iii.207-211)

The technique of discovery in this fine scene recalls the *sotties* presented by the French fool societies on their holidays, where the outer garments of various types of dignified pretension were plucked off to reveal parti-colored cloaks and long-eared caps beneath.[3] The similarity need not be from literary influence but from a common genesis in games and dances and in the conception that natural impulse, reigning on festive occasions, brings out folly. Berowne summarizes it all with "O, what a scene of fool'ry I have seen!"

Such comedy is at the opposite pole from most comedy of character. Character usually appears in comedy as an individual's way of resisting nature: it is the kill-joys, pretenders, and intruders who have character. Molière's great comedies of character distortion, *Tartuffe*, *Le Misanthrope*, are focussed primarily on the pretender or the kill-joy; the celebrants, those who can embrace nature, are generally on the periphery until the resolution. But with Shakespeare, the celebrants are at the center. And when merrimakers say yes to nature, taking the folly of the time, the joke is that they behave in exactly the same way: "More sacks to the mill." "Four woodcocks in a dish!" The festive comedies always produce this effect of a group who are experiencing together

[3] Welsford, *Fool*, pp. 218-229. Miss Welsford discusses the general relations of the sottie to misrule and the masque in *The Court Masque, A Study in the Relationship between Poetry and the Revels* (Cambridge, 1927), pp. 376 ff.

a force larger than their individual wills. Berowne hails it, when the treason of all has been discovered, with

> Sweet lords, sweet lovers. O, let us embrace!
> As true are we as flesh and blood can be.
> The sea will ebb and flow, heaven shows his face;
> Young blood doth not obey an old decree.
> (IV.iii.214-217)

In the early festive plays, one touch of nature makes the lovers rather monotonously akin; they tend to be differentiated only by accidental traits. But Shakespeare gradually learned to exhibit variety not only in the way people resist nature but also in the way they accept it.

Already in *Love's Labour's Lost* Berowne stands out, not by not doing what all do, but by being conscious of it in a different way. Where clownish wit calls a spade a spade, Berowne calls a game a game. He plays the game, but he calls it too, knowing what it is worth because he knows where it fits within a larger rhythm:

> At Christmas I no more desire a rose
> Than wish a snow in May's newfangled shows,
> But like of each thing that in season grows.
> (I.i.105-107)

It is Berowne who is ordered by Navarre to "prove / Our loving lawful and our faith not torn" (IV.iii.284-285). The set speech he delivers is Praise of Folly such as we have seen in Nashe. It is often quoted as "the young Shakespeare's philosophy," despite the fact that it is deliberately introduced as equivocation, "flattery for this evil . . . quillets, how to cheat the devil" (IV.iii.288). In proving that it is women's eyes which "sparkle still the right Promethean fire" (IV.iii.351), Berowne adopts the same mock-academic manner and uses many of the same genial arguments as Nashe's Bacchus, the same used later by Falstaff in proving sack "the first humane principle."[4] The high point of Berowne's speech

[4] See above, pp. 67-73, for the relation of Falstaff's praise of folly to that of Nashe's Bacchus. Berowne's points, and even his phrasing, are often remarkably close to Falstaff's: "abstinence engenders maladies" goes with Falstaff's "fall into a kind of male greensickness" (*2 H.IV* IV.iii.100); "other slow arts entirely keep the brain" fits with "learning a mere hoard of gold kept by the devil, till

has a fine lyric force as he pleads the case for the creative powers that go with release in love. Then as he moves into his formal peroration, he heaps up reduplicative sanctions in a recklessly punning way which keeps us aware that his oration is special pleading—true, yet only a part of the truth:

> Then fools you were these women to foreswear;
> Or keeping what is sworn, you will prove fools.
> For wisdom's sake, a word that all men love;
> Or for love's sake, a word that loves all men;
> Or for men's sake, the authors of these women;
> Or women's sake, by whom we men are men—
> Let us once lose our oaths to find ourselves,
> Or else we lose ourselves to keep our oaths.
> It is religion to be thus forsworn;
> For charity itself fulfills the law,
> And who can sever love from charity?
>
> (IV.iii.355-365)

He has turned the word "fool" around, in the classic manner of Erasmus in his *Praise of Folly*; it becomes folly not to be a fool. After reciprocally tumbling men and women around (and alluding to the sanctioning fact of procreation), the speech concludes with overtones of Christian folly in proclaiming the logic of their losing themselves to find themselves and in appealing from the law to charity. But Berowne merely leaps up to ring these big bells lightly; there is no coming to rest on sanctities; everything is in motion. The groups are swept into action by the speech—holiday action. Longaville breaks off the game of the oration with

> Now to plain-dealing. Lay these glozes by.
> Shall we resolve to woo these girls of France?
> *King.* And win them too! Therefore let us devise
> Some entertainment for them in their tents.
> *Berowne.* First from the park let us conduct them thither;
> Then homeward every man attach the hand

Sack commences it"; "love . . . not alone immured in the brain . . . courses as swift as thought in every power" parallels "the sherris warms [the blood] and makes it course from the inwards to the parts extreme."

Of his fair mistress. In the afternoon
We will with some strange pastime solace them,
Such as the shortness of the time can shape,
For revels, dances, masques, and merry hours
Forerun fair Love, strewing her way with flowers.

(IV.iii.370-380)

"sport by sport o'erthrown"

The final joke is that in the end "Love" does not arrive, despite the lords' preparations for a triumphal welcome. That the play should end without the usual marriages is exactly right, in view of what it is that is released by its festivities. Of course what the lords give way to is, in a general sense, the impulse to love; but the particular form that it takes for them is a particular sort of folly—what one could call the folly of amorous masquerade, whether in clothes, gestures, or words. It is the folly of acting love and talking love, without being in love. For the festivity releases, not the delights of love, but the delights of expression which the prospect of love engenders—though those involved are not clear about the distinction until it is forced on them; the clarification achieved by release is this recognition that love is not wooing games or love talk. And yet these sports are not written off or ruled out; on the contrary the play offers their delights for our enjoyment, while humorously putting them in their place.

It is in keeping with this perspective that masquerade and show are made fiascos. Of course, to put shows or masques on the stage effectively, things must go in an unexpected way. Benvolio glances at the hazard of boredom in planning the masque in *Romeo and Juliet*, a play written only a year or two after *Love's Labour's Lost*:

The date is out of such prolixity.
We'll have no Cupid hoodwink'd with a scarf,
Bearing a Tartar's painted bow of lath,
Scaring the ladies like a crowkeeper;
Nor no without-book prologue, faintly spoke
After the prompter, for our entrance . . .

(*Romeo* I.iv.3-8)

One way to make pageantry dramatic is to have what is pretended in masque or game actually happen in the play. This is what Shakespeare did with the masque in *Romeo and Juliet*, where the conventional pretense that the masquers were strangers asking hospitality is used in earnest, along with the fiction that, once disguise is assumed, anything can happen.

> *Benvolio.* Away, be gone; the sport is at the best.
> *Romeo.* Ay, so I fear; the more is my unrest.
> (I.iv.121-122)

The other way to make masquerades dramatic is to have the fiction of the game break down, which is the way things consistently go in *Love's Labour's Lost.* Moth, drilled to introduce the Muscovite masquers, is just such a halting prologue as Benvolio scorns. And the masquers' dance scarcely gets started:

> *Rosaline.* Since you are strangers, and come here
> by chance,
> We'll not be nice. Take hands. We will not dance.
> *King.* Why take we hands then?
> *Rosaline.* Only to part friends.
> Curtsy, sweet hearts—and so the measure ends.
> (V.ii.218-221)

In breaking off the dance before it begins, Rosaline makes a sort of dance on her own terms, sudden and capricious; and clearly the other ladies, in response to her nodded signals—"Curtsy, sweet hearts"—are doing the same pirouette at the same time. The princess describes this way of making a variation on a theme:

> There's no such sport as sport by sport o'erthrown—
> To make theirs ours, and ours none but our own.
> (V.ii.153-154)

Though there is a certain charm in this patterned crossing of purposes, it is itself too often predicted and predictable. The king and his company, returning without their Muscovite disguises after being shamed hence, are unbelievably slow to believe that they were "descried." Berowne especially ought not to take so long to see the game:

I see the trick on't. Here was a consent,
Knowing aforehand of our merriment,
To dash it like a Christmas comedy.
(V.ii.460-462)

When the commoners in their turn put on the Show of the Nine Worthies, the lords have their chance to join the ladies in dashing it, and the Princess gives a rationale for enjoying another kind of comic failure:

Their form confounded makes most form in mirth
When great things labouring perish in their birth.
(V.ii.520-521)

"a great feast of languages"

If all we got were sports that fail to come off, the play would indeed be nothing but labor lost. What saves it from anticlimax is that the most important games in which the elation of the moment finds expression are games with words, and the wordplay does for the most part work, conveying an experience of festive liberty. It is all conducted with zest and with constant exclamations about how well the game with words is going. Wordplay is compared to all sorts of other sports, tilting, dueling—or tennis: "Well bandied both! a set of wit well played." Or a game of dice:

Berowne. White-handed mistress, one sweet word with thee.
Princess. Honey, and milk, and sugar: there is three.
Berowne. Nay then, two treys, an if you grow so nice—
Metheglin, wort, and malmsey. Well run, dice!
There's half a dozen sweets.
Princess. Seventh sweet, adieu.
Since you can cog, I'll play no more with you.
(V.ii.230-236)

Besides this sort of repartee, another aristocratic wooing game is the sonneteering. The lords each "turn sonnet" (I.ii.190); love produces rhyme by reflex. "I do love, and it hath taught me to rhyme," Berowne confides to the audience, holding up a paper.

The aristocratic pastimes with language are set against the fantastic elaborations of the braggart and the schoolmaster, Armado puffing up versions of Euphuistic tautology and periphrasis, Holofernes complacently showing off his inkhorn terms, rhetorical and grammatical terminology, even declensions and alternate spellings. To play up to these fantasts, there are Moth, a quick wit, and Costard, a slow but strong one. And there is Sir Nathaniel, the gull curate, who eagerly writes down in his table-book the schoolmaster's redundancies. Dull and Jaquenetta, by usually keeping silent, prove the rule of Babel. But even Dull has a riddle in his head which he tries out on the schoolmaster. The commoners normally speak prose, the lords and ladies verse; most of the prose is as artificial in its way as the rhymed, end-stopped verses. The effect is that each social level and type is making sport with words in an appropriate way, just as the lords' infatuation with the ladies is paralleled by Costard's and then Armado's attentions to Jaquenetta. "Away," says the schoolmaster, as he invites the curate to dinner, "the gentles are at their game, and we will to our recreation" (IV.ii.171). And when they come from dinner, still babbling, Moth observes aside to Costard that "They have been at a great feast of languages and stol'n the scraps" (V.i.39).

This comedy is often described as a satire on various kinds of overelaborate language. It is certainly true that the exhibition of different sorts of far-fetched verbal play becomes almost an end in itself. Armado is introduced as a buffoon of new fashions and "fire-new words." He and the schoolmaster do make ridiculous two main Elizabethan vices of style. But each carries his vein so fantastically far that it commands a kind of gasping admiration—instead of being shown up, they turn the tables and show off, converting affectation and pedantry into ingenious games. "Be it as the style shall give us cause to climb in the merriness," says Berowne in anticipation of Armado's letter (I.i.201). For a modern reader, the game with high or learned words is sometimes tedious, because we have not ourselves tried the verbal exercises on which the gymnastic exhibition is based. Even the princess and her ladies in waiting, when they talk in terms of copy-book letters, seem just freshly out of school:

> *Rosaline*. O, he hath drawn my picture in his
> letter! . . .
> *Princess*. Beauteous as ink—a good conclusion.

Katherine. Fair as a text B in a copy-book.
Rosaline. Ware pencils, ho! Let me not die your debtor,
My red dominical, my golden letter.
(V.ii.38-44)

This kind of thing does weigh down parts of the play; it is dated by catering to a contemporary rage, a failure rare in Shakespeare's works, and one that suggests that he was writing for a special audience.

But the more one reads the play, the more one is caught up by the extraordinary excitement it expresses about what language can do—the excitement of the historical moment when English, in the hands of its greatest master, suddenly could do anything. Zest in the power of words comes out particularly clearly in the clown's part, as the chief motifs so often do in Shakespeare. As Armado gives Costard a letter to carry to Jaquenetta, he gives him a small tip with big words: "There is remuneration; for the best ward of mine honor is rewarding my dependents." When he has gone out, Costard opens his palm:

> Now I will look to his remuneration. Remuneration—O, that's the Latin word for three farthings. Three farthings—remuneration. 'What's the price of this inkle?' 'One penny.' 'No, I'll give you a remuneration!' Why, it carries it! Remuneration. Why, it is a fairer name than French crown. I will never buy and sell out of this word.
> (III.i.137-144)

O brave new world, that has *remuneration* in it! But the clown's next exchange, with Berowne, promptly demonstrates that three farthings is three farthings still.

> *Berowne.* O my good knave Costard, exceedingly well met!
> *Costard.* Pray you, sir, how much carnation ribbon may a man buy for a remuneration?
> *Berowne.* O, what is a remuneration?
> *Costard.* Marry, sir, halfpenny farthing.
> *Berowne.* O, why then, three-farthing worth of silk.
> *Costard.* I thank your worship, God be wi' you!
> *Berowne.* O, stay, slave; I must employ thee.
> (III.i.145-152)

Berowne has a letter of his own, for Rosaline, and he too gives money with it, a whole bright shilling: "There's thy guerdon. Go." Costard again opens his palm: "Gardon—O sweet gardon! better than remuneration! a 'levenpence-farthing better" (III.i.171-173). So words are good when they go with good things. By getting so literal a valuation of the words, Costard both imitates and burlesques the way his superiors value language.

Everybody in the play, however vain about themselves, is ready always with applause for another's wit. "Now by the salt wave of the Mediterranean, a sweet touch, a quick venew of wit" Spanish Armado exclaims in praise of Moth, appropriately using dueling terms. "Snip, snap, quick and home! It rejoiceth my intellect. True wit!" (V.i.61-64) Costard is equally delighted, after his own fashion:

> An I had but one penny in the world, thou shouldst have it to buy gingerbread. Hold, there is the very remuneration I had of thy master, thou halfpenny purse of wit, thou pigeon egg of discretion.
>
> (V.i.74-78)

Holofernes has the grace to applaud a pass of wit of Costard's, in a patronizing way, even though it turns against him a blunt thrust of his own, aimed at Jaquenetta:

> *Jacquenetta.* God give you good morrow, Master Person.
>
> *Holofernes.* Master Person, quasi pers-one. And if one should be pierc'd, which is the one?
>
> *Costard.* Marry, Master Schoolmaster, he that is likest to a hogshead.
>
> *Holofernes.* Of piercing a hogshead! A good lustre of conceit in a turf of earth; fire enough for a flint, pearl enough for a swine. 'Tis pretty, it is well.
>
> (IV.ii.84-91)

Holofernes is fascinated by a release in language he himself heavily fails to find. After his absurd alliterative poem, his gull Nathaniel exclaims "A rare talent." Dull throws in the dry aside: "If a talent be a claw, look how he claws him with a talent." But Holofernes has been carried away by the joy of creation:

> This is a gift that I have, simple, simple; a foolish extravagant

> spirit, full of forms, figures, shapes, objects, ideas, apprehensions, motions, revolutions. These are begot in the ventricle of memory, nourished in the womb of pia mater, and delivered upon the mellowing of occasion. But the gift is good in those in whom it is acute, and I am thankful for it. (IV.ii.67-74)

Here, as so often in Shakespeare, the outlines of a caricature are filled in with the experience of a man: Holofernes has a rhapsody of his own, an experience of the "fiery numbers" Berowne talks about—strange as his productions may be.

Wit

In a world of words, the wine is wit. Festivity in social life always enjoys, without effort, something physical from the world outside that is favorable to life, whether it be food and drink, or the warmth of the fields when they breathe sweet. Exhilaration comes when the world proves ready and willing, reaching out a hand, passing a brimming bowl; festivity signals the realization that we *belong* in the universe. Now in wit, it is language that gives us this something for nothing; unsuspected relations between words prove to be ready to hand to make a meaning that serves us. All of the comedies of Shakespeare, of course, depend on wit to convey the exhilaration of festivity. But *Love's Labour's Lost*, where the word *wit* is used more often than in any of the other plays, is particularly dependent on wit and particularly conscious in the way it uses and talks about it. So it will be useful to consider general functions of wit as they appear in this comedy.

When Moth speaks of "a great feast of languages," Costard continues the figure with "I marvel thy master hath not eaten thee for a word; for thou art not so long by the head as honorificabilitudinitatibus; thou art easier swallowed than a flapdragon" (V.i.42-45).

This is excellent fooling, and sense, too. For the people in *Love's Labour's Lost* get a lift out of fire-new words equivalent to what a tavern-mate would get from swallowing a "flapdragon"—a raisin floating in flaming brandy. Eating words is apt because the *physical* attributes of words are used by wit: a witticism capitalizes on "external associations," that is to say, it develops a meaning by connecting words through relations or likenesses not noted or used in the situation until found. The "physical," for our purpose here, is whatever had not been noticed, had not been given meaning, until wit caught hold of it and made it signify. The exploitation of physical features of language is most obvious where the wit is forced, where what is found does not really do very well after all. Little or nothing is really found when Jaquenetta mispronounces Parson as "Person," and Holofernes tries to make an innuendo by wrenching: "Master Person, quasi pers-one. And if one should be pierc'd, which is the one?" By contrast, consider Berowne's zooming finale in the speech justifying oath breaking, where successive lines seem to explode meaning already present in what went just before:

> Let us once lose our oaths to find ourselves,
> Or else we lose ourselves to keep our oaths.
> (IV.iii.361-362)

To appropriate physical relations of sound and position in language, so that it seems that language makes your meaning for you, as indeed it partly does, gives an extraordinary exhilaration, far more intense than one would expect—until one considers how much of what we are is what we can find words for. When wit flows happily, it is as though the resistance of the objective world had suddenly given way. One keeps taking words from "outside," from the world of other systems or orders, and making them one's own, making them serve one's meaning as they form in one's mouth.

In repartee, each keeps jumping the other's words to take them away and make them his own, finding a meaning in them which was not intended. So elusive yet crucial is this subject that it will be worth while to quote a passage of wit where much that is involved in repartee is almost laboriously exhibited. As constantly happens in this play, the nature of wit is talked about in the process of being witty, here by hunting and sexual metaphors:

> *Boyet.* My lady goes to kill horns; but if thou marry,
> Hang me by the neck if horns that year miscarry.
> Finely put on!
> *Rosaline.* Well then, I am the shooter.
> *Boyet.* And who is your deer?

Rosaline. If we choose by the horns, yourself. Come not near.

Finely put on indeed!

Maria. You still wrangle with her, Boyet, and she strikes at the brow.

Boyet. But she herself is hit lower. Have I hit her now?

Rosaline. Shall I come upon thee with an old saying, that was a man when King Pippen of France was a little boy, as touching the hit it?

Boyet. So I may answer thee with one as old, that was a woman when Queen Guinover of Britain was a little wench, as touching the hit it.

Rosaline. 'Thou canst not hit it, hit it, hit it,
Thou canst not hit it, my good man.'

Boyet. 'An I cannot, cannot, cannot,
An I cannot, another can.'

Costard. By my troth, most pleasant. How both did fit it.

(IV.i.112-131)

To reapply or develop a given metaphor has the same effect as to reapply or develop the pattern of sound in a given set of words. Costard's comment describes the give and take of the repartee by the sexual metaphor—which the party go on to develop far more explicitly than even our freest manners would allow. The point they make is that to use one another's words in banter is like making love; each makes meaning out of what the other provides physically. They notice in *medias res* that there is the same sort of sequence of taking advantage and acquiescing: the process of taking liberties with each other's words goes with a kind of verbal hiding and showing. Boyet can go especially far in this way because he is the safe elderly attendant of the royal party of ladies, limited by his age and role to such peeping-Tom triumphs as "An I cannot, another can." When there is a real prospect of going from words to deeds, words are more dangerous. So when the ladies encounter the lords, their game is to stand them off by denying them the "three sweet words" for which the men ask to get started.

A single speaker can of course develop his thought by witty re-use of verbal situations he himself lays out. Consider, for example, the soliloquy in which Berowne, at the opening of the discovery scene, confesses that he is in love:

> The King he is hunting the deer; I am coursing myself. They have pitch'd a toil; I am toiling in a pitch—pitch that defiles. Defile! a foul word. Well, 'set thee down, sorrow!' for so they say the fool said, and so say I, and I the fool. Well proved, wit. By the Lord, this love is as mad as Ajax: it kills sheep; it kills me—I a sheep.
> (IV.iii.1-8)

This is almost dialogue in the way it moves, like repartee, from a statement to the reapplication of the statement to "prove" something. The process of setting up and exploiting verbal situations is less obtrusive in more successful witty talk, but crucial in giving an exhilarating sense of power. Berowne has some excellent couplets mocking Boyet:

> This fellow pecks up wit as pigeons pease,
> And utters it again when God doth please.
> He is wit's pedlar, and retails his wares
> At wakes and wassails, meetings, markets, fairs;
> And we that sell by gross, the Lord doth know
> Have not the grace to grace it with such show.
> (V.ii.315-320)

How nicely the extension of the pigeon and pedlar metaphors goes with a complex pattern of alliteration, *pecks* to *pease* to *pedlar*, *wares* to *wakes* to *wassails*. It seems as though language had conspired with Berowne to mock Boyet. In such exploitation of the physical qualities of words, there are no hard and fast lines between wit and eloquence and poetry, a fact which is reflected in the broad Renaissance usage of the word wit. But one can observe that we now think of expressions as witty, rather than eloquent or poetic, when one is conscious of the physical character of the links through which the discourse moves to its meanings. And one must add that some of the wit in *Love's Labour's Lost* is, to our modern taste, tediously "conceited." The play occasionally deserved Dryden's strictures about Shakespeare's "comic art degenerating into clenches."

Putting Witty Folly in Its Place

But though one cannot blink the fact that the wit is often a will-o'-the-wisp, the play *uses* its witty extravagance, moves through it to clarification about what one sort of wit is and where it fits in human experience. There are a number of descriptions of the process of being witty which locate such release as an event in the whole sensibility. These usually go with talk about brightening eyes: typically in this play a lover's eyes catch fire just before he bursts into words. There is a remarkable description of the King's first response to the Princess which defines precisely a gathering up of the faculties for perception and expression:

> *Boyet.* If my observation (which very seldom lies),
> By the heart's still rhetoric, disclosed with eyes,
> Deceive me not now, Navarre is infected.
> *Princess.* With what?
> *Boyet.* With that which we lovers entitle 'affected.'
> (II.i.227-232)

Notice that Boyet does not answer simply "with love." Shakespeare is out to define a more limited thing, a galvanizing of sensibility which may or may not be love; and so Boyet goes round about to set up a special term, "affected." He goes on to describe his observation of "the heart's still rhetoric":

> Why, all his behaviours did make their retire
> To the court of his eye, peeping thorough desire. . . .
> His tongue, all impatient to speak and not see,
> Did stumble with haste in his eyesight to be;
> All senses to that sense did make their repair,
> To feel only looking on fairest of fair.
> Methought all his senses were lock'd in his eye,
> As jewels in crystal for some prince to buy,
> Who, tend'ring their own worth from where they were glass'd,
> Did point you to buy them along as you pass'd.
> (II.i.234-245)

This is extremely elaborate; but the dislocation of the language, for example in "to feel only looking" (which bothered Dr. Johnson),[5] catches a special movement of feeling important for the whole play, a movement of awareness into the senses and toward expression. The next step, from eye to tongue, is described in Rosaline's account of Berowne.

a merrier man
Within the limit of becoming mirth,
I never spent an hour's talk withal.
His eye begets occasion for his wit;
For every object that the one doth catch
The other turns to a mirth-moving jest,
Which his fair tongue (conceit's expositor)
Delivers in such apt and gracious words
That aged ears play truant at his tales
And younger hearings are quite ravished,
So sweet and voluble is his discourse.
(II.i.66-76)

The rhythm here, even some of the phrasing, anticipate, in a sketchy way, the description of the enchanting power of the mermaid in *A Midsummer Night's Dream*:

Uttering such dulcet and harmonious breath
That the rude sea grew civil at her song,

[5] *A New Variorum Edition of Shakespeare*, ed. H. H. Furness (Philadelphia, 1904), p. 79. A few lines later we get a drastic collapse into a characteristic vice of this play, a kind of chop-logic with images:

I only have made a mouth of his eye
By adding a tongue which I know will not lie.
(II.i.252-253)

This is bad taste, one of a number of places where the elaboration of fanciful paradox produces a result which can only be read abstractly: to form a physical image of a tongue in an eye spoils everything. An even more dramatic case is the draggle end of a wit combat over the beauty of Berowne's "black" lady, Rosaline.

Longaville. Look, here's thy love, my foot and her face see.
Berowne. O, if the streets were paved with thine eyes,
Her feet were much too dainty for such tread.
(IV.iii.277-279)

To read Berowne's talk of walking on eyeballs with full imaginative participation "would be to experiment in mania," as I. A. Richards remarked about certain stanzas of Dryden's *Annus Mirabilis* in *Coleridge on Imagination* (New York, 1935), p. 95. But one can forgive such failures in so enterprising a writer as the young author of *Love's Labour's Lost*; he is trying everything.

And certain stars shot madly from their spheres
To hear the sea-maid's music.
(*Dream* II.i.151-154)

There are a series of such descriptions of the Orphic power of musical discourse in the plays of this period, including Berowne's own climactic speech in this play. In Rosaline's lines, as elsewhere, there is a metaphor of conveying meaning out into language, perhaps with a glance at child-bearing in "delivers."[6] When Rosaline is characterized, in her turn, the power of nimble expression to free the heart of its burdens is charmingly described. Katherine contrasts her with a sister who died of Love. Love

made her melancholy, sad and heavy,
And so she died. Had she been light like you,
Of such a merry, nimble, stirring spirit,
She might 'a' been a grandam ere she died.
And so may you; for a light heart lives long.
(V.ii.14-18)

The fullest description of this kindling into Orphic wit and eloquence, at the climax of Berowne's speech justifying folly, centers on the process of awareness moving out into the senses and powers:

For when would you, my liege, or you, or you,
In leaden contemplation, have found out
Such fiery numbers as the prompting eyes
Of beauty's tutors have enrich'd you with?
Other slow arts entirely keep the brain,
And therefore finding barren practisers,
Scarce show a harvest of their heavy toil;
But love, first learned in a lady's eyes,
Lives not alone immured in the brain,
But with the motion of all elements
Courses as swift as thought in every power,
And gives to every power a double power
Above their functions and their offices.
(IV.iii.320-332)

[6] This meaning Holofernes also develops in talking of wit "nourish'd in the womb of pia mater, and delivered" (IV.ii.70-71).

The speech is a perfectly fitting counter-statement to the ascetic resolutions with which the play began. The "doctrine" it derives from "women's eyes" is a version of the Renaissance cult of love as an educational force, especially for the courtier. But notice how little Berowne is concerned with love as an experience between two people. All his attention is focussed on what happens within the lover, the heightening of his powers and perceptions. He is describing a youthful response of elation; the mere sight of "the prompting eyes" of the tutor beauty is enough to whirl pupil love into an almost autonomous rhapsody:

> It adds a precious seeing to the eye:
> A lover's eyes will gaze an eagle blind.
> A lover's ear will hear the lowest sound
> When the suspicious head of theft is stopp'd.
> Love's feeling is more soft and sensible
> Than are the tender horns of cockled snails.
> Love's tongue proves dainty Bacchus gross in taste.
> For valour, is not Love a Hercules,
> Still climbing trees in the Hesperides?
> Subtle as Sphinx; as sweet and musical
> As bright Apollo's lute, strung with his hair.
> And when Love speaks, the voice of all the gods
> Make heaven drowsy with the harmony.
> Never durst poet touch a pen to write
> Until his ink were temp'red with Love's sighs.
> O, then his lines would ravish savage ears
> And plant in tyrants mild humility.
>
> (IV.iii.333-349)

Can such delightful poetry, such rhapsody, be folly? There is a romantic response ready that would like to let go completely and simply endorse these lovely, vital lines. But the strength of Shakespeare's comic form is precisely that the attitude Berowne expresses can be presented as at once delightfully vital, *and* foolish. The foolishness is of a young and benign sort, in which the prospect of love sets off a rhapsody that almost forgets the beloved. Consummation in physical union of the sexes is not envisaged; the lady is involved only as her eyes start another sort of physical union by which the senses and powers are invested with amorous meaning.

The lords' quality of youthful elation and absorption in their own responses is what lays them open to being fooled as they are by the ladies when they try to set about revelry wholeheartedly. The game they are playing, without quite knowing it, tries to make love happen by expressing it, to blow up a sort of forced-draft passion by capering volubility and wit. A remarkable set-piece by Moth describes an Elizabethan hep-cat version of such courting: he tells Armado how to "win your love with a French brawl":

> . . . jig off a tune at the tongue's end, canary to it with your feet, humour it with turning up your eyelids; sigh a note and sing a note, sometime through the throat, as if you swallow'd love with singing love, sometime through the nose, as if you snuff'd up love by smelling love, with your hat penthouse-like o'er the shop of your eyes, with your arms cross'd on your thin-belly doublet, like a rabbit on a spit, or your hands in your pocket, like a man after the old painting; and keep not too long in one tune, but a snip and away. These are complements; these are humours; these betray nice wenches that would be betrayed without these, and make them men of note—do you note me?—that most are affected to these. (III.i.11-26)

Such antics are more plebeian than the lords' revels, but tellingly alike in purpose. The Princess and her ladies are not in any case the sort of nice wenches to be betrayed. The ladies believe, indeed, rather too little than too much. "They do it but in mocking merriment," says the Princess. "And mock for mock is only my intent." When the men have been "dry-beaten with pure scoff," Berowne eats humble pie in an effort to get started on a new basis:

> O, never will I trust to speeches penn'd
>   Nor to the motion of a schoolboy's tongue,
> Nor never come in vizard to my friend,
>   Nor woo in rhyme like a blind harper's song!
> Taffeta phrases, silken terms precise,
>   Three-pil'd hyperboles, spruce affectation,
> Figures pedantical—these summer flies
>   Have blown me full of maggot ostentation.

I do forswear them; and I here protest,
  By this white glove (how white the hand, God knows!)
Henceforth my wooing mind shall be express'd
  In russet yea's and honest kersey no's.
(V.ii.402-412)

Berowne abjures elaborate language, and it is for this alone that the lines are usually quoted. Part of the point of them lay in criticism of affected style. But a final, settled attitude toward such style has not been established. The lords' trusting in speeches penn'd, with three-piled hyperboles, has been part and parcel of trusting in the masquerade way of making love, coming in a vizard, in a three-piled Russian habit. And these pastimes are not being dismissed for good, but put in their place: they are festive follies, relished as they show the power of life, but mocked as they run out ahead of the real, the everyday situation. The point, dramatically, is that the lords had hoped that festivity would "carry it," as Costard hoped Armado's fancy word "remuneration" would carry it. Now they must start again, because, as Berowne's better judgment foresaw

Light wenches may prove plagues to men forsworn:
  If so, our copper buys no better treasure.
(IV.iii.385-386)

Perhaps the most delightful touch in the whole play is the exchange that concludes Berowne's reformation, in which he playfully betrays the fact that his mockery of sophistication is sophisticated, and Rosaline underscores the point as she deftly withdraws the hand he has taken:

And to begin: wench, so God help me, law!
My love to thee is sound, sans crack or flaw.
  Rosaline. Sans 'sans,' I pray you!
(V.ii.414-416)

Miss M. C. Bradbrook observes that "Berowne, who is both guilty of courtly artifice and critical of it, plays a double game with language throughout; the same double game that the author himself is playing. He runs with the hare and hunts with the hounds."[7] His control and poise in moving in this way goes with being able to call a game a game, as I have been saying. Another source of his mastery is the social perspective on the courtly pleasures which he gets by ironically dropping, at intervals, into homespun, proverbial speech. Of course there is a sort of affectation too in doing the downright in this way, and Berowne's humor recognizes that he himself is no common man. But he does get the power to stand apart from elegant folly by being able to say things like

> Sow'd cockle reap'd no corn,
> And justice always whirls in equal measure.
> (IV.iii.383-384)

The roles of the commoners provide the same sort of perspective, especially the illiterate commoners, who almost always come out best in the exchanges. No sooner has the Duke proclaimed his "continent cannon" than Costard proves its absurdity by being taken with Jaquenetta:

> In manner and form following, sir—all those three. I was seen with her in the manor house, sitting with her upon the form, and taken following her into the park; which put together is in manner and form following. Now, sir, for the manner—it is the manner of a man to speak to a woman; for the form—in some form. (I.i.207-215)

"In some form," the truth about human nature comes out, despite the way Costard wrests the categories in a physical direction, or indeed because of this physical tendency. "I suffer for the truth, sir," is the swain's fine summary, "for true it is I was taken with Jaquenetta, and Jaquenetta is a true girl" (I.i.313-314). He is a thoroughly satisfactory "downright" style of clown, ironical about the follies of his betters half out of naïveté and half out of shrewdness. His role embodies the proverbial, homespun perspective Berowne can occasionally borrow. Moth, a pert page in the manner of Lyly, is less rich, but he too contributes comments which help to place what the lords are doing.

All of the commoners' parts, indeed, contribute to placing the festivities. Almost all of them make telling comments, even

[2] *Shakespeare and Elizabethan Poetry* (London, 1951), p. 215.

Holofernes, who has the courage, when he is mercilessly ragged as Judas in his Show of Worthies, to say "This is not generous, not gentle, not humble" (V.ii.632). But comments are less important than the sense Shakespeare creates of people living in a settled group, where everyone is known and to be lived with, around the clock of the year. Though the different figures may have been shaped to some degree by examples in the *commedia dell' arte*—the braggart and his quick zani, the pedant, the parasite priest, the rustic clown—the group function together to represent "his lordship's simple neighbours." Through them we feel a world which exists before and after to the big moment of the entertainment, and we see the excitement of the smaller people about the big doings. Holofernes honors the Princess's success in hunting in strange, pedantical verse: "The preyful princess pierc'd and prick'd a pretty pleasing pricket" (IV.ii.58). Schoolmasters in real entertainments often furnished shows; Sidney wrote out a part for a comically pedantic schoolmaster in making an entertainment for Elizabeth, "The Lady of the May," 1579. We see Armado courteously enlisting the help of Holofernes in designing "some delightful ostentation, or show, or pageant, or antic, or firework" (V.i.120). He understands, he says, that "the curate and your sweet self are good at such eruptions and sudden breaking-out of mirth." Their talk is absurdly affected, but it is also winningly positive and hopeful. Goodman Dull, "his grace's farborough," wants to take part too:

> Via, goodman Dull! Thou hast spoken no word all this while.
> *Dull.* Nor understood none neither, sir.
> *Holofernes.* Alons! we will employ thee,
> *Dull.* I'll make one in a dance, or so; or I will play
> On the tabor to the Worthies, and let them dance the hay.
> *Holofernes.* Most dull, honest Dull! To our sport, away!
> (V.i.156-162)

Such a little scrap illustrates something that happens repeatedly in Shakespeare's festive comedies. Characters who might be merely butts also win our sympathy by taking part, each after his fashion, in "eruptions and sudden breaking-out of mirth" (V.i.121). This genial quality goes with dramatizing, not merely a story, nor merely characters, but a community occasion: "I'll make one," says laggard Dull; "to *our* sport" says vain Holofernes.

When the show is actually produced, what we watch are not the Worthies but the people who are presenting them. Costard is self-respecting and humble enough to accept correction:

> I Pompey am. Pompey surnam'd the Big—
> *Dumain.* 'The Great.'
> *Costard.* It is 'Great,' sir.
> . . . I here am come by chance,
> And lay my arms before the legs of this sweet lass of France.
> If your ladyship would say 'Thanks, Pompey,' I had done.
> *Princess.* Great thanks, great Pompey.
> *Costard.* 'Tis not so much worth. But I hope I was perfect. I made a little fault in 'Great.' (V.ii.553-562)

What poise and sense of proportion, from which the lords could learn something, is concentrated in " 'Tis not so much worth!" When the poor curate, Sir Nathaniel, is non-plussed in trying to be Alexander the conqueror, Costard makes an apology for him that has become a by-word:

> Run away for shame, Alisander. [*Sir Nathaniel stands aside*] There, an't shall please you! a foolish mild man; an honest man, look you, and soon dash'd. He is a marvellous good neighbour, faith, and a very good bowler; but for Alisander—alas! you see how 'tis—a little o'erparted. (V.ii.583-589)

Shakespeare presents a gulf fixed, and then spans it by touches like "and a very good bowler." It was part of his genius that he could do this; but it was also the genius of the society which he expressed and portrayed. As we have seen, festivities were occasions for communicating across class lines and realizing the common humanity of every level. And the institution of the holidays and entertainments was a function of community life where people knew their places and knew the human qualities of each in his place—knew, for example, that an illiterate Costard was more intelligent and more constructive than a polyliterate Holofernes.

Shakespeare can do without marriages at the end, and still end affirmatively, because he is dramatizing an occasion in a community, not just private lives. News of the French King's death breaks off the wooing game. In deferring the question of marriage, the princess says frankly but graciously that what has passed has been only "courtship, pleasant jest, and courtesy . . . bombast . . . and lining to the time . . . a merriment" (V.ii.789-793). When the King urges that the suits be granted "Now at the latest minute of the hour," she can answer with common-sense tempered by goodwill:

> A time, methinks, too short
> To make a world-without-end bargain in.
> No, no, my lord! Your Grace is perjur'd much,
> Full of dear guiltiness; and therefore this:—
> If for my love (as there is no such cause)
> You will do aught, this shall you do for me:
> (V.ii.797-802)

(Part of the delight of Shakespeare is that some of his people have such beautiful, generous manners! They can "do and say the kindest things in the kindest way.") So the king must spend a year in a hermitage to test his love. And Rosaline prescribes that Berowne must spend a twelvemonth visiting the sick, trying to make them smile by "the fierce endeavour of your wit." So he will have to recognize something beyond games and words, and learn the limits of a gibing spirit

> Whose influence is begot of that loose grace
> Which shallow laughing hearers give to fools.
> (V.ii.868-869)

The ladies' bizarre commands, by insisting that the men confront other types of experience, invite them to try separating their affections from the occasion to see whether or not their feelings are more than courtly sports. In the elation of the festive moment, the game of witty wooing seemed to be love: now comes clarification.

To draw the line between a pastime and a play is another way of marking limits. Berowne's final ironic joke shows how conscious Shakespeare was that he had made a play out of social pastimes, and one which differed from regular drama.

> Our wooing doth not end like an old play:
> Jack hath not Jill. These ladies' courtesy

> Might well have made our sport a comedy.
> (V.ii.883-885)

Sport would have become drama if something had happened. Berowne almost says what Will Fool said of Nashe's pageant: " 'tis not a play neither, but a show." *Love's Labour's Lost* is not a show, because the sports in it are used, dramatically, by people in a kind of history; it is comedy, precisely because Berowne can stand outside the sport and ruefully lament that it is only sport. Berowne's last line recognizes explicitly that to have brought these people from these festivities to the full-fledged event of marriage would have required a whole new development. The king observes hopefully about their unfinished courtship:

> Come, sir, it wants a twelvemonth and a day,
> And then 'twill end.
> *Berowne.* That's too long for a play.
> (V.ii.886-888)

"When . . . Then . . ."—The Seasonal Songs

The pageant and songs of summer and winter are the finale Shakespeare used instead of a wedding dance or masque; and they are exactly right, not an afterthought but a last, and full, expression of the controlling feeling for community and season. The songs evoke pleasures of the most traditional sort, at the opposite pole from facile improvisations. Nobody improvised the outgoing to the fields in spring or the coming together around the fire in winter. After fabulous volubility, we are looking and listening only; after conceits and polysyllables, we are told a series of simple facts in simple words:

> When daisies pied and violets blue
> And lady-smocks all silver-white
> And cuckoo-buds of yellow hue
> Do paint the meadows with delight,
> The cuckoo then on every tree. . . .
> (V.ii.904-908)

We have observed in connection with the songs in Nashe's seasonal pageant that the songs in Shakespeare's festive comedies are usually composed with explicit or implicit reference to a holiday occasion. The cuckoo and owl songs are cognate to such compositions, a very high order of poetry and of imaginative abstraction. We can briefly summarize Shakespeare's practice in composing festive songs to relate these in *Love's Labour's Lost* to simpler, more directly festive lyrics. When Silence suddenly sings out

> Be merry, be merry, my wife has all,
> For women are shrows, both short and tall,
> 'Tis merry in hall when beards wag all,
>   And welcome merry Shrovetide!
> Be merry, be merry. (2 *H.IV* V.iii.35-39)

he is singing a traditional drinking song customarily used on the occasion which it names. Usually, however, Shakespeare wrote songs *like* those used on holiday but serving more exactly and richly his own imaginative purposes. For example, he developed from the women's vantage the same Shrovetide gesture, by which the sexes mock and dismiss each other, in the song that nettles Benedict in *Much Ado about Nothing*:

> Sigh no more, ladies, sigh no more!
>   Men were deceivers ever,
> One foot in sea, and one on shore;
>   To one thing constant never.
>   Then sigh not so,
>   But let them go,
>   And be you blithe and bonny,
> Converting all your sounds of woe
>   Into Hey nonny, nonny.
> (*Much* II.iii.64-71)

How well this fits Beatrice's attitude—until the tide turns and she and Benedict experience a reconciliation all the more freehearted for coming after their merry version of the war between men and women. The development of traditional moments of feeling into songs for particular moments in particular plays is of course a very complex process, sometimes random, and mostly beyond analysis. (No doubt Shakespeare did not think out what he was doing systematically; had he needed to, he could not have done what he did.)

One can see clearly enough where "It was a lover and his lass" comes from and how it fits into *As You Like It* at the moment (V.iii) when love is about to be "crowned with the prime." So too with Feste's love song in the reveling scene of *Twelfth Night*:

> O mistress mine, where are you roaming?
> O, stay and hear! your true-love's coming,
> That can sing both high and low.
> (*Twel.* II.iii.40-42)

The "roaming" here may be to the woods; the true lover commends himself simply for the festive accomplishments of singing high and low, and addresses his mistress simply as "sweet and twenty." What is mentioned and not mentioned gives the sense of neglecting individuality because of being wholly taken up in the festive moment, the "present mirth" and "present laughter." There is a deliberate variation from the expected in the fact that it is a love song, about spring pleasures, and not the within-doors drinking song that would go with Toby's Twelfth-Night-style drinking party. This is noticed by the dialogue:

> *Clown.* Would you have a love song, or a song of good life?
> *Toby.* A love song, a love song.
> *Andrew.* Ay, ay! I care not for good life.
> (*Twel.* II.iii.36-38)

By a similar variation, it is songs of good life that provide the pattern for "Blow, blow thou winter wind," which is sung outdoors in the Forest of Arden.

> Then, heigh-ho, the holly!
> This life is most jolly.
> (*A.Y.L.* II.vii.182-183)

is a crystallization of the mood of Christmas cheer, when it was customary for the men to sing songs in praise of the holly as their emblem, against songs by the women in praise of ivy: "Ivy is soft, and meek of speech."[8] This custom explains why the *As You Like*

[8] Chambers and Sigwick, *Lyrics*, no. CXXXVIII. See also nos. CXXXIX-CXLI. The association developed in these songs is behind Titania's lines when she says

> the female ivy so
> Enrings the barky fingers of the elm.
> (*Dream* IV.i.46-47)

It chorus begins with a vocative: "Heigh-ho, sing heigh-ho, unto the green holly!" Shakespeare uses the gesture of groups singing in the hall together to express the solidarity of the banished Duke and his merry men in Arden. And he takes the Christmas feeling of mastering the cold by good life around a great fire and uses it to convey the exiles' feeling of mastering ingratitude by pastoral fellowship.

Now the spring and winter songs in *Love's Labour's Lost* primarily define moments in the year rather than particular festivals; they are a *débat*, conducted not by argument but by "praise of the Owl and the Cuckoo," as the debate between men and women could go forward by matching praises of the holly and the ivy. It seems clear, as Mr. Dover Wilson points out,[9] that Armado stage manages several disguised persons who form in two groups. The original stage direction reads "Enter all," and Armado presents pageant figures of Winter and Spring as well as of the two birds:

> This side is Hiems, Winter; this Ver, the Spring: the one maintained by the Owl, th' other by the Cuckoo. Ver, begin.
> (V.ii.901-903)

On the title page of the early Tudor printing of *The Debates or Stryfes Betwene Somer and Wynter*,[10] Somer is shown as a gallant with a hawk; Wynter as an old man. Somer describes his antagonist with "Thou art very old, . . . go shave thy hair!" (Perhaps Shakespeare was thinking of the pageant figure in *Love's Labour's Lost* when he wrote of "old Hiems" in *A Midsummer Night's Dream*, II.i.109.) *The Debates* is a writing down of a kind of formal game of argument which had long been customary as a pastime at feasts. It is interesting in this connection that Armado introduces the songs as "the Dialogue that the two learned men have compiled in praise of the Owl and the Cuckoo." The interchange between Somer and Wynter frequently turns on the pleasures of the two seasons:

[9] *Love's Labour's Lost*, ed. Sir Arthur Quiller-Couch and John Dover Wilson (Cambridge, 1923), p. 184. Mr. Wilson refers to Armado's remark to Holofernes, while they are planning the Show of the Nine Worthies: "We will have, if this fadge not, an antic" (V.i.154).

[10] Ed. J. O. Halliwell-Phillips (London, 1860). The original printer was Lawrence Andrew; S. T. C. estimates the original publication date as 1530.

Wynter. I love better good wines/ and good sweet meats upon my table . . .
Somer. Wynter, I have young damsels that have their breast white,
To go gather flowers with their lovers.

Wynter speaks of St. Martin's feast, when great and small drink wine. Somer answers with "the month of May," when there are "primroses and daisies and violet flowers" for "The true lover and his sweet leman," who "go home singing and make good cheer."

The magic of "When daisies pied and violets blue" and of "When icicles hang by the wall" is partly that they seem to be merely lists, and each thing seems to be dwelt on simply for itself; and yet each song says, in a marvelously economical way, where people are in the cycle of the year, the people of farm, manor or village who live entirely in the turning seasons. The only syntax that matters is "When . . . Then . . ."

When icicles hang by the wall,
  And Dick the shepherd blows his nail,
And Tom bears logs into the hall,
  And milk comes frozen home in pail,
When blood is nipp'd, and ways be foul,
Then nightly sings the staring owl:
                    'Tu-who!
Tu-whit, tu-who!' a merry note,
While greasy Joan doth keel the pot.[11]
                    (V.ii.931-939)

Of course these songs are not simply *of* the world they describe, not folk songs; they are art songs, consciously pastoral, sophisticated enjoyment of simplicity.[12] Their elegance and humor convey pleasure in life's being reduced to so few elements and yet being

[11] The first "Tu-who," set out alone as a line, is not in the original texts, but was added by Capell in order that both songs might be sung to the same tune (*Variorum*, p. 318). Once a rhythm has established itself for everyone the way this one has, there is no point in pedantically restoring the original reading, though it may well be the correct one.

[12] See Walter W. Greg, *Pastoral Poetry and Pastoral Drama* (London, 1906), pp. 1-8. I believe that "the sophisticated enjoyment of simplicity" is Sir Walter's phrase, but I cannot now find it in the fine introduction where he makes that point.

so delightful. Each centers on vitality, and moves from nature to man. The spring song goes from lady smocks to the maidens' summer smocks, both showing white against the green of the season, from turtle cocks who "tread" to implications about people. The old joke about the cuckoo is made so delightful because its meaning as a "word," as a call to the woods, is assumed completely as a matter of course.[13] In the winter song, the center of vitality is the fire. (Wynter says in *The Debates*, "For me they make a great fire to cheer my bonys old.") The fire is enjoyed "nightly," after the day's encounter with the cold. Gathered together "When roasted crabs hiss in the bowl," it is merry to hear the owl outside in the cold—his "Tu-whit, tu-who" come to mean this moment. Even the kitchen wench, greasy Joan, keeling the pot to keep it from boiling over, is one of us, a figure of affection. The songs evoke the daily enjoyments and the daily community out of which special festive occasions were shaped up. And so they provide for the conclusion of the comedy what marriage usually provides: an expression of the going-on power of life.

[13] Bottom handles the old cuckoo joke just the other way:

> The finch, the sparrow, and the lark,
> The plain-song cuckoo gray,
> Whose note full many a man doth mark,
> And dares not answer nay.
> For, indeed, who would set his wit to so foolish
> a bird? Who would give a bird the lie, though
> he cry 'cuckoo' never so?
> (*Dream* III.i.133-139)

The stress on "who would give a *bird* the lie" separates men and nature with a comic literalness; and Bottom has a part of the right: one can worry too much. But the other part of the truth is in the *Love's Labour's Lost* song: that "cuckoo" is not just a bird's song—it is a "word of fear," because it means that all those flowers have sprung up, asking to be gathered.

Chapter 6

MAY GAMES AND METAMORPHOSES ON A MIDSUMMER NIGHT

Such shaping fantasies, that apprehend
More than cool reason ever comprehends.

IF Shakespeare had called *A Midsummer Night's Dream* by a title that referred to pageantry and May games, the aspects of it with which I shall be chiefly concerned would be more often discussed. To honor a noble wedding, Shakespeare gathered up in a play the sort of pageantry which was usually presented piece-meal at aristocratic entertainments, in park and court as well as in hall. And the May game, everybody's pastime, gave the pattern for his whole action, which moves "from the town to the grove" and back again, bringing in summer to the bridal. These things were familiar and did not need to be stressed by a title.

Shakespeare's young men and maids, like those Stubbes described in May games, "run gadding over night to the woods, . . . where they spend the whole night in pleasant pastimes—" and in the fierce vexation which often goes with the pastimes of falling in and out of love and threatening to fight about it. "And no marvel," Stubbes exclaimed about such headlong business, "for there is a great Lord present among them, as superintendent and Lord over their pastimes and sports, namely, Satan, prince of hell."[1] In making Oberon, prince of fairies, into the May king, Shakespeare urbanely plays with the notion of a supernatural power at work in holiday: he presents the common May game presided over by an aristocratic garden god. Titania is a Summer Lady who "waxeth wounder proud":

[1] The passage in Stubbes is quoted more fully above, pp. 21-22, in the course of a summary of May day custom.

I am a spirit of no common rate,
The summer still doth tend upon my state . . .
(III.i.157-158)

And Puck, as jester, promotes the "night-rule" version of misrule over which Oberon is superintendent and lord in the "haunted grove." The lovers originally meet

in the wood, a league without the town,
Where I did meet thee once with Helena
To do observance to a morn of May.
(I.i.165-167)

Next morning, when Theseus and Hippolyta find the lovers sleeping, it is after their own early "observation is performed"—presumably some May-game observance, of a suitably aristocratic kind, for Theseus jumps to the conclusion that

No doubt they rose up early to observe
The rite of May; and, hearing our intent,
Came here in grace of our solemnity.
(IV.i.135-137)

These lines need not mean that the play's action happens on May Day. Shakespeare does not make himself accountable for exact chronological inferences; the moon that will be new according to Hippolyta will shine according to Bottom's almanac. And in any case, people went Maying at various times, "Against May, Whitsunday, and other time" is the way Stubbes puts it. This Maying can be thought of as happening on a midsummer night, even on Midsummer Eve itself, so that its accidents are complicated by the delusions of a magic time. (May Week at Cambridge University still comes in June.) The point of the allusions is not the date, but the *kind* of holiday occasion.[2] The Maying is completed when Oberon and Titania with their trains come into the great chamber to bring the blessings of fertility. They are at once common and

[2] A great deal of misunderstanding has come from the assumption of commentators that a Maying must necessarily come on May Day, May 1. The confusion that results is apparent throughout Furness' discussion of the title and date in his preface to the *Variorum* edition. He begins by quoting Dr. Johnson downright "I know not why Shakespeare calls this play 'A *Midsummer* Night's Dream' when he so carefully informs us that it happened on the night preceding *May* day" (p. v.).

special, a May king and queen making their good luck visit to the manor house, and a pair of country gods, half-English and half-Ovid, come to bring their powers in tribute to great lords and ladies.

The play's relationship to pageantry is most prominent in the scene where the fairies are introduced by our seeing their quarrel. This encounter is the sort of thing that Elizabeth and the wedding party might have happened on while walking about in the park during the long summer dusk. The fairy couple accuse each other of the usual weakness of pageant personages—a compelling love for royal personages:

> Why art thou here,
> Come from the farthest steep of India,
> But that, forsooth, the bouncing Amazon,
> Your buskin'd mistress and your warrior love,
> To Theseus must be wedded, and you come
> To give their bed joy and prosperity?
>
> (II.i.68-73)

Oberon describes an earlier entertainment, very likely one in which the family of the real-life bride or groom had been concerned:

> My gentle Puck, come hither. Thou rememb'rest
> Since once I sat upon a promontory
> And heard a mermaid, on a dolphin's back . . .
> That very time I saw (but thou couldst not)
> Flying between the cold moon and the earth
> Cupid, all arm'd. A certain aim he took
> At a fair Vestal, throned by the West,
> And loos'd his love-shaft smartly from his bow,
> As it should pierce a hundred thousand hearts.
> But I might see young Cupid's fiery shaft
> Quench'd in the chaste beams of the wat'ry moon,
> And the imperial vot'ress passed on,
> In maiden meditation, fancy-free.
>
> (II.i.147-164)

At the entertainment at Elvetham in 1591, Elizabeth was throned by the west side of a garden lake to listen to music from the water; the fairy queen came with a round of dancers and spoke of herself as wife to Auberon. These and other similarities make it quite possible, but not necessary, that Shakespeare was referring to the Elvetham occasion.[3] There has been speculation, from Warburton on down, aimed at identifying the mermaid and discovering in Cupid's fiery shaft a particular bid for Elizabeth's affections; Leicester's Kenilworth entertainment in 1575 was usually taken as the occasion alluded to, despite the twenty years that had gone by when Shakespeare wrote.[4] No one, however, has cogently demonstrated any reference to court intrigue—which is to be expected in view of the fact that the play, after its original performance, was on the public stage. The same need for discretion probably accounts for the lack of internal evidence as to the particular marriage the comedy originally celebrated.[5] But what is not in doubt, and what matters for our purpose here, is the *kind* of occasion Oberon's speech refers to, the kind of occasion Shakespeare's scene is shaped by. The speech describes, in retrospect, just such a joyous overflow of pleasure into music and make-believe as is happening in Shakespeare's own play. The fact that what Shakespeare handled with supreme skill was just what was most commonplace no doubt contributes to our inability to connect what he produced with particular historical circumstances.

As we have seen, it was commonplace to imitate Ovid. Ovidian fancies pervade *A Midsummer Night's Dream*, and especially the scene of the fairy quarrel: the description of the way Cupid "loos'd his love shaft" at Elizabeth parallels the Metamorphoses' account of the god's shooting "his best arrow, with the golden head" at Apollo; Helena, later in the scene, exclaims that "The story shall be chang'd:/ Apollo flies, and Daphne holds the chase"—and proceeds to invert animal images from Ovid.[6] The game was not so much to lift things gracefully from Ovid as it was to make up fresh things in Ovid's manner, as Shakespeare here, by playful mythopoesis, explains the bad weather by his fairies' quarrel and makes up a metamorphosis of the little Western flower to motivate

[3] See E. K. Chambers, *Shakespearean Gleanings* (Oxford, 1944), pp. 63-64; and Venezky, *Pageantry*, pp. 140ff.

[4] The conjectures are summarized in *Variorum*, pp. 75-91.

[5] Chambers, *Gleanings*, pp. 61-67.

[6] Ovid, *Metamorphoses*, with an English translation by Frank Justus Miller (New York, 1916), pp. 34 and 36-37, Bk. I, ll. 465-474 and 505-506.

the play's follies and place Elizabeth superbly above them.[7] The pervasive Ovidian influence accounts for Theseus' putting fables and fairies in the same breath when he says, punning on ancient and antic,

> I never may believe
> These antique fables nor these fairy toys.
> (V.i.2-3)

The humor of the play relates superstition, magic and passionate delusion as "fancy's images." The actual title emphasizes a sceptical attitude by calling the comedy a "dream." It seems unlikely that the title's characterization of the dream, "a midsummer night's dream," implies association with the specific customs of Midsummer Eve, the shortest night of the year, except as "midsummer night" would carry suggestions of a magic time. The observance of Midsummer Eve in England centered on building bonfires or "bonefires," of which there is nothing in Shakespeare's moonlight play. It was a time when maids might find out who their true love would be by dreams or divinations. There were customs of decking houses with greenery and hanging lights, which just possibly might connect with the fairies' torches at the comedy's end. And when people gathered fern seed at midnight, sometimes they spoke of spirits whizzing invisibly past. If one ranges through the eclectic pages of *The Golden Bough*, guided by the index for Midsummer Eve, one finds other customs suggestive of Shakespeare's play, involving moonlight, seeing the moon in water, gathering dew, and so on, but in Sweden, Bavaria, or still more remote places, rather than England.[8] One can assume that

[7] See above, pp. 83f., for a similar compliment to the Queen by Nashe in *Summer's Last Will and Testament*. Nashe also elaborates meteorology into make-believe: Summer blames the drying up of the Thames and earlier flooding of it on the pageant figure, Sol (McKerrow, *Nashe*, III, 250, ll. 541-565).

[8] A good summary of English Midsummer Eve customs is in *Brand's Antiquities*, ed. Ellis, pp. 298-337, which gives simply and briefly examples of almost all the English customs included in Frazer's far more complete survey (see *The Golden Bough*, Vol. XII, *Bibliography and General Index*, London, 1915, pp. 370-371). Ellis cites (p. 319) a song from Penzance which describes what is in many respects a Maying, held on Midsummer Eve with a Midsummer bonfire for the men and maids to dance around (such a local combination of the customs is to be expected):

> Bright Luna spreads its light around,
> The gallants for to cheer,

parallel English customs have been lost, or one can assume that Shakespeare's imagination found its way to similarities with folk cult, starting from the custom of Maying and the general feeling that spirits may be abroad in the long dusks and short nights of midsummer. Olivia in *Twelfth Night* speaks of "midsummer madness" (III.iv.61). In the absence of evidence, there is no way to settle just how much comes from tradition. But what *is* clear is that Shakespeare was not *simply* writing out folklore which he heard in his youth, as Romantic critics liked to assume. On the contrary, his fairies are produced by a complex fusion of pageantry and popular game, as well as popular fancy. Moreover, as we shall see, they are not serious in the menacing way in which the people's fairies were serious. Instead they are serious in a very different way, as embodiments of the May-game experience of eros in men and women and trees and flowers, while any superstitious tendency to believe in their literal reality is mocked. The whole night's action is presented as a release of shaping fantasy which brings clarification about the tricks of strong imagination. We watch a dream; but we are awake, thanks to pervasive humor about the tendency to take fantasy literally, whether in love, in superstition, or in Bottom's mechanical dramatics. As in *Love's Labour's Lost* the folly of wit becomes the generalized comic subject in the course of an astonishing release of witty invention, so here in the course of a more inclusive release of imagination, the folly of fantasy becomes the general subject, echoed back and forth between the strains of the play's imitative counterpoint.

The Fond Pageant

We can best follow first the strain of the lovers; then the fairies,

---

As they lay sporting on the ground,
  At the fair June bonfire.

All on the pleasant dewy mead,
  They shared each other's charms,
Till Phoebus' beams began to spread,
  And coming day alarms.

Although reported as "sung for a long series of years at Penzance and the neighbourhood," the piece obviously was written after Shakespeare's period. But the customs it describes in its rather crude way are interesting in relation to *A Midsummer Night's Dream*, particularly the moonlight and dew, and the sun's beams coming to end it all.

their persuasive and then their humorous aspects; and finally the broadly comic strain of the clowns. We feel what happens to the young lovers in relation to the wedding of the Duke. Theseus and Hippolyta have a quite special sort of role: they are principals without being protagonists; the play happens for them rather than to them. This relation goes with their being stand-ins for the noble couple whose marriage the play originally honored. In expressing the prospect of Theseus' marriage, Shakespeare can fix in ideal form, so that it can be felt later at performance in the theater, the mood that would obtain in a palace as the "nuptial hour / Draws on apace." Theseus looks towards the hour with masculine impatience, Hippolyta with a woman's happy willingness to dream away the time. Theseus gives directions for the "four happy days" to his "usual manager of mirth," his Master of the Revels, Philostrate:

> Go, Philostrate,
> Stir up the Athenian youth to merriments,
> Awake the pert and nimble spirit of mirth,
> Turn melancholy forth to funerals;
> The pale companion is not for our pomp.
> (I.i.11-15)

The whole community is to observe a decorum of the passions, with Philostrate as choreographer of a pageant where Melancholy's float will not appear. After the war in which he won Hippolyta, the Duke announces that he is going to wed her

> in another key,
> With pomp, with triumph, and with revelling.
> (I.i.18-19)

But his large, poised line is interrupted by Egeus, panting out vexation. After the initial invocation of nuptial festivity, we are confronted by the sort of tension from which merriment is a release. Here is Age, standing in the way of Athenian youth; here are the locked conflicts of everyday. By the dwelling here on "the sharp Athenian law," on the fate of nuns "in shady cloister mew'd," we are led to feel the outgoing to the woods as an escape from the inhibitions imposed by parents and the organized community. And this sense of release is also prepared by looking for just a moment at the tragic potentialities of passion. Lysander and Hermia, left alone in their predicament, speak a plaintive, symmetrical duet on the theme, learned "from tale or history," that "The course of true love never did run smooth":

> *Lysander.* But, either it was different in blood—
> *Hermia.* O cross! too high to be enthrall'd to low!
> *Lysander.* Or else misgraffed in respect of years—
> *Hermia.* O spite! too old to be engag'd to young!
> (I.i.135-138)

Suddenly the tone changes, as Lysander describes in little the sort of tragedy presented in *Romeo and Juliet*, where Juliet exclaimed that their love was "Too like the lightning, which doth cease to be / Ere one can say 'It lightens'" (II.ii.119-120).

> *Lysander.* Or, if there were a sympathy in choice,
> War, death, or sickness did lay siege to it,
> Making it momentany as a sound,
> Swift as a shadow, short as any dream,
> Brief as the lightning in the collied night,
> That, in a spleen, unfolds both heaven and earth,
> And ere a man hath power to say 'Behold!'
> The jaws of darkness do devour it up:
> So quick bright things come to confusion.
> (I.i.141-149)

But Hermia shakes herself free of the tragic vision, and they turn to thoughts of stealing forth tomorrow night to meet in the Maying wood and go on to the dowager aunt, where "the sharp Athenian law / Cannot pursue us."

If they had reached the wealthy aunt, the play would be a romance. But it is a change of heart, not a change of fortune, which lets love have its way. The merriments Philostrate was to have directed happen inadvertently, the lovers walking into them blind, so to speak. This is characteristic of the way game is transformed into drama in this play, by contrast with the disabling of the fictions in *Love's Labour's Lost*. Here the roles which the young people might play in a wooing game, they carry out in earnest.

And nobody is shown setting about to play the parts of Oberon or Titania. Instead the pageant fictions are presented as "actually" happening—at least so it seems at first glance.

We see the fairies meet by moonlight in the woods before we see the lovers arrive there, and so are prepared to see the mortals lose themselves. In *The Winter's Tale*, Perdita describes explicitly the transforming and liberating powers of the spring festival which in *A Midsummer Night's Dream* are embodied in the nightwood world the lovers enter. After Perdita has described the spring flowers, she concludes with

O, these I lack
To make you garlands of; and my sweet friend,
To strew him o'er and o'er!
Florizel. What, like a corse?
Perdita. No, like a bank for love to lie and play on;
Not like a corse; or if—not to be buried,
But quick, and in mine arms. Come, take your flow'rs.
Methinks I play as I have seen them do
In Whitsun pastorals. Sure this robe of mine
Does change my disposition.

(*WT* IV.iv.127-135)

Her recovery is as exquisite as her impulse towards surrender: she comes back to herself by seeing her gesture as the expression of the occasion. She makes the festive clothes she wears mean its transforming power. Florizel has told her that

These your unusual weeds to each part of you
Do give a life—no shepherdess but Flora
Peering in April's front!

(IV.iv.1-3)

Holiday disguising, her humility suggests, would be embarrassing but for the license of the sheep-shearing feast:

But that our feasts
In every mess have folly, and the feeders
Digest it with a custom, I should blush
To see you so attired.

(IV.iv.10-13)

The lovers in *A Midsummer Night's Dream* play "as in Whitsun pastorals," but they are entirely without this sort of consciousness of their folly. They are unreservedly *in* the passionate protestations which they rhyme at each other as they change partners:

> *Helena.* Lysander, if you live, good sir, awake.
> *Lysander.* And run through fire I will for thy sweet sake
> Transparent Helena! (II.ii.102-104)

The result of this lack of consciousness is that they are often rather dull and undignified, since however energetically they elaborate conceits, there is usually no qualifying irony, nothing withheld. And only accidental differences can be exhibited, Helena tall, Hermia short. Although the men think that "reason says" now Hermia, now Helena, is "the worthier maid," personalities have nothing to do with the case: it is the flowers that bloom in the spring. The life in the lovers' parts is not to be caught in individual speeches, but by regarding the whole movement of the farce, which swings and spins each in turn through a common pattern, an evolution that seems to have an impersonal power of its own. Miss Enid Welsford describes the play's movement as a dance:

> The plot is a pattern, a figure, rather than a series of human events occasioned by character and passion, and this pattern, especially in the moonlight parts of the play, is the pattern of a dance.
>
> "Enter a Fairie at one doore, and Robin Goodfellow at another. . . . Enter the King of Fairies, at one doore, with his traine; and the Queene, at another with hers."
>
> The appearance and disappearance and reappearance of the various lovers, the will-o'-the-wisp movement of the elusive Puck, form a kind of figured ballet. The lovers quarrel in a dance pattern: first, there are two men to one woman and the other woman alone, then a brief space of circular movement, each one pursuing and pursued, then a return to the first figure with the position of the woman reversed, then a cross-movement, man quarrelling with man and woman with woman, and then,

> as finale, a general setting to partners, including not only the lovers but fairies and royal personages as well.[9]

This is fine and right, except that one must add that the lovers' evolutions have a headlong and helpless quality that depends on their not being *intended* as dance, by contrast with those of the fairies. (One can also contrast the courtly circle's intended though abortive dances in *Love's Labour's Lost.*) The farce is funniest, and most meaningful, in the climactic scene where the lovers are most unwilling, where they try their hardest to use personality to break free, and still are willy-nilly swept along to end in pitch darkness, trying to fight. When both men have arrived at wooing Helena, she assumes it must be voluntary mockery, a "false sport" fashioned "in spite." She appeals to Hermia on the basis of their relation as particular individuals, their "sister's vows." But Hermia is at sea, too; names no longer work: "Am I not Hermia? Are not you Lysander?" So in the end Hermia too, though she has held off, is swept into the whirl, attacking Helena as a thief of love. She grasps at straws to explain what has happened by something manageably related to their individual identities:

> *Helena.* Fie, fie! You counterfeit, you puppet you.
> *Hermia.* Puppet? Why so! Ay, that way goes the game.
> Now I perceive that she hath made compare
> Between our statures; she hath urg'd her height . . .
> How low am I, thou painted maypole? Speak!
> (III.ii.289-296)

In exhibiting a more drastic helplessness of will and mind than anyone experienced in *Love Labour's Lost*, this farce conveys a sense of people being tossed about by a force which puts them beside themselves to take them beyond themselves. The change that happens is presented simply, with little suggestion that it involves a growth in insight—Demetrius is not led to realize something false in his diverted affection for Hermia. But one psycho-

[9] *The Court Masque*, pp. 331-332. Although Miss Welsford's perceptions about dance and revel make her account of *A Midsummer Night's Dream* extremely effective, the court masque, to which she chiefly refers it, is not really a formal prototype for this play. It *is* a direct and large influence in shaping *The Tempest*, and her account of that play brings out fundamental structure such as the early masterpiece gets from entertainment and outdoor holiday, not the court masque.

logical change, fundamental in growing up, is presented. Helena tries at first to move Hermia by an appeal to "schooldays friendship, childhood innocence," described at length in lovely, generous lines:

> So we grew together,
> Like to a double cherry, seeming parted,
> But yet an union in partition—
> Two lovely berries molded on one stem . . .
> And will you rent our ancient love asunder
> To join with men in scorning your poor friend?
> (III.ii.208-216)

"To join with men" has a plaintive girlishness about it. But before the scramble is over, the two girls have broken the double-cherry bond, to fight each without reserve for her man. So they move from the loyalties of one stage of life to those of another. When it has happened, when they wake up, the changes in affections seem mysterious. So Demetrius says

> But, my good lord, I wot not by what power
> (But by some power it is) my love to Hermia,
> Melted as the snow, seems to me now
> As the remembrance of an idle gaud
> Which in my childhood I did dote upon . . .
> (IV.i.167-171)

The comedy's irony about love's motives and choices expresses love's power not as an attribute of special personality but as an impersonal force beyond the persons concerned. The tragedies of love, by isolating Romeo and Juliet, Antony and Cleopatra, enlist our concern for love as it enters into unique destinies, and convey its subjective immensity in individual experience. The festive comedies, in presenting love's effect on a group, convey a different sense of its power, less intense but also less precarious.

In *Love's Labour's Lost* it was one of the lovers, Berowne, who was aware, in the midst of folly's game, that it was folly and a game; such consciousness, in *A Midsummer Night's Dream*, is lodged outside the lovers, in Puck. It is he who knows "which way goes the game," as poor Hermia only thought she did. As a jester, and as Robin Goodfellow, games and practical jokes are his great delight: his lines express for the audience the mastery that comes from seeing folly as a pattern:

> Then will two at once woo one.
> That must needs be sport alone.
> (III.ii.118-119)

Like Berowne, he counts up the sacks as they come to Cupid's mill:

> Yet but three? Come one more.
> Two of both kinds makes up four.
> Here she comes, curst and sad.
> Cupid is a knavish lad
> Thus to make poor females mad.
> (III.ii.437-441)

Females, ordinarily a graceless word, works nicely here because it includes *every* girl. The same effect is got by using the names Jack and Jill, *any* boy and *any* girl:

> And the country proverb known,
> That every man should take his own,
> In your waking shall be shown:
> Jack shall have Jill;
> Nought shall go ill:
> The man shall have his mare again and all shall be well.
> (III.ii.457-463)

The trailing off into rollicking doggerel is exactly right to convey a country-proverb confidence in common humanity and in what humanity have in common. The proverb is on the lovers' side, as it was not for Berowne, who had ruefully to accept an ending in which "Jack hath not Jill." A festive confidence that things will ultimately go right supports the perfect gayety and detachment with which Puck relishes the preposterous course they take:

> Shall we their fond pageant see?
> Lord, what fools these mortals be!
> (III.ii.114-115)

The pageant is "fond" because the mortals do not realize they are in it, nor that it is sure to come out right, since nature will have its way.

Bringing in Summer to the Bridal

Spenser's *Epithalamion*, written at about the same time as *A Midsummer Night's Dream*, about 1595, is very like Shakespeare's play in the way it uses a complex literary heritage to express native English customs. In the course of fetching the bride to church and home again, Spenser makes the marriage a fulfillment of the whole countryside and community:

> So goodly all agree with sweet consent,
> To this dayes merriment.
>
> (83-84)

A gathering in, like that of the May game, is part of this confluence:

> Bring with you all the Nymphes that you can heare
> Both of the riuers and the forrests greene:
> And of the sea that neighbours to her neare,
> Al with gay girlands goodly well beseene.
>
> (37-40)

The church of course is decked with garlands, and the bride, "being crowned with a girland greene," seems "lyke some mayden Queene." It is Midsummer. The pervasive feeling for the kinship of men and nature is what rings in the refrain:

> That all the woods them answer and their echo ring.

Shakespeare, in developing a May-game action at length to express the will in nature that is consummated in marriage, brings out underlying magical meanings of the ritual while keeping always a sense of what it is humanly, as an experience. The way nature is felt is shaped, as we noticed in an earlier chapter, by the things that are done in encountering it.[10] The woods are a region of passionate excitement where, as Berowne said, love "adds a precious seeing to the eye." This precious seeing was talked about but never realized in *Love's Labour's Lost*; instead we got wit. But now it is realized; we get poetry. Poetry conveys the experience of amorous tendency diffused in nature; and poetry, dance, gesture, dramatic fiction, combine to create, in the fairies, creatures who embody the passionate mind's elated sense of its own omnipo-

[10] See above, p. 20.

tence. The woods are established as a region of metamorphosis, where in liquid moonlight or glimmering starlight, things can change, merge and melt into each other. Metamorphosis expresses both what love sees and what it seeks to do.

The opening scene, like an overture, announces this theme of dissolving, in unobtrusive but persuasive imagery. Hippolyta says that the four days until the wedding will "quickly *steep* themselves in night" and the nights "quickly *dream* away the time" (I.i.6-7)—night will dissolve day in dream. Then an imagery of wax develops as Egeus complains that Lysander has bewitched his daughter Hermia, "stol'n the *impression* of her fantasy" (I.i.32). Theseus backs up Egeus by telling Hermia that

> To you your father should be as a god;
> One that compos'd your beauties; yea, and one
> To whom you are but as a form in wax,
> By him imprinted, and within his power
> To leave the figure, or disfigure it.
>
> (I.i.47-51)

The supposedly moral threat is incongruously communicated in lines that relish the joy of composing beauties and suggests a god-like, almost inhuman freedom to do as one pleases in such creation. The metaphor of sealing as procreation is picked up again when Theseus requires Hermia to decide "by the next new moon, / The sealing day betwixt my love and me" (I.i.84-85). The consummation in prospect with marriage is envisaged as a melting into a new form and a new meaning. Helena says to Hermia that she would give the world "to be to you translated" (I.i.191), and in another image describes meanings that melt from love's transforming power:

> ere Demetrius look'd on Hermia's eyes,
> He hail'd down oaths that he was only mine;
> And when this hail some heat from Hermia felt,
> So he dissolv'd, and show'rs of oaths did melt.
>
> (I.i.242-245)

The most general statement, and one that perfectly fits what we are to see in the wood when Titania meets Bottom, is

Things base and vile, holding no quantity,
Love can transpose to form and dignity.
(I.i.232-233)

"The glimmering night" promotes transpositions by an effect not simply of light, but also of a half-liquid medium in or through which things are seen:

Tomorrow night, when Phoebe doth behold
Her silver visage in the wat'ry glass,
Decking with liquid pearl the bladed grass,
(A time that lovers' flights doth still conceal) . . .
(I.i.209-213)

Miss Caroline Spurgeon pointed to the moonlight in this play as one of the earliest sustained effects of "iterative imagery."[11] To realize how the effect is achieved, we have to recognize that the imagery is not used simply to paint an external scene but to convey human attitudes. We do not get simply "the glimmering night," but

Didst thou not lead him through the glimmering night
From Perigouna, whom he ravished?
(II.i.77-78)

The liquid imagery conveys an experience of the skin, as well as the eye's confusion by refraction. The moon "looks with a wat'ry eye" (III.i.203) and "washes all the air" (II.i.104); its sheen, becoming liquid pearl as it mingles with dew, seems to get onto the eyeballs of the lovers, altering them to reshape what they see, like the juice of the flower with which they are "streaked" by Oberon and Puck. The climax of unreason comes when Puck overcasts the night to make it "black as Acheron" (III.ii.357); the lovers now experience only sound and touch, running blind over uneven ground, through bog and brake, "bedabbled with the dew and torn with briers" (III.ii.442). There is nothing more they can do until the return of light permits a return of control: light is anticipated as "comforts from the East" (III.ii.432), "the Morning's love" (III.ii.389). The sun announces its coming in a triumph

[11] *Shakespeare's Imagery and What It Tells Us* (New York, 1935), pp. 259-263.

of red and gold over salt green, an entire change of key from the moon's "silver visage in her wat'ry glass":

> the eastern gate, all fiery red,
> Opening on Neptune, with fair blessed beams
> Turns into yellow gold his salt green streams.
> (III.ii.391-393)

Finally Theseus comes with his hounds and his horns in the morning, and the lovers are startled awake. They find as they come to themselves that

> These things seem small and undistinguishable,
> Like far-off mountains turned into clouds.
> (IV.i.190-191)

The teeming metamorphoses which we encounter are placed, in this way, in a medium and in a moment where the perceived structure of the outer world breaks down, where the body and its environment interpenetrate in unaccustomed ways, so that the seeming separateness and stability of identity is lost.

The action of metaphor is itself a process of transposing, a kind of metamorphosis. There is less direct description of external nature *in* the play than one would suppose: much of the effect of being in nature comes from imagery which endows it with anthropomorphic love, hanging a wanton pearl in every cowslip's ear. Titania laments that

> the green corn
> Hath rotted ere his youth attain'd a beard;

while

> Hoary-headed frosts
> Fall in the fresh lap of the crimson rose . . .
> (II.i.94-95, 107-108)

By a complementary movement of imagination, human love is treated in terms of growing things. Theseus warns Hermia against becoming a nun, because

> earthlier happy is the rose distill'd
> Than that which, withering on the virgin thorn
> Grows, lives and dies in single blessedness.
> (I.i.76-78)

Titania, embracing Bottom, describes herself in terms that fit her surroundings and uses the association of ivy with women of the songs traditional at Christmas:[12]

> So doth the woodbine the sweet honeysuckle
> Gently entwist; the female ivy so
> Enrings the barky fingers of the elm.
> (IV.i.45-47)

One could go on and on in instancing metamorphic metaphors. But one of the most beautiful bravura speeches can serve as an epitome of the metamorphic action in the play, Titania's astonishing answer when Oberon asks for the changeling boy:

> Set your heart at rest.
> The fairyland buys not the child of me.
> His mother was a vot'ress of my order;
> And in the spiced Indian air, by night,
> Full often hath she gossip'd by my side,
> And sat with me on Neptune's yellow sands,
> Marking th'embarked traders on the flood;
> When we have laugh'd to see the sails conceive
> And grow big-bellied with the wanton wind;
> Which she, with pretty and with swimming gait
> Following (her womb then rich with my young squire)
> Would imitate, and sail upon the land
> To fetch me trifles, and return again,
> As from a voyage, rich with merchandise.
> But she, being mortal, of that boy did die,
> And for her sake do I rear up her boy;
> And for her sake I will not part from him.
> (II.i.121-137)

The memory of a moment seemingly so remote expresses with plastic felicity the present moment when Titania speaks and we watch. It suits Titania's immediate mood, for it is a glimpse of

[12] See above, pp. 115-116. A recurrent feature of the type of pastoral which begins with something like "As I walked forth one morn in May" is a bank of flowers "for love to lie and play on," such as Perdita speaks of. This motif appears in the "bank where the wild thyme blows" where Titania sleeps "lull'd in these flowers by dances and delight." In such references there is a magical suggestion that love is infused with nature's vitality by contact.

women who gossip alone, apart from men and feeling now no need of them, rejoicing in their own special part of life's power. At such moments, the child, not the lover, is their object—as this young squire is still the object for Titania, who "crowns him with flowers, and makes him all her joy." The passage conveys a wanton joy in achieved sexuality, in fertility; and a gay acceptance of the waxing of the body (like joy in the varying moon). At leisure in the spiced night air, when the proximate senses of touch and smell are most alive, this joy finds sport in projecting images of love and growth where they are not. The mother, having laughed to see the ship a woman with child, imitates it so as to go the other way about and herself become a ship. She fetches trifles, but she is also actually "rich with merchandise," for her womb is "rich with my young squire." The secure quality of the play's pleasure is conveyed by having the ships out on the flood while she sails, safely, upon the *land*, with a pretty and swimming gait that is an overflowing of the security of make-believe. The next line brings a poignant glance out beyond this gamesome world:

> But she, being mortal, of that boy did die.

It is when the flower magic leads Titania to find a new object that she gives up the child (who goes now from her bower to the man's world of Oberon). So here is another sort of change of heart that contributes to the expression of what is consummated in marriage, this one a part of the rhythm of adult life, as opposed to the change in the young lovers that goes with growing up. Once Titania has made this transition, their ritual marriage is renewed:

> Now thou and I are new in amity,
> And will to-morrow midnight solemnly
> Dance in Duke Theseus' house triumphantly
> And bless it to all fair prosperity.
>
> (IV.i.90-93)

The final dancing blessing of the fairies, "Through the house with glimmering light" (V.i.398), after the lovers are abed, has been given meaning by the symbolic action we have been describing: the fairies have been made into tutelary spirits of fertility, so that they can promise that

> the blots of Nature's hand
> Shall not in their issue stand.
> (V.i.416-417)

When merely read, the text of this episode seems somewhat bare, but its clipped quality differentiates the fairy speakers from the mortals, and anyway richer language would be in the way. Shakespeare has changed from a fully dramatic medium to conclude, in a manner appropriate to festival, with dance and song. It seems likely that, as Dr. Johnson argued, there were two songs which have been lost, one led by Oberon and the other by Titania.[13] There were probably two dance evolutions also, the first a processional dance led by the king and the second a round led by the queen: Oberon's lines direct the fairies to dance and sing "through the house," "by the fire," "after me"; Titania seems to start a circling dance with "First rehearse your song by rote"; by contrast with Oberon's "after me," she calls for "hand in hand." This combination of processional and round dances is the obvious one for the occasion: to get the fairies in and give them something to do. But these two forms of dance are associated in origin with just the sort of festival use of them which Shakespeare is making. "The customs of the village festival," Chambers writes, "gave rise by natural development to two types of dance. One was the processional dance of a band of worshippers in progress round their boundaries and from field to field, house to house. . . . The other type of folk dance, the *ronde* or 'round,' is derived from the comparatively stationary dance of the group of worshippers around the more especially sacred objects of the festival, such as the tree or fire. The custom of dancing round the Maypole has been more or less preserved wherever the Maypole is known. But 'Thread the Needle' (a type of surviving processional dance) itself often winds up with a circular dance or *ronde*. . . ."[14] One can make too much of such analogies. But they do illustrate the rich traditional meanings available in the materials Shakespeare was handling.

Puck's broom is another case in point: it is his property as a

[13] See *Variorum*, p. 239, for Dr. Johnson's cogent note. Richmond Noble, in *Shakespeare's Use of Song* (Oxford, 1923), pp. 55-57, argues that the text as we have it *is* the text of the song, without, I think, meeting the arguments of Johnson and subsequent editors.

[14] *Mediaeval Stage*, I, 165-166.

housemaid's sprite, "to sweep the dust behind the door" (V.i.397); also it permits him to make "room," in the manner of the presenter of a holiday mummers' group. And with the dust, out go evil spirits. Puck refers to "evil sprites" let forth by graves, developing a momentary sense of midnight terrors, of spirits that walk by night; then he promises that no mouse shall disturb "this hallowed house." The exorcism of evil powers complements the invocation of good. With their "field dew consecrate," the fairies enact a lustration. Fertilizing and beneficent virtues are in festival custom persistently attributed to dew gathered on May mornings.[15] Shakespeare's handling of nature has infused dew in this play with the vital spirit of moist and verdant woods. The dew is "consecrate" in this sense. But the religious associations inevitably attaching to the word suggest also the sanctification of love by marriage. It was customary for the clergy, at least in important marriages, to bless the bed and bridal couple with holy water. The benediction included exorcism, in the Manual for the use of Salisbury a prayer to protect them from what Spenser called "evill sprights" and "things that be not" (*ab omnibus fantasmaticis demonum illusionibus*).[16] This custom may itself be an ecclesiastical adaptation of a more primitive bridal lustration, a water charm of which dew-gathering on May Day is one variant. Such a play as *A Midsummer Night's Dream* is possible because the May and Summer Spirit, despite its pagan affinities, is not conceived as necessarily in opposition to the wholeness of traditional Christian life.

Magic as Imagination: The Ironic Wit

In promoting the mastery of passion by expression, dramatic art can provide a civilized equivalent for exorcism. The exorcism represented as magically accomplished at the conclusion of the comedy is accomplished, in another sense, by the whole dramatic action, as it keeps moving through release to clarification. By embodying in the fairies the mind's proclivity to court its own omnipotence, Shakespeare draws this tendency, this "spirit," out into the open. They have the meaning they do only because we see them in the midst of the metamorphic region we have just considered—removed

[15] *Ibid.*, I, 122.

[16] *Variorum*, p. 240.

from this particular wood, most of their significance evaporates, as for example in *Nymphidia* and other pretty floral miniatures. One might summarize their role by saying that they represent the power of imagination. But to say what they *are* is to short-circuit the life of them and the humor. They present themselves moment by moment as actual persons; the humor keeps *recognizing* that the person is a personification, that the magic is imagination.

The sceptical side of the play has been badly neglected because romantic taste, which first made it popular, wanted to believe in fairies. Romantic criticism usually praised *A Midsummer Night's Dream* on the assumption that its spell should be complete, and that the absolute persuasiveness of the poetry should be taken as the measure of its success. This expectation of unreserved illusion finds a characteristic expression in Hazlitt:

> All that is finest in the play is lost in the representation. The spectacle is grand; but the spirit was evaporated, the genius was fled. Poetry and the stage do not agree well together. . . . Where all is left to the imagination (as is the case in reading) every circumstance, near or remote, has an equal chance of being kept in mind and tells according to the mixed impression of all that has been suggested. But the imagination cannot sufficiently qualify the actual impressions of the senses. Any offense given to the eye is not to be got rid of by explanation. Thus Bottom's head in the play is a fantastic illusion, produced by magic spells; on the stage it is an ass's head, and nothing more; certainly a very strange costume for a gentleman to appear in. Fancy cannot be embodied any more than a simile can be painted; and it is as idle to attempt it as to personate *Wall* or *Moonshine*. Fairies are not incredible, but Fairies six feet high are so.[17]

Hazlitt's objections were no doubt partly justified by the elaborate methods of nineteenth-century production. A superfluity of "actual impressions of the senses" came into conflict with the poetry by attempting to reduplicate it. But Hazlitt looks for a complete illusion of a kind which Shakespeare's theater did not provide and Shakespeare's play was not designed to exploit; failing to find it

[17] *Characters of Shakespeare's Plays* (1817) in *The Complete Works*, ed. P. P. Howe (London, 1930), IV, 247-248; quoted in *Variorum*, pp. 299-300.

on the stage, he retires to his study, where he is free of the discrepancy between imagination and sense which he finds troublesome. The result is the nineteenth-century's characteristic misreading, which regards "the play" as a series of real supernatural events, with a real ass's head and real fairies, and, by excluding all awareness that "the play" is a play, misses its most important humor.

The extravagant subject matter actually led the dramatist to rely more heavily than elsewhere on a flexible attitude toward representation. The circumstances of the original production made this all the more inevitable: Puck stood in a hall familiar to the audience. We have noticed how in holiday shows, it was customary to make game with the difference between art and life by witty transitions back and forth between them. The aim was not to make the auditors "forget they are in a theater," but to extend reality into fiction. The general Renaissance tendency frankly to accept and relish the artificiality of art, and the vogue of formal rhetoric and "conceited" love poetry, also made for sophistication about the artistic process. The sonneteers mock their mythological machinery, only to insist the more on the reality of what it represents:

> It is most true, what we call Cupid's dart,
> An image is, which for ourselves we carve.

Yet it is

> True and most true, that I must Stella love.[18]

Shakespeare's auditors had not been conditioned by a century and a half of effort to achieve sincerity by denying art. Coleridge has a remark about the advantages that Shakespeare enjoyed as a dramatist which is particularly illuminating in connection with this feeling for art in *A Midsummer Night's Dream*. He observes that "the circumstances of acting were altogether different from ours; it was more of recitation," with the result that "the idea of the poet was always present."[19] The nearly bare stage worked as Proust observed that the bare walls of an art gallery work, to isolate "the essential thing, the act of mind."

[18] Sir Philip Sidney, *Astrophel and Stella*, No. V, in *Arcadia, 1593, and Astrophel and Stella*, ed. Albert Feuillerat (Cambridge, 1922), p. 244.

[19] Coleridge, *Select Poetry and Prose*, ed. Stephen Potter (London, 1933), p. 342.

It is "the act of mind" and "the idea of the poet" which are brought into focus when, at the beginning of the relaxed fifth act, Theseus comments on what the lovers have reported of their night in the woods. I shall quote the passage in full, despite its familiarity, to consider the complex attitude it conveys:

> The lunatic, the lover, and the poet
> Are of imagination all compact.
> One sees more devils than vast hell can hold:
> That is the madman. The lover, all as frantic,
> Sees Helen's beauty in a brow of Egypt.
> The poet's eye, in a fine frenzy rolling,
> Doth glance from heaven to earth, from earth to heaven;
> And as imagination bodies forth
> The forms of things unknown, the poet's pen
> Turns them to shapes, and gives to airy nothing
> A local habitation and a name.
> Such tricks hath strong imagination
> That, if it would but apprehend some joy,
> It comprehends some bringer of that joy;
> Or in the night, imagining some fear,
> How easy is a bush suppos'd a bear! (V.i.7-22)

The description of the power of poetic creation is so beautiful that these lines are generally taken out of context and instanced simply as glorification of the poet. But the praise of the poet is qualified in conformity with the tone Theseus adopts towards the lover and the madman. In his comment there is wonder, wonderfully expressed, at the power of the mind to create from airy nothing; but also recognition that the creation may be founded, after all, merely on airy nothing. Neither awareness cancels out the other. A sense of the plausible life and energy of fancy goes with the knowledge that often its productions are more strange than true.

Scepticism is explicitly crystallized out in the *détente* of Theseus' speech; but scepticism is in solution throughout the play. There is a delicate humor about the unreality of the fairies even while they are walking about in a local habitation with proper names. The usual production, even now, rides rough-shod over this humor by trying to act the fairies in a "vivid" way that will compel belief—with much fluttery expressiveness that has led many to conclude that the fairies are naïve and silly. Quite the contrary—the fairy business is exceedingly sophisticated. The literal and figurative aspects of what is presented are both deliberately kept open to view. The effect is well described by Hermia's remark when she looks back at her dream:

> Methinks I see these things with parted eye,
> When everything seems double.
>
> (IV.i.192-193)

As we watch the dream, the doubleness is made explicit to keep us aware that strong imagination is at work:

> And I serve the Fairy Queen,
> To dew her orbs upon the green.
> The cowslips tall her pensioners be;
> In their gold coats spots you see.
> Those be rubies, fairy favours;
> In those freckles live their savours.
>
> (II.i.8-13)

These conceits, half botany, half personification, are explicit about remaking nature's economy after the pattern of man's: "spots you see. / Those be rubies . . ." The same conscious double vision appears when Puck introduces himself:

> sometime lurk I in a gossip's bowl
> In very likeness of a roasted crab . . .
> The wisest aunt, telling the saddest tale,
> Sometime for three-foot stool mistaketh me;
>
> (II.i.47-52)

The plain implication of the lines, though Puck speaks them, is that Puck does not really exist—that he is a figment of naïve imagination, projected to motivate the little accidents of household life.

This scepticism goes with social remoteness from the folk whose superstitions the poet is here enjoying. Puck's description has the aloof detachment of genre painting, where the grotesqueries of the subject are seen across lines of class difference. As a matter of fact there is much less popular lore in these fairies than is generally assumed in talking about them. The fairies do, it is true, show all the main characteristics of fairies in popular belief: they appear in the forest, at midnight, and leave at sunrise; they take children, dance in ringlets. But as I have remarked already, their whole quality is drastically different from that of the fairies "of the villagery," creatures who, as Dr. Minor White Latham has shown, were dangerous to meddle with, large enough to harm, often malicious, sometimes the consorts of witches.[20] One can speak of Shakespeare's having changed the fairies of popular superstition, as Miss Latham does. Or one can look at what he did in relation to the traditions of holiday and pageantry and see his creatures as pageant nymphs and holiday celebrants, colored by touches from popular superstition, but shaped primarily by a very different provenance. Most of the detailed popular lore concerns Puck, not properly a fairy at all; even he is several parts Cupid and several parts mischievous stage page (a cousin of Moth in *Love's Labour's Lost* and no doubt played by the same small, agile boy). And Puck is only *using* the credulity of the folk as a jester, to amuse a king.

Titania and Oberon and their trains are very different crea-

[20] *The Elizabethan Fairies, The Fairies of Folklore and the Fairies of Shakespeare* (New York, 1930), Ch. V and passim. Professor Latham's excellent study points out in detail how Shakespeare, in keeping such features of popular superstition as, say, the taking of changelings, entirely alters the emphasis, so as to make the fairies either harmless or benign, as Titania is benign in rearing up the child of her dead vot'ress "for her sake." Dr. Latham develops and documents the distinction, recognized to a degree by some commentators from the time of Sir Walter Scott, between the fairies of popular belief and those of *Dream*. In particular she emphasizes that, in addition to being malicious, the fairies of common English belief were large enough to be menacing (Ch. II and passim). This difference in size fits with everything else—though it is not borne out by quite all of the evidence, especially if one considers, as Dr. Louis Wright has suggested to me in conversation, that Warwick is close enough to Wales to have possibly been influenced by Welsh traditions. (We have no direct knowledge, one way or the other, about Warwickshire lore in the Elizabethan period.)

Although Dr. Latham summarizes the appearances of fairies in entertainment pageantry, she does not consider the influence of this tradition, nor of the May game, in shaping what Shakespeare made of his fairies—or more accurately, in shaping what Shakespeare made of his play and so of the fairies in it. But her book made a decisive, cogent contribution to a subject that is often treated with coy vagueness. She surveys in Ch. VI the traditions current before Shakespeare about Robin Goodfellow, pointing out that he had not been a native of fairyland until Shakespeare made him so, but "occupied the unique position of the national practical joker" (p. 223).

tures from the *gemütlich* fairies of middleclass folklore enthusiasm in the nineteenth century. The spectrum of Shakespeare's imagination includes some of the warm domestic tones which the later century cherished. But the whole attitude of self-abnegating humility before the mystery of folk imagination is wrong for interpreting this play. His fairies are creatures of pastoral, varied by adapting folk superstitions so as to make a new sort of arcadia. Though they are not shepherds, they lead a life similarly occupied with the pleasures of song and dance and, for king and queen, the vexations and pleasures of love. They have not the pastoral "labours" of tending flocks, but equivalent duties are suggested in the tending of nature's fragile beauties, killing "cankers in the musk-rose buds." They have a freedom like that of shepherds in arcadias, but raised to a higher power: they are free not only of the limitations of place and purse but of space and time.

The settled content of regular pastoral is possible because it is a "low" content, foregoing wealth and position; Shakespeare's fairies too can have their fine freedom because their sphere is limited. At times their tiny size limits them, though this is less important than is generally suggested by summary descriptions of "Shakespeare's fairy race." The poet plays the game of diminution delightfully, but never with Titania and Oberon, only with their attendants, and not all the time with them. It seems quite possible that Peaseblossom, Cobweb, Moth, and Mustardseed were originally played by children of the family—their parts seem designed to be foolproof for little children: "Ready.—And I.—And I.—And I." Diminutiveness is *the* characteristic of the Queen Mab Mercutio describes in *Romeo and Juliet*, and, as Dr. Latham has shown, it quickly became the hallmark of the progeny of literary fairies that followed;[21] but it is only occasionally at issue in *A Midsummer Night's Dream*. More fundamental is their limited time. Oberon can boast that, by contrast with horrors who must "wilfully themselves exile from light,"

[21] Dr. Latham (*Fairies*, pp. 194-216) traces the way fairies derived from Shakespeare were perpetuated by Drayton and William Browne and others by elaborating conceits about their small size and their relationship to flowers. She develops the point that other writers had suggested earlier, that Shakespeare's influence soon altered popular conceptions of the fairies—and in the process of making them benign and tiny, made them purely literary creatures, without a hold on belief.

we are spirits of another sort.
I with the Morning's love have oft made sport;
And, like a forester, the groves may tread
Even till the eastern gate, all fiery red,
Opening on Neptune, with fair blessed beams
Turns into yellow gold his salt green streams.
(III.ii.388-393)

But for all his pride, full daylight is beyond him: "But notwithstanding, haste; . . . We must effect this business yet ere day." The enjoyment of any sort of pastoral depends on an implicit recognition that it presents a hypothetical case as if it were actual. Puck's lines about the way the fairies run

From the presence of the sun,
Following darkness like a dream,
(V.i.392-393)

summarizes the relation between their special time and their limited sort of existence.

This explicit summary comes at the close, when the whole machinery is being distanced to end with "If we shadows have offended. . . ." But the consciousness and humor which I am concerned to underline are present throughout the presentation of the fairies. It has been easy for production and criticism to ignore, just because usually amusement is not precipitated out in laughter but remains in solution with wonder and delight. In the scene of the quarrel between Titania and Oberon, the fragility of the conceits correspond finely to the half-reality of their world and specialness of their values. The factitiousness of the causes Titania lays out for the weather is gently mocked by the repeated *therefore's*: "Therefore the winds . . . Therefore the moon . . . The ox hath therefore. . . ." Her account makes it explicit that she and Oberon are tutelary gods of fertility, but with an implicit recognition like Sidney's about Cupid's dart—"an image . . . which for ourselves we carve." And her emphasis makes the wheat blight a disaster felt most keenly not for men who go hungry but for the green wheat itself, because it never achieves manhood:

and the green corn
Hath rotted ere his youth attain'd a beard.
(II.i.94-95)

Her concern for the holiday aspect of nature is presented in lines which are poised between sympathy and amusement:

The human mortals want their winter cheer;
No night is now with hymn or carol blest . . .
The seasons alter. Hoary-headed frosts
Fall in the fresh lap of the crimson rose;
And on old Hiems' thin and icy crown
An odorous chaplet of sweet summer buds
Is, as in mockery, set.
(II.i.101-102, 107-111)

Part of the delight of this poetry is that we can enjoy without agitation imaginative action of the highest order. It is like gazing in a crystal: what you see is clear and vivid, but on the other side of the glass. Almost unnoticed, the lines have a positive effect through the amorous suggestion implicit in the imagery, even while letting it be manifest that those concerned are only personifications of flowers and a pageant figure wearing the livery of the wrong season. Titania can speak of "the human mortals" as very far off indeed; the phrase crystallizes what has been achieved in imaginative distance and freedom. But Titania is as far off from us as we are from her.

The effect of wit which in such passages goes along with great imaginative power is abetted by the absence of any compelling interest in passion or plot. Producers utterly ruin the scene when they have the fairy couple mouth their lines at each other as expressively as possible. Titania, after all, leaves before that point is reached: "Fairies, away! / We shall chide downright if I longer stay" (II.i.144-145). At moments of dramatic intensity, the most violent distortion can go unnoticed; what the poet is doing is ignored in responding to what his people are doing. But here a great part of the point is that we *should* notice the distortion, the action of the poet, the wit. Plot tension launches flights of witty poetry which use it up, so to speak, just as the tensions in broad comedy are discharged in laughter. Rhetorical schematizations, or patterns of rhyme, are often used in *A Midsummer Night's Dream* to mark off the units of such verse. But blank verse paragraphs are also constructed so as to form autonomous bravura passages which reach a climax and come to rest while actor and audience catch their breath. Oberon's description of the mermaid, and his tribute to Elizabeth (II.i.148-164), are two such flights, each a rhythmical unit, the first punctuated by Puck's "I remember," the second by Oberon's change of tone at "Yet mark'd I where the bolt of Cupid fell." The formal and emotional isolation of the two passages is calculated to make the audience respond with wonder to the effortless reach of imagination which brings the stars madly shooting from their spheres. In a tribute to Elizabeth, the prominence of "the idea of the poet" in the poetry obviously was all to the good. By Oberon's remark to Puck, "that very time I saw, but thou couldst not," courtly Shakespeare contrived to place the mythology he was creating about Elizabeth on a level appropriately more sublime and occult than that about the mermaid.

Moonlight and Moonshine: The Ironic Burlesque

The consciousness of the creative or poetic act itself, which pervades the main action, explains the subject-matter of the burlesque accompaniment provided by the clowns. If Shakespeare were chiefly concerned with the nature of love, the clowns would be in love, after their fashion. But instead, they are putting on a play. That some commoners should honor the wedding, in their own way, along with the figures from pageantry, is of course in keeping with the purpose of gathering into a play the several sorts of entertainments usually presented separately. But an organic purpose is served too: the clowns provide a broad burlesque of the mimetic impulse to become something by acting it, the impulse which in the main action is fulfilled by imagination and understood by humor. Bottom feels he can be anything: "What is Pyramus, a lover, or a tyrant? . . . An I may hide my face, let me play Thisby too . . . Let me play the lion too." His soul would like to fly out into them all; but he is *not* Puck! In dealing with dramatic illusion, he and the other mechanicals are invincibly literal-minded, carrying to absurdity the tendency to treat the imaginary as though it were real. They exhibit just the all-or-nothing attitude towards fancy which would be fatal to the play as a whole.

When the clowns think that Bottom's transformation has deprived them of their chief actor, their lament seems pointedly allusive to Shakespeare's company and their play.

> *Snug.* Masters, the Duke is coming from the temple, and there is two or three lords and ladies more married. If our sport had gone forward, we had all been made men.
>
> *Flute.* O sweet bully Bottom! Thus hath he lost sixpence a day during his life. He could not have scaped sixpence a day. An the Duke had not given him sixpence a day for playing Pyramus, I'll be hanged! He would have deserved it. Sixpence a day in Pyramus, or nothing!
>
> (IV.ii.15-24)

The repetition of "sixpence a day" seems loaded: if Bottom in Pyramus is worth sixpence, what is Kempe in Bottom worth? For Bottom is to Theseus as Kempe was to the nobleman for whom the play was first produced. The business about moonshine brings this out:

> *Quince.* . . . But there is two hard things: that is, to bring the moonlight into a chamber; for, you know, Pyramus and Thisby meet by moonlight.
>
> *Snout.* Doth the moon shine that night we play our play?
>
> *Bottom.* A calendar, a calendar! Look in the almanac. Find out moonshine, find out moonshine!
>
> *Quince.* Yes, it doth shine that night.
>
> *Bottom.* Why, then may you leave a casement of the great chamber window, where we play, open, and the moon may shine in at the casement.
>
> *Quince.* Ay; or else one must come in with a bush of thorns and a lantern, and say he comes to disfigure, or to present, the person of Moonshine.
>
> (III.i.47-63)

Shakespeare, in *his* play, triumphantly accomplishes just this hard thing, "to bring the moonlight into a chamber." The moonshine, here and later, shows how aware Shakespeare was of what his plastic imagination was doing with moonlight. Since the great chamber Bottom speaks of was, at the initial private performance, the very chamber in which the Chamberlain's men were playing, "Pyramus and Thisby" adorns Theseus' fictitious wedding just as *A Midsummer Night's Dream* adorns the real wedding. Bottom's proposal to open a casement reduces the desire for realism to the absurdity of producing the genuine article. Translated out of irony, it suggests, that "if you want real moonlight, you put yourself in Bottom's class." It is amusing how later producers have labored with ever greater technical resources to achieve Bottom's ideal. Hollywood's Max Reinhardt version omitted most of the poetry to make room for cellophane-spangled fairies standing in rows on ninety-foot moonbeams.

The difference between art and life is also what the clowns forget in their parlous fear lest "the ladies be afeared of the lion" and the killing. Bottom's solution is to tell the ladies in plain language that fiction is not fact:

> Write me a prologue; and let the prologue seem to say, we will do no harm with our swords, and that Pyramus is not kill'd indeed; and for the more better assurance, tell them that I Pyramus am not Pyramus, but Bottom the weaver. This will put them out of fear. (III.i.18-23)

Now this expresses Bottom's vanity, too. But producers and actors, bent on showing "character," can lose the structural, ironic point if they let the lines get lost in Bottom's strutting. What the clowns forget, having "never labour'd in their minds till now," is that a killing or a lion in a play, however plausibly presented, is a mental event.[22] Because, like children, they do not discriminate between

[22] What Shakespeare exhibits in Bottom's dramatics by reduction to absurdity is expressed directly in the Prologues of *H.V.* There the dramatist is dealing with heroic events which cannot be presented "in their huge and proper life" (Pro. V, l. 5) and so appeals to his audience repeatedly to "eke out our performance with your minds," . . . "minding true things by what their mock'ries be" (Pro. III, l. 35, and Pro. IV, l. 53). The prologues insist continually on the mental process by which alone a play comes to life (Pro. I, ll. 23-25 and 28):

> Piece out our imperfections with your thoughts:
> Into a thousand parts divide one man
> And make imaginary puissance . . .
> For 'tis your thoughts that now must deck our kings . . .

In reference to the rapid shifting of his locale, Shakespeare uses an image which might describe Puck's powers to do what men can only conceive (Pro. III, ll. 1-3):

> Thus with imagin'd wing our swift scene flies,
> In motion of no less celerity
> Than that of thought . . .

Even in a play where, by contrast with *Dream*, Shakespeare is concerned to realize

imaginary and real events, they are literal about fiction. But they are not *un*imaginative: on the contrary they embody the stage of mental development before the discipline of facts has curbed the tendency to equate what is "in" the mind with what is "outside" it. They apply to drama the same sort of mentality that supports superstition—it is in keeping that the frightening sort of folk beliefs about changelings are for them an accepted part of life: "Out of doubt he is transported."[23] Because this uncritical imaginativeness is the protoplasm from which all art develops, the clowns are as delightful and stimulating as they are ridiculous. Even while we are laughing at them, we recover sympathetically the power of fantasy enjoyed by children, who, like Bottom, can be anything, a train, an Indian or a lion.

In the performance of *Pyramus and Thisby*, Shakespeare captures the naïveté of folk dramatics and makes it serve his controlling purpose as a final variant of imaginative aberration. The story from Ovid, appropriate for a burlesque in an Ovidian play, is scarcely the kind of thing the simple people would have presented in life; but their method and spirit in putting it on, and the spirit in which the noble company take it, are not unlike what is suggested by Laneham's account of the bride-ale show at Kenilworth. "If we imagine no worse of them than they of themselves," Theseus observes of the Athenian artisans, "they may pass for excellent men" (V.i.218). The comedy of the piece centers not so much on what is acted in it as in the continual failure to translate actor into character. Shakespeare's skill is devoted to keeping both the players and their would-be play before us at the same time, so that we watch, not Pyramus alone, nor Bottom alone, but Bottom "in Pyramus," the fact of the one doing violence to the fiction of the other.

Almost half of *Pyramus and Thisby* is taken up with prologues of the sort one gets in the mummers' plays:

---

actual historical events, he insists that this realization must be by imaginative projection, not literal reproduction.

[23] IV.ii.2. In their terrified response to Puck's intervention, Bottom's companions are like the colored man in the Hollywood ghost thriller. In showing the whites of his eyes and running without even an effort at courage, he is more credulous than the heroes are, and more than we are. For a moment we laugh at the fear of the uncanny which we ourselves have just experienced, and this comic relief prepares us for another spell of the creeps.

I am king of England,
As you may plainly see.[24]

Such prologues suit Shakespeare's purpose, because they present the performer openly climbing in the window of aesthetic illusion, where he can get stuck midway:

In this same enterlude it doth befall
That I, one Snout by name, present a wall . . .
This loam, this roughcast, and this stone doth show
That I am that same wall. The truth is so.
(V.i.156-163)

"The truth is so," by warranting that fiction is fact, asks for a laugh, as does the Prologue's "At the which let no man wonder," or Moon's

Myself the man i' the moon *do seem to be.*

The incarnation of Wall is a particularly "happy-unhappy" inspiration, because the more Wall does, the less he is a wall and the more he is Snout.

There is a great deal of incidental amusement in the parody and burlesque with which *Pyramus and Thisby* is loaded. It burlesques the substance of the death scene in *Romeo and Juliet* in a style which combines ineptitudes from Golding's translation of Ovid with locutions from the crudest doggerel drama.[25] What is most

[24] J. M. Manly, *Specimens of Pre-Shakespearean Drama* (Boston, 1897), I, 293, from *The Lutterworth Christmas Play.*

[25] The familiar Ovidian story which Shakespeare elected to make into "very tragic mirth" is extremely similar, on the face of it, to the story of *Romeo*, which also hinges on surreptitious meetings and an accidental misunderstanding leading to double suicide. The similarity seems to be underscored by allusions (V.i.355-359):

Theseus. Moonshine and Lion are left to bury the dead.
Demetrius. Ay, and Wall too.
Bottom. [starts up] No, I assure you; the wall is down that parted their fathers.

Perhaps there is another allusion to *Romeo* when, after Wall's earlier exit (V.i.210), Theseus makes the mock-sententious observation: "Now is the mural down between the two neighbours." There is nothing in Ovid about a reconciliation, but there is a great deal at the end of *Romeo*. Parts for Thisby's mother and father and Pyramus' father are assigned by Peter Quince in first mustering his actors (I.ii.62). Perhaps Shakespeare planned to make tragical mirth of their laments before he thought of Wall and Moonshine. Miss M. C. Bradbrook, in *Elizabethan Stage Conditions* (Cambridge, 1932), p. 39, notes that when Romeo, before the

remarkable about it, however, is the way it fits hilarious fun into the whole comedy's development of attitude and understanding. After the exigent poise of the humorous fantasy, laughs now explode one after another; and yet they are still on the subject, even

---

balcony scene, "ran this way and leap'd this orchard wall" to get away from his friends and into the Capulets' orchard, the staging of the wall presented an unusual problem. She adds that "it is amusing to note the parody of this same orchard wall" in *Dream*. Snout's "you can never bring in a wall" certainly seems a likely by-product of Shakespeare's having recent experience with the difficulty. The effect of the burlesque does not, of course, hinge on specifically recognizing *Romeo* as a prototype. An awareness of the connection adds point; but the remarks about reconciliation are funny enough simply as comic versions of the *kind* of sentiment to be expected at the end of a tragedy.

The style of *Pyramus and Thisby* imitates with a shrewd eye for characteristic defects what Marlowe, in the Prologue to *Tamburlaine*, called the "jigging veins of rhyming mother wits." The most common devices used by inept early poets "to plump their verse withall" turn up in Shakespeare's parody. The leaden ring of the expletives "same" ("This *same* wall") and "certaine" ("This beauteous Lady, Thisby is *certaine*") recalls many pieces in Dodsley's *Old English Plays* and many passages in Golding's translation of Ovid. Golding's style may well have been Shakespeare's most immediate model. The comic possibilities of the story are very obvious indeed in the translation, whose fourteeners here are often incapable of carrying the elaborate rhetoric. One bit of this high-flown rhetoric is the apostrophizing of the wall, which appears in Golding thus (*Shakespeare's Ovid / Being Arthur Golding's Translation of the Metamorphoses*, ed. W.H.D. Rouse [London, 1904], pp. 83-84, Bk. IV, ll. 90-100):

> O thou envious wall (they sayd) why letst thou lovers thus?
> What matter were it if that thou permitted both of us
> In armes eche other to embrace? Or if that thou think this
> Were overmuch, yet mightest thou at least make roume to kisse.
> And yet thou shalt not finde us churles: we think
> ourselves in det
> For this same piece of courtesie, in vouching safe to let
> Our sayings to our friendly ears thus freely to come and goe,
> Thus having where they stood in vaine complayned of their woe,
> When night drew nere, they bade adew and eche gave
> kisses sweete
> Unto the parget on their side, the which did never meete.

In addition to the top-heavy personification which in Golding makes the wall into a sort of stubborn chaperon, Shakespeare's version exploits the fatuous effect of suddenly reversing the wall's attributes from envious to courteous, when the wall, after all, is perfectly consistent. Bottom at first wheedles a "courteous Wall" and then storms at a "wicked Wall." The would-be pathetic touch about kissing the parget (plaster) instead of each others' lips also reappears (V.i.204).

To fill out a line, or to make a rhyme as false as "Thisby . . . secretly," the mother wits often elaborate redundancies, so that technical ineptitude results in a most inappropriate and unpoetical factuality. Shakespeare exploits this effect repeatedly:

> My cherry lips have often kiss'd thy stones,
> Thy stones with lime and hair knit up in thee.
> (V.i.192-193)

There are also many redundant synonyms, like "Did scare away, or rather did

though now we are romping reassuringly through easy-to-make distinctions. Theseus can say blandly

> The best in this kind are but shadows; and the worst are no worse, if imagination amend them. (V.i.214-216)

Although we need not agree (Hippolyta says "It must be your imagination then, and not theirs."), Theseus expresses part of our response—a growing detachment towards imagination, moving towards the distance from the dream expressed in Puck's epilogue.

The meeting in the woods of Bottom and Titania is the climax of the polyphonic interplay; it comes in the middle of the dream, when the humor has the most work to do. Bottom in the ass's head provides a literal metamorphosis, and in the process brings in the element of grotesque fantasy which the Savage Man or Woodwose furnished at Kenilworth, a comic version of an animal-headed dancer or of the sort of figure Shakespeare used in Herne the Hunter, "with great ragged horns," at the oak in *The Merry Wives of Windsor.* At the same time he is the theatrical company's clown "thrust in by head and shoulder to play a part in majestical

---

affright." In imitating the use of such homemade stuffing, Shakespeare goes far back (or down) for his models, notably skipping an intermediate, more pretentious level of sophistication in bad Tudor poetry, where fustian classical allusions, "English Seneca read by Candlelight," replace bald redundancy as the characteristic means of plumping verse. Pistol's discharges are Shakespeare's burlesque of such bombast. Most of Bottom's rhetoric is a step down the ladder: the "Shafalus" and "Limander" of *Pyramus* are classical names as these appear in such pieces as *Thersites.*

Perhaps when Bottom starts up, very much alive despite his emphatic death, to correct the Duke in the matter of the wall, his comic resurrection owes something, directly or via the jig, to the folk play. When the St. George, or Fool, or whoever, starts up, alive again, after the miraculous cure, the reversal must have been played as a moment of comical triumph, an upset, more or less grotesque or absurd, no doubt, but still exhilarating—to come back alive is the ultimate turning of the tables on whatever is an enemy of life. The most popular of Elizabethan jigs, "The Jig of Rowland," involves a device of playing dead and pretending to come back to life which may well be a rationalized development of this primitive resurrection motif. Rowland wins back Margaret from the Sexton by getting into a grave and playing dead; she laments him and then starts to go off with his rival; but Rowland jumps up behind them, astonishes the Sexton, sends him packing and wins the wench. (Baskervill, *Jig*, pp. 220-222.) Such brief comic song and dance dramas as this were used as afterpieces following the regular play. *Pyramus and Thisby* almost amounts to a developed jig which has been brought into the framework of the play instead of being presented as an afterpiece, in the usual fashion. The dance element comes in when Bottom, after coming back alive, concludes by dancing a bergomasque.

matters" and remaining uproariously literal and antipoetic as he does so. Titania and he are fancy against fact, not beauty and the beast. She makes all the advances while he remains very respectful, desiring nothing bestial but "a peck of provender." Clownish oblivion to languishing beauty is sure-fire comedy on any vaudeville stage. Here it is elaborated in such a way that when Titania is frustrated, so is the transforming power of poetry:

> *Titania.* I pray thee, gentle mortal, sing again.
> Mine ear is much enamoured of thy note;
> So is mine eye enthralled to thy shape;
> And thy fair virtue's force (perforce) doth move me,
> On the first view, to say, to swear, I love thee.
> *Bottom.* Methinks, mistress, you should have little reason for that. And yet, to say the truth, reason and love keep little company together now-a-days. The more the pity that some honest neighbours will not make them friends. Nay, I can gleek, upon occasion.
> *Titania.* Thou art as wise as thou art beautiful.
> *Bottom.* Not so, neither . . .
> (III.i.140-152)

From a vantage below romance, the clown makes the same point as sceptical Theseus, that reason and love do not go together. Titania tells him that she

> . . . will purge thy mortal grossness so
> That thou shalt like an airy spirit go.
> (III.i.163-164)

But even her magic cannot "transpose" Bottom.

The "low" or "realistic" effect which he produces when juxtaposed with her is much less a matter of accurate imitation of common life than one assumes at first glance. Of course the homely touches are telling—forms of address like "Methinks, mistress" or words like *gleek* suggest a social world remote from the elegant queen's. But the realistic effect does not depend on Bottom's being like real weavers, but on the *détente* of imaginative tension, on a downward movement which counters imaginative lift. This antipoetic action involves, like the poetic, a high degree of abstraction from real life, including the control of rhythm which can establish a blank verse movement in as little as a single line, "Thou art as wise as thou art beautiful," and so be able to break the ardent progression of the queen's speech with "Not so, neither" When Bottom encounters the fairy attendants, he reduces the fiction of their existence to fact:

Bottom. I cry your worships mercy, heartily. I beseech your worship's name.
Cobweb. Cobweb.
Bottom. I shall desire you of more acquaintance, good Master Cobweb. If I cut my finger, I shall make bold with you.
(III.i.182-187)

Cobwebs served the Elizabethans for adhesive plaster, so that when Bottom proposes to "make bold with" Cobweb, he treats him as a *thing*, undoing the personification on which the little fellow's life depends. To take hold of Cobweb in this way is of course a witty thing to do, when one thinks about it. But since the wit is in the service of a literal tendency, we can take it as the expression of a "hempen homespun." There is usually a similar incongruity between the "stupidity" of a clown and the imagination and wit required to express such stupidity. Bottom's charming combination of ignorant exuberance and oblivious imaginativeness make him the most humanly credible and appealing personality Shakespeare had yet created from the incongruous qualities required for the clown's role. The only trouble with the part, in practice, is that performers become so preoccupied with bringing out the weaver's vanity as an actor that they lose track of what the role is expressing as part of the larger imaginative design.

For there is an impersonal, imaginative interaction between the clowning and the rest of the play which makes the clowns mean more than they themselves know and more than they are as personalities. Bottom serves to represent, in so aware a play, the limits of awareness, limits as limitations—and also, at moments, limits as form and so strength.

Bottom. Where are these lads? Where are these hearts?
Quince. Bottom! O most courageous day! O most happy hour!

Bottom. Masters, I am to discourse wonders; but ask me not what. For if I tell you, I am no true Athenian. I will tell you everything, right as it fell out.

Quince. Let us hear, sweet Bottom.

Bottom. Not a word of me. All that I will tell you is, that the Duke hath dined. Get your apparel together, good strings to your beards . . .

(IV.ii.26-36)

It is ludicrous for Bottom to be so utterly unable to cope with the "wonders," especially where he is shown boggling in astonishment as he wordlessly remembers them: "I have had a most rare vision. I have had a dream past the wit of man to say what dream it was" (IV.i.207-209). But there is something splendid, too, in the way he exuberantly rejoins "these lads" and takes up his particular, positive life as a "true Athenian." Metamorphosis cannot faze him for long. His imperviousness, indeed, is what is most delightful about him with Titania: he remains so completely himself, even in her arms, and despite the outward change of his head and ears; his confident, self-satisfied tone is a triumph of consistency, persistence, existence.

The Sense of Reality

The value of humor, and the finest pleasure in it, depends on the seriousness of what it makes into fun. It is easy to be gay by taking a trivial theme, or by trivializing an important theme. The greatness of comedy, as of every other art form, must rest, to use Henry James' phrase, on the amount of "felt life" with which it deals in its proper fashion. After examining the structure and artifice of *A Midsummer Night's Dream*, we can now ask how much reality it masters by its mirth. This comedy is the first that is completely, triumphantly successful; but it has the limitations, as well as the strength, of a youthful play.

The role of imagination in experience is a major preoccupation in other plays of the same period. Dreams are several times presented as oracles of irrational powers shaping life, and inspire dread and awe. In the death scene of Clarence, in *Richard III*, the poet had presented the experience of oppression and helplessness on waking from the grip of nightmare. *A Midsummer Night's Dream* presents a resolution of the dream forces which so often augur conflict. To indulge dreamlike irrationality with impunity is, as Freud pointed out, one of the basic satisfactions of wit. The action of *A Midsummer Night's Dream* shows the same pattern on a large scale: it suggests the compulsion of dream, and then reconciles night's motives with the day's as the lovers conclude, "Why then, we are awake":

> *Demetrius.* These things seem small and undistinguishable,
> Like far-off mountains turned into clouds . . .
> *Helena.* And I have found Demetrius like a jewel,
> Mine own, and not mine own.
> *Demetrius.* Are you sure
> That we are awake? It seems to me
> That yet we sleep, we dream. Do not you think
> The Duke was here, and bid us follow him?
> *Hermia.* Yea, and my father.
> *Helena.* And Hippolyta.
> *Lysander.* And he did bid us follow to the temple.
> *Demetrius.* Why then, we are awake. Let's follow him,
> And by the way let us recount our dreams.
> (IV.i.190-202)

The fun which Mercutio makes of dreams and fairies in *Romeo and Juliet* is an attempt to do in a single speech what the whole action does in *A Midsummer Night's Dream.* His excursion on Queen Mab is designed to laugh away Romeo's dream-born misgivings about their fatal visit to the Capulets.

> *Romeo.* . . . we mean well, in going to this masque;
> But 'tis no wit to go.
> *Mercutio.* Why, may one ask?
> *Romeo.* I dreamt a dream to-night.
> *Mercutio.* And so did I.
> *Romeo.* Well, what was yours?
> *Mercutio.* That dreamers often lie.
> *Romeo.* In bed asleep, while they do dream things true.
> *Mercutio.* O, then I see Queen Mab hath been with you.
> (*Romeo* I.iv.47-53)

—and then follow the delightfully plausible impossibilities about the fairies' midwife, implying that dreams accord with the dreamer's wishes, and huddled rapidly one on another, to prevent Romeo's interrupting. The implication is that to believe in dreams is as foolish as to believe in Queen Mab's hazel-nut chariot. When Romeo finally interrupts, Mercutio dismisses his own fairy toys almost in the spirit of Duke Theseus:

> *Romeo.* Peace, peace, Mercutio, peace!
> Thou talk'st of nothing.
> *Mercutio.* True, I talk of dreams;
> Which are the children of an idle brain,
> Begot of nothing but vain fantasy;
> Which is as thin of substance as the air . . .
> (I.iv.95-99)

Romeo's dream, however, in spite of Mercutio, is not to be dismissed so easily as airy nothing:

> . . . my mind misgives
> Some consequence, yet hanging in the stars . . .
> (I.iv.106-107)

A Midsummer Night's Dream is a play in the spirit of Mercutio: the dreaming in it includes the knowledge "that dreamers often lie." The comedy and tragedy are companion pieces: the one moves away from sadness as the other moves away from mirth.

One can feel, indeed, that in the comedy, as compared with Shakespeare's later works, mastery comes a little too easily, because the imaginary and the real are too easy to separate. The same thing can be said of the other plays of the period, *Titus Andronicus, Romeo and Juliet*, and *Richard II*. Theseus makes a generalization that

> The lunatic, the lover, and the poet
> Are of imagination all compact.
> (*Dream* V.i.7-8)

In all these plays the young author gives dramatic urgency to poetic language by putting his heroes in situations which give the lie to what their minds imagine under the influence of passion. Tragedy is conceived chiefly as the contradiction between a warm inner world of feeling and impulse and a cold outer world of fact. Imagination, as the voice of this inner world, has a crucial significance, but its felt reality is limited by the way the imaginary and the real are commonly presented as separate realms. Imagination tends to be *merely* expressive, an evidence of passion rather than a mode of perception. This is true almost without qualification of *Titus Andronicus*, the earliest play of the group. In presenting the madness of Titus, Shakespeare's assumptions about reality are altogether those of Theseus' speech, empirical and fact-minded. The psychological factor is always kept in the foreground when the young poet, following, with more imagination but less profundity, Kyd's method in *The Spanish Tragedy*, expresses the intensity of Titus' grief by having his distraction take literally hyperboles and imaginative identifications. His delusions are very deliberately manipulated to conform to his predominant emotion; in the almost comical scene about killing the fly, Titus first bemoans the act because the fly is a fellow victim, then exults at the creature's death because its blackness links it with the Moor who has wronged him. Even in *Romeo and Juliet*, while the emotional reality of love is triumphantly affirmed we remain always aware of what in the expression is factual and what imaginary, and of how the poetry is lifting us from one plane to the other:

> A grave? O, no, a lanthorn, slaught'red youth,
> For here lies Juliet, and her beauty makes
> This vault a feasting presence full of light.
>
> (*Romeo* V.iii.84-86)

In the poetry of this period, there is room beside metaphor and hyperbole to insert a phrase like "so to speak." Marcus exclaims of Titus' distraction:

> Alas, poor man! Grief has so wrought on him
> He takes false shadows for true substances.
>
> (*Tit.* III.ii.79-80)

The same remark could be made about Richard II, whose hosts of grief-begotten angels prove so inadequate against the "true substances" mobilized by Bolingbroke. The plays present passionate expression or delusion by the use of relatively simple contrasts between fact and fiction, reason and feeling, keeping an orientation outside the passionate characters' imaginative expression.

In *Richard II*, however, the simple shadow-substance antithesis becomes something more: the divine right of kings gives one sort of objective validity to Richard's imaginings—although his guardian angels are ineffective immediately, they are grounded in moral perception, and Bolingbroke eventually finds their avenging power. Later in Shakespeare's work, the imagination becomes in its own right a way of knowing "more things in heaven and earth" than cool reason ever comprehends. Contrasts between real and imaginary are included in and superseded by contrasts between appearance and reality, as these unfold at various levels of awareness. How different Shakespeare's sense of reality finally became is evident if we set the proud scepticism of Theseus beside the humble scepticism of Prospero. The presiding genius of Shakespeare's latest fantasy also turns from a pageant-like work of imagination to reflect on its relation to life. But for him life itself is like the insubstantial pageant, and *we*, not just the Titanias and Oberons, are such stuff as dreams are made on.

The greater profundity of the later work, however, should not blind us to the different virtues of the earlier. The confident assumption dominant in *A Midsummer Night's Dream*, that substance and shadow can be kept separate, determines the peculiarly unshadowed gaiety of the fun it makes with fancy. Its organization by polarities—everyday-holiday, town-grove, day-night, waking-dreaming—provides a remarkable resource for mastering passionate experience. By a curious paradox, the full dramatization of holiday affirmations permitted "that side" of experience to be boxed off by Theseus. If we take our stand shoulder to shoulder with Theseus, the play can be an agency for distinguishing what is merely "apprehended" from what is "comprehended." Shakespeare's method of structuring is as powerful, in its way, as Descartes' distinction between mind and body, the formidable engine by which the philosopher swept away "secondary qualities" so that mathematical mind might manipulate geometrical extension. If we do not in our age want to rest in Theseus' rationalistic position (any more than in Descartes'), it remains a great achievement to have got there, and wherever we are going in our sense of reality, we have come via that standing place.

Theseus, moreover, does not quite have the last word, even in this play: his position is only one stage in a dialectic. Hippolyta will not be reasoned out of her wonder, and answers her new Lord with

> But all the story of the night told over,
> And all their minds transfigur'd so together,
> More witnesseth than fancy's images
> And grows to something of great constancy;
> But howsoever, strange and admirable.
>
> (V.i.23-27)

Did it happen, or didn't it happen? The doubt is justified by what Shakespeare has shown us. We are not asked to think that fairies exist. But imagination, by presenting these figments, has reached to something, a creative tendency and process. What is this process? Where is it? What shall we call it? It is what happens in the play. It is what happens in marriage. To name it requires many words, words in motion—the words of *A Midsummer Night's Dream.*

Chapter 7

THE MERCHANTS AND THE JEW OF VENICE: WEALTH'S COMMUNION AND AN INTRUDER

Should I go to church
And see the holy edifice of stone
And not bethink me straight of dangerous rocks,
Which, touching but my gentle vessel's side,
Would scatter all her spices on the stream,
Enrobe the roaring waters with my silks,
And, in a word, but even now worth this,
And now worth nothing?

WHEN Nashe, in *Summer's Last Will and Testament*, brings on a Christmas who is a miser and refuses to keep the feast, the kill-joy figure serves, as we have noticed,[1] to consolidate feeling in support of holiday. Shakespeare's miser in *The Merchant of Venice* has the same sort of effect in consolidating the gay Christians behind Portia's "The quality of mercy is not strained." The comic antagonist as we get him in Nashe's churlish Christmas, uncomplicated by such a local habitation as Shakespeare developed for Shylock, is a transposed image of the pageant's positive spokesmen for holiday. Summer reminds him, when he first comes on, of the role he ought to play, and his miserliness is set off against the generosity proper to festivity:

Summer. Christmas, how chance thou com'st not as the rest,
Accompanied with some music, or some song?
A merry carol would have grac'd thee well;
Thy ancestors have us'd it heretofore.
Christmas. Aye, antiquity was the mother of ignorance: this

[1] See above, p. 60.

latter world, that sees but with her spectacles, hath spied a pad in those sports more than they could.

Summer. What, is't against thy conscience for to sing?

Christmas. No, nor to say, by my troth, if I may get a good bargain.

Summer. Why, thou should'st spend, thou should'st not to care to get. Christmas is god of hospitality.

Christmas. So will he never be of good husbandry. I may say to you, there is many an old god that is now grown out of fashion. So is the god of hospitality.

Summer. What reason canst thou give he should be left?

Christmas. No other reason, but that Gluttony is a sin, and too many dunghills are infectious. A man's belly was not made for a powdering beef tub: to feed the poor twelve days, and let them starve all the year after, would but stretch out the guts wider than they should be, and so make famine a bigger den in their bellies than he had before. . . .

Autumn. [Commenting on Christmas]
A fool conceits no further than he sees,
He hath no sense of aught but what he feels.

Christmas. Aye, aye, such wise men as you come to beg at such fool's doors as we be.

Autumn. Thou shut'st thy door; how should we beg of thee? . . .

Christmas. Liberalitas liberalitate perit; . . . our doors must have bars, our doublets must have buttons. . . . Not a porter that brings a man a letter, but will have his penny. I am afraid to keep past one or two servants, lest, hungry knaves, they should rob me: and those I keep, I warrant I do not pamper up too lusty; I keep them under with red herring and poor John all the year long. I have damned up all my chimnies. . . .[2]

Here is the stock business about denying food and locking up which appears also in Shylock's part, along with a suggestion of the harsh ironical humor that bases itself on "the facts"—"aye, such wise men as you come to beg at such fool's doors as we be"—and also a moment like several in *The Merchant of Venice* where

[2] Lines 1627-1710 in McKerrow, *Nashe*, III, 284-287.

the fangs of avarice glint naked—"if I may get a good bargain." Shylock, moreover, has the same attitude as Nashe's miser about festivity:

> What, are there masques? Hear you me, Jessica.
> Lock up my doors; and when you hear the drum
> And the vile squealing of the wry-neck'd fife,
> Clamber not you up to the casements then,
> Nor thrust your head into the public street
> To gaze on Christian fools with varnish'd faces;
> But stop my house's ears—I mean my casements.
> Let not the sound of shallow fopp'ry enter
> My sober house.
> (II.v.28-36)

Lorenzo's enterprise in stealing Jessica wins our sympathy partly because it is done in a masque, as a merriment:

> *Bassanio.* . . . put on
> Your boldest suit of mirth, for we have friends
> That purpose merriment . . .
> (II.ii.210-212)

> *Lorenzo.* Nay, we will slink away at supper time,
> Disguise us at my lodging, and return
> All in an hour.
> *Gratiano.* We have not made good preparation.
> *Salerio.* We have not spoke us yet of torchbearers.
> *Solanio.* 'Tis vile, unless it may be quaintly ordered. . . .
> (II.iv.1-6)

The gallants are sophisticated, like Mercutio, about masquerade; but this masque *is* "quaintly ordered," because, as Lorenzo confides to Gratiano,

> Fair Jessica shall be my torchbearer.
> (II.iv.40)

The episode is another place where Shakespeare has it come true that nature can have its way when people are in festive disguise. Shylock's "tight" opposition, "fast bind, fast find" (II.v.54) helps to put us on the side of the "masquing mates," even though what they do, soberly considered, is a gentlemanly version of raiding the Lombard quarter or sacking bawdy houses on Shrove Tuesday.[3]

Making Distinctions about the Use of Riches

The Merchant of Venice as a whole is not shaped by festivity in the relatively direct way that we have traced in *Love's Labour's Lost* and *A Midsummer Night's Dream.* The whirling away of daughter and ducats is just one episode in a complex plot which is based on story materials and worked out with much more concern for events, for what happens next, than there is in the two previous comedies. This play was probably written in 1596, at any rate fairly early in the first period of easy mastery which extends from *Romeo and Juliet, A Midsummer Night's Dream*, and *Richard II* through the Henry IV and V plays and *As You Like It* to *Julius Caesar* and *Twelfth Night.* At the opening of this period, the two comedies modeled directly on festivities represent a new departure, from which Shakespeare returns in *The Merchant of Venice* to write a comedy with a festive emphasis, but one which is rather more "a kind of history" and less "a gambold." The play's large structure is developed from traditions which are properly theatrical; it is not a theatrical adaptation of a social ritual. And yet analogies to social occasions and rituals prove to be useful in understanding the symbolic action. I shall be pursuing such analogies without suggesting, in most cases, that there is a direct influence from the social to the theatrical form. Shakespeare here is working with autonomous mastery, developing a style of comedy that makes a festive form for feeling and awareness out of all the theatrical elements, scene, speech, story, gesture, role which his astonishing art brought into organic combination.

Invocation and abuse, poetry and railing, romance and ridicule—we have seen repeatedly how such complementary gestures go to the festive celebration of life's powers, along with the complementary roles of revellers and kill-joys, wits and butts, insiders and intruders. What is mocked, what kind of intruder disturbs the revel and is baffled, depends on what particular sort of beneficence is being celebrated. *The Merchant of Venice*, as its title indicates, ex-

[3] See above, p. 38.

hibits the beneficence of civilized wealth, the something-for-nothing which wealth gives to those who use it graciously to live together in a humanly knit group. It also deals, in the role of Shylock, with anxieties about money, and its power to set men at odds. Our econometric age makes us think of wealth chiefly as a practical matter, an abstract concern of work, not a tangible joy for festivity. But for the new commercial civilizations of the Renaissance, wealth glowed in luminous metal, shone in silks, perfumed the air in spices. Robert Wilson, already in the late eighties, wrote a pageant play in the manner of the moralities, *Three Lords and Three Ladies of London*, in which instead of Virtues, London's Pomp and London's Wealth walked gorgeously and smugly about the stage.[4] Despite the terrible sufferings some sections of society were experiencing, the 1590's were a period when London was becoming conscious of itself as wealthy and cultivated, so that it could consider great commercial Venice as a prototype. And yet there were at the same time traditional suspicions of the profit motive and newly urgent anxieties about the power of money to disrupt human relations.[5] Robert Wilson also wrote, early in the eighties, a play called *The Three Ladies of London*, where instead of London's Wealth and Pomp we have Lady Lucar and the attitude towards her which her name implies. It was in expressing and so coping with these anxieties about money that Shakespeare developed in Shylock a comic antagonist far more important than any such figure had been in his earlier comedies. His play is still centered in the celebrants rather than the intruder, but Shylock's part is so fascinating that already in 1598 the comedy was entered in the stationer's register as "a book of the Merchant of Venice, or otherwise called the Jew of Venice." Shylock's name has become a byword because of the superb way that he embodies the evil side of the power of money, its ridiculous and pernicious consequences in anxiety and destructiveness. In creating him and setting him over against Antonio, Bassanio, Portia, and the rest, Shakespeare was making dis-

[4] Printed together with *The Three Ladies of London* in Robert Dodsley, *A Select Collection of Old Plays*, ed. W. C. Hazlett (London, 1874-76), Vol. VI.

[5] A very useful background for understanding *Merch.* is provided by L. C. Knight's *Drama and Society in the Age of Jonson* (London, 1937) and by the fundamental social history which Mr. Knight used as one point of departure, R. H. Tawney's *Religion and the Rise of Capitalism* (New York, 1926).

tinctions about the use of riches, not statically, of course, but dynamically, as distinctions are made when a social group sorts people out, or when an organized social ritual does so. Shylock is the opposite of what the Venetians are; but at the same time he is an embodied irony, troublingly like them. So his role is like that of the scapegoat in many of the primitive rituals which Frazer has made familiar, a figure in whom the evils potential in a social organization are embodied, recognized and enjoyed during a period of licence, and then in due course abused, ridiculed, and expelled.

The large role of the antagonist in *The Merchant of Venice* complicates the movement through release to clarification: instead of the single outgoing of *A Midsummer Night's Dream*, there are two phases. Initially there is a rapid, festive movement by which gay youth gets something for nothing, Lorenzo going masquing to win a Jessica gilded with ducats, and Bassanio sailing off like Jason to win the golden fleece in Belmont. But all this is done against a background of anxiety. We soon forget all about Egeus' threat in *A Midsummer Night's Dream*, but we are kept aware of Shylock's malice by a series of interposed scenes. Will Summer said wryly about the Harvest merrymakers in *Summer's Last Will and Testament*, "As lusty as they are, they run on the score with George's wife for their posset."[6] We are made conscious that running on the score with Shylock is a very dangerous business, and no sooner is the joyous triumph accomplished at Belmont than Shylock's malice is set loose. It is only after the threat he poses has been met that the redemption of the prodigal can be completed by a return to Belmont.

The key question in evaluating the play is how this threat is met, whether the baffling of Shylock is meaningful or simply melodramatic. Certainly the plot, considered in outline, seems merely a prodigal's dream coming true: to have a rich friend who will set you up with one more loan so that you can marry a woman both beautiful and rich, girlishly yielding and masterful; and on top of that to get rid of the obligation of the loan because the old money bags from whom your friend got the money is proved to be so villainous that he does not deserve to be paid back! If one adds humanitarian and democratic indignation at anti-semitism, it is

[6] Lines 943-944 in McKerrow, *Nashe*, III, 263.

hard to see, from a distance, what there can be to say for the play: Shylock seems to be made a scapegoat in the crudest, most dishonest way. One can apologize for the plot, as Middleton Murry and Granville-Barker do, by observing that it is based on a fairy-story sort of tale, and that Shakespeare's method was not to change implausible story material, but to invent characters and motives which would make it acceptable and credible, moment by moment, on the stage.[7] But it is inadequate to praise the play for delightful and poetic incoherence. Nor does it seem adequate to say, as E. E. Stoll does, that things just do go this way in comedy, where old rich men are always baffled by young and handsome lovers, lenders by borrowers.[8] Stoll is certainly right, but the question is whether Shakespeare has done something more than merely appeal to the feelings any crowd has in a theater in favor of prodigal young lovers and against old misers. As I see it, he has expressed important things about the relations of love and hate to wealth. When he kept to old tales, he not only made plausible protagonists for them, but also, at any rate when his luck held, he brought up into a social focus deep symbolic meanings. Shylock is an ogre, as Middleton Murry said, but he is the ogre of money power. The old tale of the pound of flesh involved taking literally the proverbial metaphors about money-lenders "taking it out of the hide" of their victims, eating them up. Shakespeare keeps the unrealistic literal business, knife-sharpening and all; we accept it, because he makes it express real human attitudes:

> If I can catch him once upon the hip,
> I will feed fat the ancient grudge I bear him.[9]
> (I.iii.47-48)

So too with the fairy-story caskets at Belmont: Shakespeare makes Bassanio's prodigal fortune meaningful as an expression of the

[7] John Middleton Murry, *Shakespeare* (New York, 1936), pp. 154-157; Harley Granville-Barker, *Prefaces to Shakespeare* (Princeton, 1946-47), I, 335-336.

[8] *Shakespeare Studies* (New York, 1927), pp. 293-295.

[9] It is striking that, along with the imagery of the money-lender feeding on his victims, there is the complementary prohibition Shylock mentions against eating with Christians; Shakespeare brings alive a primitive anxiety about feasting *with* people who might feast *on* you. And when Shylock violates his own taboo ("But yet I'll go in hate, to feed upon / The prodigal Christian." II.v.14-15) it is he who is caught upon the hip!

triumph of human, social relations over the relations kept track of by accounting. The whole play dramatizes the conflict between the mechanisms of wealth and the masterful, social use of it. The happy ending, which abstractly considered as an event is hard to credit, and the treatment of Shylock, which abstractly considered as justice is hard to justify, *work* as we actually watch or read the play because these events express relief and triumph in the achievement of a distinction.

To see how this distinction is developed, we need to attend to the tangibles of imaginative design which are neglected in talking about plot. So, in the two first scenes, it is the seemingly incidental, random talk that establishes the gracious, opulent world of the Venetian gentlemen and of the "lady richly left" at Belmont, and so motivates Bassanio's later success. Wealth in this world is something profoundly social, and it is relished without a trace of shame when Salerio and Salanio open the play by telling Antonio how rich he is:

> Your mind is tossing on the ocean;
> There where your argosies with portly sail—
> Like signiors and rich burghers on the flood,
> Or, as it were, the pageants of the sea—
> Do overpeer the petty traffickers,
> That cursy to them, do them reverence,
> As they fly by them with their woven wings.
> (I.i.8-14)

Professor Venezky points out that Elizabethan auditors would have thought not only of the famous Venetian water ceremonies but also of "colorfully decorated pageant barges" on the Thames or of "pageant devices of huge ships which were drawn about in street shows."[10] What is crucial is the ceremonial, social feeling for wealth. Salerio and Salanio do Antonio reverence just as the petty traffickers of the harbor salute his ships, giving way to leave him "with better company" when Bassanio and Gratiano arrive. He stands at ease, courteous, relaxed, melancholy (but not about his fortunes, which are too large for worry), while around him moves a shifting but close-knit group who "converse and waste the time

[10] Venezky, *Pageantry*, p. 172.

together" (III.iv.12), make merry, speak "an infinite deal of nothing" (I.i.114), propose good times: "Good signiors, both, when shall we laugh? say, when?" (I.i.66). When Bassanio is finally alone with the royal merchant, he opens his mind with

> To you, Antonio,
> I owe the most, in money and in love.
> (I.i.130-131)

Mark Van Doren, in his excellent chapter on this play, notes how these lines summarize the gentleman's world where "there is no incompatibility between money and love."[11] So too, one can add, in this community there is no conflict between enjoying Portia's beauty and her wealth: "her sunny locks / Hang on her temples like a golden fleece." When, a moment later, we see Portia mocking her suitors, the world suggested is, again, one where standards are urbanely and humanly social: the sad disposition of the county Palatine is rebuked because (unlike Antonio's) it is "unmannerly." Yet already in the first scene, though Shylock is not in question yet, the anxiety that dogs wealth is suggested. In the lines which I have taken as an epigraph for this chapter, Salerio's mind moves from attending church—from safety, comfort and solidarity—through the playful association of the "holy edifice of stone" with "dangerous rocks," to the thought that the sociable luxuries of wealth are vulnerable to impersonal forces:

> rocks,
> Which, touching but my gentle vessel's side,
> Would scatter all her spices on the stream,
> Enrobe the roaring waters with my silks . . .
> (I.i.31-34)

The destruction of what is cherished, of the civic and personal, by ruthless impersonal forces is sensuously immediate in the wild waste of shining silk on turbulent water, one of the magic, summary lines of the play. Earlier there is a tender, solicitous suggestion that the vessel is the more vulnerable because it is "gentle"—as later Antonio is gentle and vulnerable when his ships encoun-

[11] *Shakespeare* (New York, 1939), p. 96.

ter "the dreadful touch / Of merchant-marring rocks" (III.ii.270-271) and his side is menaced by a "stony adversary" (IV.i.4).

When Shylock comes on in the third scene, the easy, confident flow of colorful talk and people is checked by a solitary figure and an unyielding speech:

> *Shylock.* Three thousand ducats—well.
> *Bassanio.* Ay, sir, for three months.
> *Shylock.* For three months—well.
> *Bassanio.* For the which, as I told you, Antonio shall be bound.
> *Shylock.* Antonio shall become bound—well.
> *Bassanio.* May you stead me? Will you pleasure me? Shall I know your answer?
> *Shylock.* Three thousand ducats for three months, and Antonio bound.
> (I.iii.1-10)

We can construe Shylock's hesitation as playing for time while he forms his plan. But more fundamentally, his deliberation expresses the impersonal logic, the mechanism, involved in the control of money. Those *well's* are wonderful in the way they bring bland Bassanio up short. Bassanio assumes that social gestures can brush aside such consideration:

> *Shylock.* Antonio is a good man.
> *Bassanio.* Have you heard any imputation to the contrary?
> *Shylock.* Ho, no, no, no, no! My meaning in saying he is a good man, is to have you understand me that he is sufficient.
> (I.iii.12-17)

The laugh is on Bassanio as Shylock drives his hard financial meaning of "good man" right through the center of Bassanio's softer social meaning. The Jew goes on to calculate and count. He connects the hard facts of money with the rocky sea hazards of which we have so far been only picturesquely aware: "ships are but boards"; and he betrays his own unwillingness to take the risks proper to commerce: "and other ventures he hath, squand'red abroad."

> . . . I think I may take his bond.
> *Bassanio.* Be assur'd you may.

Shylock. I will be assur'd I may; and, that I may be assured, I will bethink me.

(I.iii.28-31)

The Jew in this encounter expresses just the things about money which are likely to be forgotten by those who have it, or presume they have it, as part of a social station. He stands for what we mean when we say that "money is money." So Shylock makes an ironic comment—and *is* a comment, by virtue of his whole tone and bearing—on the folly in Bassanio which leads him to confuse those two meanings of "good man," to ask Shylock to dine, to use in this business context such social phrases as "Will you *pleasure* me?" When Antonio joins them, Shylock (after a soliloquy in which his plain hatred has glittered) becomes a pretender to fellowship, with an equivocating mask:

Shylock. This is kind I offer.
Bassanio. This were kindness.
Shylock. This kindness will I show.

(I.iii.143-144)

We are of course in no doubt as to how to take the word "kindness" when Shylock proposes "in a merry sport" that the penalty be a pound of Antonio's flesh.

In the next two acts, Shylock and the accounting mechanism which he embodies are crudely baffled in Venice and rhapsodically transcended in Belmont. The solidarity of the Venetians includes the clown, in whose part Shakespeare can use conventional blacks and whites about Jews and misers without asking us to take them too seriously:

To be ruled by my conscience, I should stay with the Jew my master, who (God bless the mark) is a kind of devil. . . . My master's a very Jew.

(II.ii.24-25, 111)

Even the street urchins can mock Shylock after the passion which "the dog Jew did utter in the streets":

Why, all the boys in Venice follow him,
Crying his stones, his daughter, and his ducats.

(II.viii.23-24)

Transcending Reckoning at Belmont

The simplest way to describe what happens at Belmont is to say that Bassanio is lucky; but Shakespeare gives a great deal of meaning to his being lucky. His choosing of the casket might be merely theatrical; but the play's handling of the age-old story motif makes it an integral part of the expression of relations between people and possessions. Most of the argument about gold, silver, and lead is certainly factitious, even tedious. It must necessarily be so, because the essence of a lottery is a discontinuity, something hidden so that the chooser cannot get from here to there by reasoning. Nerissa makes explicit a primitive notion of divination:

> Your father was ever virtuous; and holy men at their death have good inspirations. Therefore the lott'ry that he hath devised in these three chests of gold, silver, and lead, whereof who chooses his meaning chooses you, will no doubt never be chosen by any rightly but one who shall rightly love. (I.ii.30-36)

The elegant phrasing does not ask us to take the proposition very seriously, but Nerissa is pointing in the direction of a mystery. Part of the meaning is that love is not altogether a matter of the will, however willing. Portia recognizes this even when her heart is in her mouth as Bassanio is about to choose:

> Away then! I am lock'd in one of them.
> If you do love me, you will find me out.
> Nerissa and the rest, stand all aloof.
> Let music sound while he doth make his choice . . .
> (III.ii.40-43)

The song, "Tell me, where is fancy bred," serves to emphasize the break, the speechless pause while Bassanio chooses. The notion that it serves as a signal to warn Bassanio off gold and silver is one of those busy-body emendations which eliminate the dramatic in seeking to elaborate it. The dramatic point is precisely that there is no signal: "Who chooseth me must give and hazard all he hath" (II.vii.16).

If we look across for a moment at Shylock, thinking through

opposites as the play's structure invites us to do, his discussion with Antonio about the "thrift" of Jacob and the taking of interest proves to be relevant to the luck of the caskets. Antonio appeals to the principle that interest is wrong because it involves no risk:

> This was a venture, sir, that Jacob serv'd for;
> A thing not in his power to bring to pass,
> But sway'd and fashion'd by the hand of heaven.
> (I.iii.92-94)

One way to get a fortune is to be fortunate: the two words fall together significantly at the conclusion of the opening scene:

> *Bassanio.* O my Antonio, had I but the means
> To hold a rival place with one of them,
> I have a mind presages me such thrift
> That I should questionless be fortunate!
> *Antonio.* Thou know'st that all my fortunes are at sea . . .
> (I.i.173-177)

Antonio's loan is venture capital. It fits with this conception that Bassanio, when at Belmont he goes "to my fortune and the caskets," turns away from money, from "gaudy gold, / Hard food for Midas," and from silver, the "pale and common drudge / 'Tween man and man" (III.ii.101-104). Money is not used to get money; that is the usurer's way:

> *Antonio.* Or is your gold and silver ewes and rams?
> *Shylock.* I cannot tell; I make it breed as fast.
> (I.iii.96-97)

Instead Bassanio's borrowed purse is invested in life—including such lively things as the "rare new liveries" (II.ii.117) that excite Launcelot, and the "gifts of rich value" which excite Nerissa to say

> A day in April never came so sweet
> To show how costly summer was at hand
> As this fore-spurrer comes before his lord.
> (II.ix.93-95)

With the money, Bassanio invests *himself*, and so risks losing himself—as has to be the case with love. (Antonio's commitment of his body for his friend is in the background.) It is a limitation of the scene where he makes his choice that the risk has to be conveyed largely by the poetry, since the outward circumstances are not hazardous. Portia describes Bassanio as

> young Alcides when he did redeem
> The virgin tribute paid by howling Troy
> To the sea monster. . . . Go, Hercules!
> Live thou, I live.
>
> (III.ii.55-61)

Of course we know that these are lover's feelings. But the moment of choice is expressed in terms that point beyond feelings to emphasize discontinuity; they convey the experience of being lost and giddily finding oneself again in a new situation. The dramatic shift is all the more vividly rendered in the language since gesture here can do little. Portia speaks of an overwhelming ecstasy of love when "all the other passions fleet to air" (III.ii.108). Bassanio likens himself to an athlete

> Hearing applause and universal shout,
> Giddy in spirit, still gazing in a doubt
> Whether those peals of praise be his or no.
>
> (III.ii.143-145)

He describes in a wonderful way the experience of being disrupted by joy:

> Madam, you have bereft me of all words,
> Only my blood speaks to you in my veins;
> And there is such confusion in my powers
> As, after some oration fairly spoke
> By a beloved prince, there doth appear
> Among the buzzing pleased multitude,
> Where every something, being blent together,
> Turns to a wild of nothing, save of joy,
> Express'd and not express'd.
>
> (III.ii.175-183)

This poetry is remarkable for the conscious way that it describes being carried beyond expression, using words to tell of being beyond them. The lines in which Portia gives herself and her possessions to Bassanio make explicit, by an elaborate metaphor of accounting, that what is happening sets the accounting principle aside:

> You see me, Lord Bassanio, where I stand,
> Such as I am. Though for myself alone
> I would not be ambitious in my wish
> To wish myself much better, yet for you
> I would be trebled twenty times myself,
> A thousand times more fair, ten thousand times more rich,
> That, only to stand high in your account,
> I might in virtues, beauties, livings, friends,
> Exceed account. But the full sum of me
> Is sum of nothing, which, to term in gross,
> Is an unlesson'd girl, unschool'd, unpractic'd. . . .
>
> (III.ii.149-159)

This is extravagant, and extravagantly modest, as fits the moment; but what is telling is the way the lines move from possessions, through the paradox about sums, to the person in the midst of them all, "where I stand," who cannot be added up. It is she that Bassanio has won, and with her a way of living for which his humanity, breeding, and manhood can provide a center:

> Happiest of all is that her gentle spirit
> Commits itself to yours to be directed,
> As from her lord, her governor, her king.
>
> (III.ii.163-165)

The possessions *follow* from this human, social relation.

Comical/Menacing Mechanism in Shylock

But the accounting mechanism which has been left behind by Bassanio and Portia has gone on working, back at Venice, to put Antonio at Shylock's mercy, and the anxiety it causes has to be mastered before the marriage can be consummated,

> For never shall you lie by Portia's side
> With an unquiet soul.
>
> (III.ii.305-306)

Historical changes in stock attitudes have made difficulties about Shylock's role as a butt, not so much in the theater, where it works perfectly if producers only let it, but in criticism, where winds of doctrine blow sentiments and abstractions about. The Elizabethans almost never saw Jews except on the stage, where Marlowe's Barabas was familiar. They did see *one*, on the scaffold, when Elizabeth's unfortunate physician suffered for trumped-up charges of a poisoning plot. The popular attitude was that to take interest for money was to be a loan shark—though limited interest was in fact allowed by law. An aristocrat who like Lord Bassanio ran out of money commanded sympathy no longer felt in a middle-class world. Most important of all, suffering was not an absolute evil in an era when men sometimes embraced it deliberately, accepted it as inevitable, and could watch it with equanimity. Humanitarianism has made it necessary for us to be much more thoroughly insulated from the human reality of people if we are to laugh at their discomfiture or relish their suffering. During the romantic period, and sometimes more recently, the play was presented as a tragi-comedy, and actors vied with one another in making Shylock a figure of pathos. I remember a very moving scene, a stock feature of romantic productions, in which George Arliss came home after Bassanio's party, lonely and tired and old, to knock in vain at the door of the house left empty by Jessica. How completely unhistorical the romantic treatment was, E. E. Stoll demonstrated overwhelmingly in his essay on Shylock in 1911, both by wide-ranging comparisons of Shylock's role with others in Renaissance drama and by analysis of the *optique du théâtre*.[12]

To insert a humanitarian scene about Shylock's pathetic home-coming prevents the development of the scornful amusement with which Shakespeare's text presents the miser's reaction in Solanio's narrative:

> I never heard a passion so confus'd,
> So strange, outrageous, and so variable,
> As the dog Jew did utter in the streets.
> "My daughter! O my ducats! O my daughter!
> Fled with a Christian! O my Christian ducats! . . ."
> (II.viii.12-16)

[12] In *Shakespeare Studies.*

Marlowe had done such a moment already with Barabas hugging in turn his money bags and his daughter—whom later the Jew of Malta poisons with a pot of porridge, as the Jew of Venice later wishes that Jessica "were hears'd at my foot, and the ducats in her coffin" (III.i.93-94). But the humanitarian way of playing the part develops suggestions that are *also* in Shakespeare's text:

> I am bid forth to supper, Jessica.
> There are my keys. But wherefore should I go?
> I am not bid for love; they flatter me.
> But yet I'll go in hate, to feed upon
> The prodigal Christian.
> (II.v.11-15)

Shakespeare's marvelous creative sympathy takes the stock role of Jewish usurer and villain and conveys how it would feel to be a man living inside it. But this does not mean that he shrinks from confronting the evil and the absurdity that go with the role; for the Elizabethan age, to understand did not necessarily mean to forgive. Shylock can be a thorough villain and yet be allowed to express what sort of treatment has made him what he is:

> You call me misbeliever, cutthroat dog,
> And spet upon my Jewish gaberdine,
> And all for use of that which is mine own.
> (I.iii.112-114)

We can understand his degradation and even blame the Antonios of Venice for it; yet it remains degradation:

> Thou call'dst me dog before thou hadst a cause,
> But, since I am a dog, beware my fangs.
> (III.iii.6-7)

Shylock repeatedly states, as he does here, that he is only finishing what the Venetians started. He can be a drastic ironist, because he carries to extremes what is present, whether acknowledged or not, in their silken world. He insists that money is money—and they cannot do without money either. So too with the rights of property. The power to give freely, which absolute property confers and Antonio and Portia so splendidly exhibit, is also a power to refuse, as Shylock so logically refuses:

You have among you many a puchas'd slave,
Which, like your asses and your dogs and mules,
You use in abject and in slavish parts,
Because you bought them. Shall I say to you,
"Let them be free, marry them to you heirs! . . ."
You will answer,
"The slaves are ours." So do I answer you.
The pound of flesh which I demand of him
Is dearly bought, 'tis mine, and I will have it.
(IV.i.90-100)

At this point in the trial scene, Shylock seems a juggernaut that nothing can stop, armed as he is against a pillar of society by the principles of society itself: "If you deny me, fie upon your law! . . . I stand for judgement. Answer. Shall I have it." Nobody does answer him here, directly; instead there is an interruption for Portia's entrance. To answer him is the function of the whole dramatic action, which is making a distinction that could not be made in direct, logical argument.

Let us follow this dramatic action from its comic side. Shylock is comic, so far as he is so, because he exhibits what should be human, degraded into mechanism. The reduction of life to mechanism goes with the miser's wary calculation, with the locking up, with the preoccupation with "that which is mine own." Antonio tells Bassanio that

My purse, my person, my extremest means
Lie all unlock'd to your occasions.
(I.i.138-139)

How open! Antonio has to live inside some sort of rich man's melancholy, but at least he communicates with the world through outgoing Bassanio (and, one can add, through the commerce which takes his fortunes out to sea). Shylock, by contrast, who breeds barren metal, wants to keep "the vile squeeling of the wry-neck'd fife" out of his house, and speaks later, in a curiously revealing, seemingly random illustration, of men who "when the bag-pipe sings i'th'nose, / Cannot contain their urine" (V.i.49-50). Not only is he closed up tight inside himself, but after the first two scenes, we are scarcely allowed by his lines to feel with him. And we never encounter him alone; he regularly comes on to join a group whose talk has established an outside point of view towards him. This perspective on him does not exclude a potential pathos. There is always potential pathos, behind, when drama makes fun of isolating, anti-social qualities. Indeed, the process of *making fun of* a person often works by exhibiting pretensions to humanity so as to show that they are inhuman, mechanical, not validly appropriate for sympathy. With a comic villain such as Shylock, the effect is mixed in various degrees between our responding to the mechanism as menacing and laughing at it as ridiculous.

So in the great scene in which Solanio and Salerio taunt Shylock, the potentiality of pathos produces effects which vary between comedy and menace:

> *Shylock.* You knew, none so well, none so well as you, of my daughter's flight.
>
> *Salerio.* That's certain. I, for my part, knew the tailor that made the wings she flew withal.
>
> (III.i.27-30)

Shylock's characteristic repetitions, and the way he has of moving ahead through similar, short phrases, as though even with language he was going to use only what was his own, can give an effect of concentration and power, or again, an impression of a comically limited, isolated figure. In the great speech of self-justification to which he is goaded by the two bland little gentlemen, the iteration conveys the energy of anguish:

> —and what's his reason? I am a Jew. Hath not a Jew eyes? Hath not a Jew hands, organs, dimensions, senses, affections, passions? fed with the same food, hurt with the same weapons, subject to the same diseases, healed by the same means, warmed and cooled by the same winter and summer as a Christian is? If you prick us, do we not bleed? If you tickle us, do we not laugh? If you poison us, do we not die? And if you wrong us, shall we not revenge? If we are like you in the rest, we will resemble you in that.
>
> (III.i.60-71)

Certainly no actor would deliver this speech without an effort at pathos; but it is a pathos which, as the speech moves, converts to menace. And the pathos is qualified, limited, in a way which is badly falsified by humanitarian renderings that open all the stops at "Hath not a Jew hands, etc. . . ." For Shylock thinks to claim only a *part* of humanness, the lower part, physical and passional. The similar self-pitying enumeration which Richard II makes differs significantly in going from "live with bread like you" to social responses and needs, "Taste grief, / Need friends" (*R.II* III.ii.175-176). The passions in Shylock's speech are conceived as reflexes; the parallel clauses draw them all towards the level of "tickle . . . laugh." The same assumption, that the passions and social responses are mechanisms on a par with a nervous tic, appears in the court scene when Shylock defends his right to follow his "humor" in taking Antonio's flesh:

> As there is no firm reason to be rend'red
> Why he cannot abide a gaping pig,
> Why he a harmless necessary cat,
> Why he a woollen bagpipe—but of force
> Must yield to such inevitable shame
> As to offend himself, being offended;
> So can I give no reason, nor I will not,
> More than a lodg'd hate and a certain loathing
> I bear unto Antonio . . .
> (IV.i.52-61)

The most succinct expression of this assumption about man is Shylock's response to Bassanio's incredulous question:

> *Bassanio.* Do all men kill the things they do not love?
> *Shylock.* Hates any man the thing he would not kill?
> (IV.i.66-67)

There is no room in this view for mercy to come in between "wrong us" and "shall we not revenge?" As Shylock insists, there is Christian example for him: the irony is strong. But the mechanism of stimulus and response is only a part of the truth. The reductive tendency of Shylock's metaphors, savagely humorous in Iago's fashion, goes with this speaking only the lower part of the truth. He is not cynical in Iago's aggressive way, because as an alien he simply doesn't participate in many of the social ideals which Iago is concerned to discredit in self-justification. But the two villains have the same frightening, ironical power from moral simplification.

Shylock becomes a clear-cut butt at the moments when he is himself caught in compulsive, reflexive responses, when instead of controlling mechanism he is controlled by it: "O my daughter! O my ducats!" At the end of the scene of taunting, his menace and his pathos become ridiculous when he dances like a jumping jack in alternate joy and sorrow as Tubal pulls the strings:

> *Tubal.* Yes, other men have ill luck too. Antonio, as I heard in Genoa—
>
> *Shylock.* What, what, what? Ill luck, ill luck?
>
> *Tubal.* Hath an argosy cast away coming from Tripolis.
>
> *Shylock.* I thank God, I thank God!—Is it true? is it true?
>
> *Tubal.* I spoke with some of the sailors that escaped the wrack.
>
> *Shylock.* I thank thee, good Tubal. Good news, good news! Ha, ha! Where? in Genoa?
>
> *Tubal.* Your daughter spent in Genoa, as I heard, one night fourscore ducats.
>
> *Shylock.* Thou stick'st a dagger in me. I shall never see my gold again. Fourscore ducats at a sitting! Fourscore ducats!
>
> *Tubal.* There came divers of Antonio's creditors in my company to Venice that swear he cannot choose but break.
>
> *Shylock.* I am very glad of it. I'll plague him; I'll torture him. I am glad of it.
>
> *Tubal.* One of them show'd me a ring that he had of your daughter for a monkey.
>
> *Shylock.* Out upon her! Thou torturest me, Tubal. It was my turquoise; I had it of Leah when I was a bachelor. I would not have given it for a wilderness of monkeys.
>
> *Tubal.* But Antonio is certainly undone.
>
> *Shylock.* Nay, that's true, that's very true.
>
> (III.i.102-130)

This is a scene in the dry manner of Marlowe, Jonson, or Molière, a type of comedy not very common in Shakespeare: its abrupt alternations in response convey the effect Bergson describes so well in *Le Rire*, where the comic butt is a puppet in whom motives have become mechanisms that usurp life's self-determining prerogative. Some critics have left the rhythm of the scene behind to dwell on the pathos of the ring he had from Leah when he was a bachelor. It is like Shakespeare once to show Shylock putting a gentle sentimental value on something, to match the savage sentimental value he puts on revenge. There *is* pathos; but it is being fed into the comic mill and makes the laughter all the more hilarious.

The Community Setting Aside Its Machinery

In the trial scene, the turning point is appropriately the moment when Shylock gets caught in the mechanism he relies on so ruthlessly. He narrows everything down to his roll of parchment and his knife: "Till thou canst rail the seal from off my bond . . ." (IV.i.139). But two can play at this game:

> as thou urgest justice, be assur'd
> Thou shalt have justice more than thou desir'st.
> (IV.i.315-316)

Shylock's bafflement is comic, as well as dramatic, in the degree that we now see through the threat that he has presented, recognizing it to have been, in a degree, unreal. For it is unreal to depend so heavily on legal form, on fixed verbal definition, on the mere machinery by which human relations are controlled. Once Portia's legalism has broken through his legalism, he can only go on the way he started, weakly asking "Is that the law?" while Gratiano's jeers underscore the comic symmetry:

> A Daniel still say I, a second Daniel!
> I thank thee, Jew, for teaching me that word.
> (IV.i.340-341)

The turning of the tables is not, of course, simply comic, except for the bold, wild and "skipping spirit" of Gratiano. The trial scene is a species of drama that uses comic movement in slow motion, with an investment of feeling such that the resolution is in elation and relief colored by amusement, rather than in the evacuation of laughter. Malvolio, a less threatening kill-joy intruder, is simply laughed out of court, but Shylock must be ruled out, with jeering only on the side lines. The threat Shylock offers is, after all, drastic, for legal instruments, contract, property are fundamental. Comic dramatists often choose to set them hilariously at naught; but Shakespeare is, as usual, scrupulously responsible to the principles of social order (however factitious his "law" may be literally). So he produced a scene which exhibits the limitations of legalism. It works by a dialectic that carries to a more general level what might be comic reduction to absurdity. To be tolerant, because we are all fools; to forgive, because we are all guilty—the two gestures of the spirit are allied, as Erasmus noted in praising the sublime folly of following Christ. Shylock says before the trial "I'll not be made a soft and dull-ey'd fool" by "Christian intercessors" (III.iii.14-15). Now when he is asked how he can hope for mercy if he renders none, he answers: "What judgement shall I dread, doing no wrong?" As the man who will not acknowledge his own share of folly ends by being more foolish than anyone else, so Shylock, who will not acknowledge a share of guilt, ends by being more guilty—and more foolish, to judge by results. An argument between Old Testament legalism and New Testament reliance on grace develops as the scene goes forward. (Shylock's references to Daniel in this scene, and his constant use of Old Testament names and allusions, contribute to the contrast.) Portia does not deny the bond—nor the law behind it; instead she makes such a plea as St. Paul made to his compatriots:

> Therefore, Jew,
> Though justice be thy plea, consider this—
> That, in the course of justice, none of us
> Should see salvation. We do pray for mercy,
> And that same prayer doth teach us all to render
> The deeds of mercy.
> (IV.i.97-102)

Mercy becomes the word that gathers up everything we have seen the Venetians enjoying in their reliance on community. What is on one side an issue of principles is on the other a matter of social solidarity: Shylock is not one of the "we" Portia refers to, the Christians who say in the Lord's Prayer "Forgive us our debts as we forgive our debtors." All through the play the word Christian has been repeated, primarily in statements that enforce the fact that the Jew is outside the easy bonds of community. Portia's plea for mercy is a sublime version of what in less intense circumstances, among friends of a single communion, can be conveyed with a shrug or a wink:

> Dost thou hear, Hal? Thou knowest in the state of innocency Adam fell; and what should poor Jack Falstaff do in the days of villany?
>
> (*1 H.IV* III.iii.185-188)

Falstaff, asking for an amnesty to get started again, relies on his festive solidarity with Hal. Comedy, in one way or another, is always asking for amnesty, after showing the moral machinery of life getting in the way of life. The machinery as such need not be dismissed—Portia is very emphatic about not doing that. But social solidarity, resting on the buoyant force of a collective life that transcends particular mistakes, can set the machinery aside. Shylock, closed off as he is, clutching his bond and his knife, cannot trust this force, and so acts only on compulsion:

> *Portia.* Do you confess the bond?
> *Antonio.* I do.
> *Portia.* Then must the Jew be merciful.
> *Shylock.* On what compulsion must I? Tell me that.
> *Portia.* The quality of mercy is not strain'd;
> It droppeth as the gentle rain from heaven
> Upon the place beneath. It is twice blest—
> It blesseth him that gives, and him that takes.
>
> (IV.i.181-187)

It has been in giving and taking, beyond the compulsion of accounts, that Portia, Bassanio, Antonio have enjoyed the something-for-nothing that Portia here summarizes in speaking of the gentle rain from heaven.

Sharing in the Grace of Life

The troth-plight rings which Bassanio and Gratiano have given away are all that remain of plot to keep the play moving after the trial. It is a slight business, but it gives the women a teasing way to relish the fact that they have played the parts of men as they give up the liberty of that disguise to become wives. And the play's general subject is continued, for in getting over the difficulty, the group provides one final demonstration that human relationships are stronger than their outward signs. Once more, Bassanio expresses a harassed perplexity about obligations in conflict; and Portia gayly pretends to be almost a Shylock about this lover's bond, carrying the logic of the machinery to absurd lengths before showing, by the new gift of the ring, love's power to set debts aside and begin over again.

No other comedy, until the late romances, ends with so full an expression of harmony as that which we get in the opening of the final scene of *The Merchant of Venice*. And no other final scene is so completely without irony about the joys it celebrates. The ironies have been dealt with beforehand in baffling Shylock; in the moment of relief after expelling an antagonist, we do not need to look at the limitations of what we have been defending. So in *Summer's Last Will and Testament*, when Summer is confronted by a miserly Christmas, he comes out wholeheartedly for festivity, whereas elsewhere, confronting spokesmen for festivity, he is always wry about it. He dismisses Christmas with

> Christmas, I tell thee plain, thou art a snudge,
> And wer't not that we love thy father well,
> Thou shouldst have felt what 'longs to Avarice.
> It is the honor of nobility
> To keep high days and solemn festivals—
> Then to set their magnificence to view,
> To frolic open with their favorites,
> And use their neighbors with all courtesy,
> When thou in hugger-mugger spend'st thy wealth.
> Amend thy manners, breathe thy rusty gold:
> Bounty will win thee love, when thou art old.[13]

The court compels Shylock to breathe his gold and give bounty to Lorenzo. He is plainly told that he is a snudge—and we are off to noble magnificence and frolic at Belmont. No high day is involved, though Shakespeare might easily have staged the solemn festival due after Portia's wedding. Instead Lorenzo and Jessica feel the harmony of the universe and its hospitality to life in a

[13] McKerrow, *Nashe*, III, 287, ll. 1722-32.

quiet moment of idle talk and casual enjoyment of music. There is an opening out to experience in their exquisite outdoor poetry which corresponds to the openness stressed by Nashe in contrast to miserly hugger-mugger.

> The moon shines bright. In such a night as this,
> When the sweet wind did gently kiss the trees
> And they did make no noise—in such a night
> Troilus methinks mounted the Troyan walls
> And sigh'd his soul towards the Grecian tents,
> Where Cressid lay that night. (V.i.1-6)

The openness to experience, the images of reaching out towards it, or of welcoming it, letting music "creep in our ears," go with the perception of a gracious universe such as Portia's mercy speech invoked:

> How sweet the moonlight sleeps upon this bank!
> Here will we sit and let the sounds of music
> Creep in our ears. Soft stillness and the night
> Become the touches of sweet harmony.
> Sit, Jessica. Look how the floor of heaven
> Is thick inlaid with patens of bright gold.
> There's not the smallest orb which thou behold'st
> But in his motion like an angel sings . . .
> (V.i.54-61)

Lorenzo is showing Jessica the graciousness of the Christian world into which he has brought her; and it is as richly golden as it is musical! Jessica is already at ease in it, to the point of being able to recall the pains of famous lovers with equanimity, rally her lover on his vows and turn the whole thing off with "I would out-night you did no body come, / But hark, I hear the footing of a man." That everybody is so perfectly easy is part of the openness:

> *Lorenzo.* Who comes so fast in silence of the night.
> *Messenger.* A friend.
> *Lorenzo.* A friend? What friend? Your name, I pray you, friend? . . .

Sweet soul, let's in, and there expect their coming.
And yet no matter. Why should we go in?
. . . bring your music forth into the air.
(V.i.25-27, 51-54)

As the actual music plays, there is talk about its Orphic power, and we look back a moment toward Shylock

The man that hath no music in himself
Nor is not mov'd with concord of sweet sounds,
Is fit for treasons, stratagems, and spoils . . .
(V.i.82-84)

A certain contemplative distance is maintained by talking *about* perception, *about* harmony and its conditions, even while enjoying it. Portia comes on exclaiming how far the candle throws its beams, how much sweeter the music sounds than by day. There are conditions, times and seasons, to be observed; but the cosmological music, which cannot be heard directly at all, is behind the buoyant decorum of the people:

How many things by season season'd are
To their right praise and true perfection!
Peace ho! The moon sleeps with Endymion
And would not be awak'd.
(V.i.107-110)

At the end of the play, there is Portia's news of Antonio's three argosies richly come to harbor, and the special deed of gift for Lorenzo—"manna in the way / Of starved people." Such particular happy events are not sentimental because Shakespeare has floated them on an expression of a tendency in society and nature which supports life and expels what would destroy it.

I must add, after all this praise for the way the play makes its distinction about the use of wealth, that *on reflection*, not when viewing or reading the play, but when thinking about it, I find the distinction, as others have, somewhat too easy. While I read or watch, all is well, for the attitudes of Shylock are appallingly inhuman, and Shakespeare makes me feel constantly how the Shylock attitude rests on a lack of faith in community and grace. But when one thinks about the Portia-Bassanio group, not in opposition to Shylock but alone (as Shakespeare does not show them), one can be troubled by their being so very very far above money:

> What, no more?
> Pay him six thousand, and deface the bond.
> Double six thousand and then treble that . . .
> (III.ii.298-300)

It would be interesting to see Portia say no, for once, instead of always yes: after all, Nashe's miser has a point, "*Liberalitas liberalitate perit.*" One can feel a difficulty too with Antonio's bland rhetorical question:

> when did friendship take
> A breed of barren metal of his friend?
> (I.iii.134-135)

Elizabethan attitudes about the taking of interest were unrealistic: while Sir Thomas Gresham built up Elizabeth's credit in the money market of Antwerp, and the government regulated interest rates, popular sentiment continued on the level of thinking Antonio's remark reflects. Shakespeare's ideal figures and sentiments are open here to ironies which he does not explore. The clown's role just touches them when he pretends to grumble

> We were Christians enow before, e'en as many as could well live by one another. This making of Christians will raise the price of hogs.
> (III.v.23-26)

In a later chapter we shall see, in *As You Like It*, a more complete confronting of ironies, which leaves, I feel, a cleaner aftertaste. Shakespeare could no doubt have gone beyond the naïve economic morality of Elizabethan popular culture, had he had an artistic need. But he did not, because in the antithetical sort of comic form he was using in this play, the ironical function was fulfilled by the heavy contrasts embodied in Shylock.

About Shylock, too, there is a difficulty which grows on reflection, a difficulty which may be felt too in reading or performance. His part fits perfectly into the design of the play, and yet he is so alive that he raises an interest beyond its design. I do not think his humanity spoils the design, as Walter Raleigh and others argued,[14] and as was almost inevitable for audiences who assumed that to be human was to be ipso-facto good. But it is true that in the small compass of Shylock's three hundred and sixty-odd lines, Shakespeare provided material that asks for a whole additional play to work itself out. Granville-Barker perceptively summarizes how much there is in the scene, not sixty lines long, in which Shylock is seen at home:

> The parting with Launcelot: he has a niggard liking for the fellow, is even hurt a little by his leaving, touched in pride, too, and shows it childishly.
>
> Thou shalt not gormandize
> As thou hast done with me . . .
>
> . . . The parting with Jessica, which we of the audience know to be a parting indeed; that constant calling her by name, which tells us of the lonely man! He has looked to her for everything, has tasked her hard, no doubt; he is her jailer, yet he trusts her, and loves her in his extortionate way. Uneasy stranger that he is within these Venetian gates; the puritan, who, in a wastrel world, will abide by law and prophets![15]

To have dramatized "he has looked to her for everything, has tasked her hard, no doubt," would have taken Shakespeare far afield indeed from the prodigal story he was concerned with—as far afield as *King Lear*. Yet the suggestion is there. The figure of Shylock is like some secondary figure in a Rembrandt painting, so charged with implied life that one can forget his surroundings. To look sometimes with absorption at the suffering, raging Jew alone is irresistible. But the more one is aware of what the play's whole design is expressing through Shylock, of the comedy's high seriousness in its concern for the grace of community, the less one wants to lose the play Shakespeare wrote for the sake of one he merely suggested.

[14] *Shakespeare* (London, 1923, first published 1907), pp. 149-151.
[15] *Prefaces*, I, 355.

Chapter 8

RULE AND MISRULE IN *HENRY IV*

> If all the year were playing holidays,
> To sport would be as tedious as to work . . .

THE two parts of *Henry IV*, written probably in 1597 and 1598, are an astonishing development of drama in the direction of inclusiveness, a development possible because of the range of the traditional culture and the popular theater, but realized only because Shakespeare's genius for construction matched his receptivity. We have noticed briefly in the introductory chapter how, early in his career, Shakespeare made brilliant use of the long standing tradition of comic accompaniment and counterstatement by the clown.[1] Now suddenly he takes the diverse elements in the potpourri of the popular chronicle play and composes a structure in which they draw each other out. The Falstaff comedy, far from being forced into an alien environment of historical drama, is begotten by that environment, giving and taking meaning as it grows. The implications of the saturnalian attitude are more drastically and inclusively expressed here than anywhere else, because here misrule is presented along with rule and along with the tensions that challenge rule. Shakespeare dramatizes not only holiday but also the need for holiday and the need to limit holiday.

It is in the Henry IV plays that we can consider most fruitfully general questions concerning the relation of comedy to analogous forms of symbolic action in folk rituals: not only the likenesses of comedy to ritual, but the differences, the features of comic form which make it comedy and not ritual. Such analogies, I think, prove to be useful critical tools: they lead us to see structure in the drama. And they also raise fascinating historical and theoretical questions about the relation of drama to other products of culture. One way in which our time has been seeing the universal in liter-

[1] See above, pp. 12-13.

ature has been to find in complex literary works patterns which are analogous to myths and rituals and which can be regarded as archetypes, in some sense primitive or fundamental. I have found this approach very exciting indeed. But at the same time, such analysis can be misleading if it results in equating the literary form with primitive analogues. When we are dealing with so developed an art as Shakespeare's, in so complex an epoch as the Renaissance, primitive patterns may be seen in literature mainly because literary imagination, exploiting the heritage of literary form, disengages them from the suggestions of a complex culture. And the primitive levels are articulated in the course of reunderstanding their nature —indeed, the primitive can be fully expressed only on condition that the artist can deal with it in a most civilized way. Shakespeare presents patterns analogous to magic and ritual in the process of redefining magic as imagination, ritual as social action.

Shakespeare was the opposite of primitivistic, for in his culture what we search out and call primitive was in the blood and bone as a matter of course; the problem was to deal with it, to master it. The Renaissance, moreover, was a moment when educated men were modifying a ceremonial conception of human life to create a historical conception. The ceremonial view, which assumed that names and meanings are fixed and final, expressed experience as pageant and ritual—pageant where the right names could march in proper order, or ritual where names could be changed in the right, the proper way. The historical view expresses life as drama. People in drama are not identical with their names, for they gain and lose their names, their status and meaning—and not by settled ritual: the gaining and losing of names, of meaning, is beyond the control of any set ritual sequence. Shakespeare's plays are full of pageantry and of action patterned in a ritualistic way. But the pageants are regularly interrupted; the rituals are abortive or perverted; or if they succeed, they succeed against odds or in an unexpected fashion. The people in the plays try to organize their lives by pageant and ritual, but the plays are dramatic precisely because the effort fails. This failure drama presents as history and personality; in the largest perspective, as destiny.

At the heart of the plays there is, I think, a fascination with the individualistic use or abuse of ritual—with magic. There is an intoxication with the possibility of an omnipotence of mind by which words might become things, by which a man might "gain a deity," might achieve, by making his own ritual, an unlimited power to incarnate meaning.[2] This fascination is expressed in the poetry by which Shakespeare's people envisage their ideal selves. But his drama also expresses an equal and complementary awareness that magic is delusory, that words can become things or lead to deeds only within a social group, by virtue of a historical, social situation beyond the mind and discourse of any one man. This awareness of limitations is expressed by the ironies, whether comic or tragic, which Shakespeare embodies in the dramatic situations of his speakers, the ironies which bring down the meanings which fly high in winged words.

In using an analogy with temporary king and scapegoat to bring out patterns of symbolic action in Falstaff's role, it will be important to keep it clear that the analogy is one we make now, that it is not Shakespeare's analogy; otherwise we falsify his relation to tradition.[3] He did not need to discriminate consciously, in our way,

[2] Fascination with the abuse of ritual is nowhere clearer than in Marlowe's *Tamburlaine* and *Dr. Faustus.*

[3] The use of analogies like the scapegoat rituals can be misleading, or merely amusing, if the pattern is not rigorously related to the imaginative process in the play. Janet Spens, a student of Gilbert Murray's, wrote in 1916 a brief study which attempted to establish the presence of ritual patterns in Shakespeare's work (*An Essay on Shakespeare's Relation to Tradition*, Oxford, 1916). She throws out some brilliant suggestions. But her method for the most part consists of leaping intuitively from folklore to the plots of the plays, via the hypothesis of lost intermediary folk plays; and the plots, abstracted from the concrete emphasis of their dramatic realization, can be adjusted to square with an almost unlimited range of analogies. Miss Spens argues, for example, that because Antonio in *The Merchant of Venice* is enigmatically detached from personal concerns, and because in accepting the prospect of death at Shylock's hands he says "I am the tainted wether of the flock," he "is" the Scapegoat. To be sure, at a very general level there is a partial analogy to scapegoat rituals, since Antonio is undertaking to bear the consequence of Bassanio's extravagance; and perhaps the pound of flesh motif goes back ultimately, through the tangle of legend and story tradition, to some such ceremonial. But there is no controlling such analogies if we go after them by catching at fragments of narrative; and one can understand, on that basis, the impulse to give up the whole approach as hopelessly capricious.

The case is altered, however, if attention is focused, not on this or that group of people in this or that story, but on the roles the persons are given in the play. When we are concerned to describe dramatic form—the rhythm of feeling and awareness in the audience which is focused through complementary roles in the fable and implemented by concrete patterns of language and gesture—then the form of rituals is relevant to the form of the plays as a parallel expression of the same kind of organization of experience.

underlying configurations which came to him with his themes and materials. His way of extending consciousness of such patterns was the drama. In creating the Falstaff comedy, he fused two main saturnalian traditions, the clowning customary on the stage and the folly customary on holiday, and produced something unprecedented. He was working out attitudes towards chivalry, the state and crown in history, in response to the challenge posed by the fate he had dramatized in *Richard II*. The fact that we find analogies to the ritual interregnum relevant to what Shakespeare produced is not the consequence of a direct influence; his power of dramatic statement, in developing saturnalian comedy, reached to modes of organizing experience which primitive cultures have developed with a clarity of outline comparable to that of his drama. The large and profound relations he expressed were developed from the relatively simple dramatic method of composing with statement and counterstatement, elevated action and burlesque. The Henry IV plays are masterpieces of the popular theater whose plays were, in Sidney's words, "neither right tragedies nor right comedies, mingling kings and clowns."

Mingling Kings and Clowns

The fascination of Falstaff as a dramatic figure has led criticism, from Morgan's essay onward, to center *1 Henry IV* on him, and to treat the rest of the play merely as a setting for him. But despite his predominating imaginative significance, the play is centered on Prince Hal, developing in such a way as to exhibit in the prince an inclusive, sovereign nature fitted for kingship. The relation of the Prince to Falstaff can be summarized fairly adequately in terms of the relation of holiday to everyday. As the non-historical material came to Shakespeare in *The Famous Victories of Henry the Fifth*, the prince was cast in the traditional role of the prodigal son, while his disreputable companions functioned as tempters in the same general fashion as the Vice of the morality plays. At one level Shakespeare keeps this pattern, but he shifts the emphasis away from simple moral terms. The issue, in his hands, is not whether Hal will be good or bad but whether he will be noble or degenerate, whether his holiday will become his everyday. The interregnum of a Lord of Misrule, delightful in its moment, might develop into the anarchic reign of a favorite dominating a dissolute king. Hal's secret, which he confides early to the audience, is that for him Falstaff is merely a pastime, to be dismissed in due course:

> If all the year were playing holidays,
> To sport would be as tedious as to work;
> But when they seldom come, they wish'd-for come . . .
> (I.ii.228-230)

The prince's sports, accordingly, express not dissoluteness but a fine excess of vitality—"as full of spirit as the month of May"—together with a capacity for occasionally looking at the world as though it were upside down. His energy is controlled by an inclusive awareness of the rhythm in which he is living: despite appearances, he will not make the mistake which undid Richard II, who played at saturnalia until it caught up with him in earnest. During the battle of Shrewsbury (when, in Hotspur's phrase, "Doomsday is near"), Hal dismisses Falstaff with "What! is it a time to jest and dally now?" (V.iii.57) This sense of timing, of the relation of holiday to everyday and doomsday, contributes to establishing the prince as a sovereign nature.

But the way Hal sees the relations is not the way other people see them, nor indeed the way the audience sees them until the end. The holiday-everyday antithesis is his resource for control, and in the end he makes it stick. But before that, the only clear-cut definition of relations in these terms is in his single soliloquy, after his first appearance with Falstaff. Indeed, it is remarkable how little satisfactory formulation there is of the relationships which the play explores dramatically. It is essential to the play that the prince should be misconstrued, that the king should see "riot and dishonor stain" (I.i.85) his brow, that Percy should patronize him as a "nimble-footed madcap" (IV.ii.95) who might easily be poisoned with a pot of ale if it were worth the trouble. But the absence of adequate summary also reflects the fact that Shakespeare was doing something which he could not summarize, which only the whole resources of his dramatic art could convey.

It is an open question, throughout *Part One*, as to just who or what Falstaff is. At the very end, when Prince John observes

"This is the strangest tale that ever I heard," Hal responds with "This is the strangest fellow, brother John" (V.iv.158-159). From the beginning, Falstaff is constantly renaming himself:

> Marry, then, sweet wag, when thou art king, let not us that are squires of the night's body be called thieves of the day's beauty. Let us be Diana's Foresters, Gentlemen of the Shade, Minions of the Moon; and let men say we be men of good government . . .
> (I.ii.26-31)

Here Misrule is asking to be called Good Government, as it is his role to do—though he does so with a wink which sets real good government at naught, concluding with "steal":

> . . . men of good government, being governed as the sea is, by our noble and chase mistress the moon, under whose countenance we steal.
> (I.ii.31-33)

I have considered in an earlier chapter how the witty equivocation Falstaff practices, like that of Nashe's Bacchus and other apologists for folly and vice, alludes to the very morality it is flouting.[4] Such "damnable iteration" is a sport that implies a rolling-eyed awareness of both sides of the moral medal; the Prince summarizes it in saying that Sir John "was never yet a breaker of proverbs. He will give the devil his due" (I.ii.131-133). It is also a game to be played with cards close to the chest. A Lord of Misrule naturally does not call himself Lord of Misrule in setting out to reign, but takes some title with the life of pretense in it. Falstaff's pretensions, moreover, are not limited to one occasion, for he is not properly a holiday lord, but a *de facto* buffoon who makes his way by continually seizing, catch as catch can, on what names and meanings the moment offers. He is not a professed buffoon—few buffoons, in life, are apt to be. In Renaissance courts, the role of buffoon was recognized but not necessarily formalized, not necessarily altogether distinct from the role of favorite. And he is a highwayman: Shakespeare draws on the euphemistic, mock-chivalric cant by which "the profession" grace themselves. Falstaff in *Part One* plays it that he is Hal's friend, a gentleman, a "gentleman of the shade," and a soldier; he even enjoys turning the tables with "Thou hast done

[4] See above, pp. 67-73.

much harm upon me, Hal . . . I must give over this life, and I will give it over . . . I'll be damn'd for never a king's son in Christendom" (I.ii.102-109). It is the essence of his character, and his role, in *Part One*, that he never comes to rest where we can see him for what he "is." He is always in motion, always adopting postures, assuming characters.

That he does indeed care for Hal can be conveyed in performance without imposing sentimental tableaux on the action, provided that actors and producer recognize that he cares for the prince after his own fashion. It is from the prince that he chiefly gets his meaning, as it is from real kings that mock kings always get their meaning. We can believe it when we hear in *Henry V* that banishment has "killed his heart" (II.i.92). But to make much of a personal affection for the prince is a misconceived way to find meaning in Falstaff. His extraordinary meaningfulness comes from the way he manages to live "out of all order, out of all compass" by his wit and his wits; and from the way he keeps reflecting on the rest of the action, at first indirectly by the mock roles that he plays, at the end directly by his comments at the battle. Through this burlesque and mockery an intelligence of the highest order is expressed. It is not always clear whether the intelligence is Falstaff's or the dramatist's; often the question need not arise. Romantic criticism went the limit in ascribing a God-like superiority to the character, to the point of insisting that he tells the lies about the multiplying men in buckram merely to amuse, that he knew all the time at Gadshill that it was with Hal and Poins that he fought. To go so far in that direction obviously destroys the drama—spoils the joke in the case of the "incomprehensible lies," a joke which, as E. E. Stoll abundantly demonstrates, must be a joke *on* Falstaff.[5] On the other hand, I see no reason why actor and producer should not do all they can to make us enjoy the intellectual mastery involved in Falstaff's comic resource and power of humorous redefinition. It is crucial that he should not be made so superior that he is never in predicaments, for his genius is expressed in getting out of them. But he does have genius, as Maurice Morgan rightly insisted though in a misconceived way. Through his part Shakespeare expressed attitudes towards experience which,

[5] *Shakespeare Studies*, pp. 403-433.

grounded in a saturnalian reversal of values, went beyond that to include a radical challenge to received ideas.

Throughout the first three acts of *Part One*, the Falstaff comedy is continuously responsive to the serious action. There are constant parallels and contrasts with what happens at court or with the rebels. And yet these parallels are not explicitly noticed; the relations are presented, not formulated. So the first scene ends in a mood of urgency, with the tired king urging haste: "come yourself with speed to us again." The second scene opens with Hal asking Falstaff "What a devil hast thou to do with the time of day?" The prose in which he explains why time is nothing to Sir John is wonderfully leisurely and abundant, an elegant sort of talk that has all the time in the world to enjoy the completion of its schematized patterns:

> Unless hours were cups of sack, and minutes capons, and clocks the tongues of bawds, and dials the signs of leaping houses, and the blessed sun himself a fair hot wench in flame-colored taffeta, I see no reason why thou shouldst be so superfluous to demand the time of day.
>
> (I.ii.7-13)

The same difference in the attitude towards time runs throughout and goes with the difference between verse and prose mediums. A similar contrast obtains about lese majesty. Thus at their first appearance Falstaff insults Hal's majesty with casual, off-hand wit which the prince tolerates (while getting his own back by jibing at Falstaff's girth):

> And I prithee, sweet wag, when thou art king, as God save thy Grace—Majesty I should say, for grace thou wilt have none—
>
> *Prince.* What, none?
>
> *Falstaff.* No, by my troth; not so much as will serve to be prologue to an egg and butter.
>
> *Prince.* Well, how then? Come, roundly, roundly.
>
> (I.ii.17-25)

In the next scene, we see Worcester calling into question the grace of Bolingbroke, "that same greatness to which our own hands / Have holp to make so portly" (I.iii.12-13). The King's response is immediate and drastic, and his lines point a moral that Hal seems to be ignoring:

> Worcester, get thee gone; for I do see
> Danger and disobedience in thine eye.
> O, sir, your presence is too bold and peremptory,
> And majesty might never yet endure
> The moody frontier of a servant brow.
>
> (I.iii.15-19)

Similar parallels run between Hotspur's heroics and Falstaff's mock-heroics. In the third scene we hear Hotspur talking of "an easy leap / To pluck bright honor from the pale-face'd moon" (I.iii.201-202). Then in the robbery, Falstaff is complaining that "Eight yards of uneven ground is threescore and ten miles afoot for me," and asking "Have you any levers to lift me up again, being down?" (II.ii.25-28, 36) After Hotspur enters exclaiming against the cowardly lord who has written that he will not join the rebellion, we have Falstaff's entrance to the tune of "A plague of all cowards" (II.iv.127). And so on, and so on. Shakespeare's art has reached the point where he makes everything foil to everything else. Hal's imagery, in his soliloquy, shows the dramatist thinking about such relations: "like bright metal on a sullen ground, / My reformation, glitt'ring o'er my fault" (I.ii.236-237).

Now it is not true that Falstaff's impudence about Hal's grace undercuts Bolingbroke's majesty, nor that Sir John's posturing as a hero among cowards invalidates the heroic commitment Hotspur expresses when he says "but I tell you, my lord fool, out of this nettle, danger, we pluck this flower, safety" (II.iii.11-12). The relationship is not one of a mocking echo. Instead, there is a certain distance between the comic and serious strains which leaves room for a complex interaction, organized by the crucial role of the prince. We are invited, by the King's unfavorable comparison in the opening scene, to see the Prince in relation to Hotspur. And Hal himself, in the midst of his Boars Head revel, compares himself with Hotspur. In telling Poins of his encounter with the drawers among the hogsheads of the wine-cellar, he says "I have sounded the very bass-string of humility," goes on to note what he has gained by it, "I can drink with any tinker in his own language during my life," and concludes with "I tell thee, Ned, thou hast lost much honour that thou wert not with me in this action" (II.iv.5, 20-24). His mock-heroic way of talking about "this action" shows how well he knows how to value it from a princely vantage. But the remark cuts two ways. For running the gamut of society *is* an important action: after their experiment with Francis and his "Anon, anon, sir," the Prince exclaims

> That ever this fellow should have fewer words than a parrot, and yet the son of a woman! . . . I am not yet of Percy's mind, the Hotspur of the North; he that kills me some six or seven dozen of Scots at a breakfast, washes his hands, and says to his wife, "Fie upon this quiet life! I want work." "O my sweet Harry," says she, "how many hast thou kill'd to-day?" "Give my roan horse a drench," says he, and answers "Some fourteen," an hour after, "a trifle, a trifle." I prithee call in Falstaff. I'll play Percy, and that damn'd brawn shall play Dame Mortimer his wife.
>
> (II.iv.110-124)

It is the narrowness and obliviousness of the martial hero that Hal's mockery brings out; here his awareness explicitly spans the distance between the separate strains of the action; indeed, the distance is made the measure of the kingliness of his nature. His "I am not *yet* of Percy's mind" implies what he later promises his father (the commercial image he employs reflects his ability to use, after his father's fashion, the politician's calculation and indirection):

> Percy is but my factor, good my lord,
> To engross up glorious deeds on my behalf . . .
>
> (III.ii.147-148)

In the Boars Head Tavern scene, Hal never carries out the plan of playing Percy to Falstaff's Dame Mortimer; in effect he has played both their parts already in his snatch of mimicry. But Falstaff provides him with a continuous exercise in the consciousness that comes from playing at being what one is not, and from seeing through such playing.

Even here, where one world does comment on another explicitly, Hotspur's quality is not invalidated; rather, his achievement is *placed*. It is included within a wider field which contains also the drawers, mine host, Mistress Quickly, and by implication, not only "all the good lads of Eastcheap" but all the estates of England.[6] When we saw Hotspur and his Lady, he was not foolish, but delightful in his headlong, spontaneous way. His Lady has a certain pathos in the complaints which serve to convey how all absorbing his battle passion is. But the joke is with him as he mocks her:

> Love? I love thee not;
> I care not for thee, Kate. This is no world
> To play with mammets and to tilt with lips.
> We must have bloody noses and crack'd crowns,
> And pass them current, too. Gods me, my horse!
> (II.iii.93-97)

One could make some very broad fun of Hotspur's preference for his horse over his wife. But there is nothing of the kind in Shakespeare: here and later, his treatment values the conversion of love into war as one of the important human powers. Hotspur has the fullness of life and the unforced integrity of the great aristocrat who has never known what it is to cramp his own style. His style shows it; he speaks the richest, freshest poetry of the play, in lines that take all the scope they need to fulfill feeling and perception:

> oft the teeming earth
> Is with a kind of colic pinch'd and vex'd
> By the imprisoning of unruly wind
> Within her womb, which, for enlargement striving,
> Shakes the old beldame earth and topples down
> Steeples and mossgrown towers. At your birth
> Our grandam earth, having this distemp'rature,
> In passion shook.
> *Glendower*. Cousin, of many men
> I do not bear these crossings. Give me leave
> To tell you once again that at my birth
> The front of heaven was full of fiery shapes,
> The goats ran from the mountains, and the herds
> Were strangely clamorous to the frighted fields.
> (III.i.28-40)

[6] See Empson, *Pastoral*, pp. 42ff.

The established life of moss-grown towers is in Percy's poetic speech, as the grazed-over Welsh mountains are in Glendower's. They are both strong; everybody in this play is strong in his own way. Hotspur's humor is untrammeled, like his verse, based on the heedless empiricism of an active, secure nobleman:

> *Glendower.* I can call spirits from the vasty deep.
> *Hotspur.* Why, so can I, or so can any man;
> But will they come when you do call for them?
> (III.i.53-55)

His unconsciousness makes him, at other moments, a comic if winning figure, as the limitations of his feudal virtues are brought out: his want of tact and judgment, his choleric man's forgetfulness, his sudden boyish habit of leaping to conclusions, the noble but also comical way he can be carried away by "imagination of some great exploit" (I.iii.199), or by indignation at "this vile politician, Bolingbroke" (I.iii.241). Professor Lily B. Campbell has demonstrated that the rebellion of the Northern Earls in 1570 was present for Shakespeare's audience in watching the Percy family in the play.[7] The remoteness of this rough north country life from the London world of his audience, as well as its aristocratic charm, are conveyed when Hotspur tells his wife that she swears "like a comfit-maker's wife,"

> As if thou ne'er walk'st further than Finsbury.
> Swear me, Kate, like a lady as thou art,
> A good mouth-filling oath; and leave 'in sooth'
> And such protest of pepper gingerbread
> To velvet guards and Sunday citizens.
> (III.i.255-259)

It is the various strengths of a stirring world, not deficiencies, which make the conflict in *1 Henry IV*. Even the humble carriers, and the professional thieves, are full of themselves and their business:

> I am joined with no foot land-rakers, no long-staff sixpenny strikers, none of these mad mustachio purple-hued maltworms;

[7] Lily B. Campbell, *Shakespeare's Histories, Mirrors of Elizabethan Policy* (San Marino, 1947), pp. 229-238.

> but with nobility and tranquillity, burgomasters and great oneyers, such as can hold in, such as will strike sooner than speak, and speak sooner than drink, and drink sooner than pray; and yet, zounds, I lie; for they pray continually to their saint, the commonwealth, or rather, not pray to her, but prey on her, for they ride up and down on her and make her their boots.
>
> (II.i.81-91)

In his early history play, *2 Henry VI*, as we have noticed, Shakespeare used his clowns to present the Jack Cade rebellion as a saturnalia ignorantly undertaken in earnest, a highly-stylized piece of dramaturgy, which he brings off triumphantly. In this more complex play the underworld is presented as endemic disorder alongside the crisis of noble rebellion: the king's lines are apposite when he says that insurrection can always mobilize

> moody beggars, starving for a time
> Of pell-mell havoc and confusion.
>
> (V.i.81-82)

Falstaff places himself in saying "Well, God be thanked for these rebels. They offend none but the virtuous. I laud them, I praise them."

The whole effect, in the opening acts, when there is little commentary on the spectacle as a whole, is of life overflowing its bounds by sheer vitality. Thieves and rebels and honest men—"one that hath abundance of charge too, God knows what" (II.i.64)—ride up and down on the commonwealth, pray to her and prey on her. Hotspur exults that "That roan shall be my throne" (II.iii.73). Falstaff exclaims, "Shall I? Content. This chair shall be my state" (II.iv.415). Hal summarizes the effect, after Hotspur is dead, with

> When that this body did contain a spirit,
> A kingdom for it was too small a bound.
>
> (V.iv.89-90)

The stillness when he says this, at the close of the battle, is the moment when his royalty is made manifest. When he stands poised above the prostrate bodies of Hotspur and Falstaff, his position on the stage and his lines about the two heroes express a nature which includes within a larger order the now subordinated parts of life which are represented in those two: in Hotspur, honor, the social obligation to courage and self-sacrifice, a value which has been isolated in this magnificently anarchical feudal lord to become almost everything; and in Falstaff, the complementary *joie de vivre* which rejects all social obligations with "I like not such grinning honour as Sir Walter hath. Give me life" (V.iii.61).

Getting Rid of Bad Luck by Comedy

But Falstaff does not stay dead. He jumps up in a triumph which, like Bottom coming alive after Pyramus is dead, reminds one of the comic resurrections in the St. George plays. He comes back to life because he is still relevant. His apology for counterfeiting cuts deeply indeed, because it does not apply merely to himself; we can relate it, as William Empson has shown, to the counterfeiting of the king. Bolingbroke too knows when it is time to counterfeit, both in this battle, where he survives because he has many marching in his coats, and throughout a political career where, as he acknowledges to Hal, he manipulates the symbols of majesty with a calculating concern for ulterior results. L. C. Knights, noticing this relation and the burlesque, elsewhere in Falstaff's part, of the attitudes of chivalry, concluded with nineteenth-century critics like Ulrici and Victor Hugo that the comedy should be taken as a devastating satire on war and government.[8] But this is obviously an impossible, anachronistic view, based on the assumption of the age of individualism that politics and war are unnatural activities that can be done without. Mr. Knights would have it that the audience should feel a jeering response when Henry sonorously declares, after Shrewsbury: "Thus ever did rebellion find rebuke." This interpretation makes a shambles of the heroic moments of the play—makes them clearly impossible to act. My own view, as will be clear, is that the dynamic relation of comedy and serious action is saturnalian rather than satiric, that the misrule works, through the whole dramatic rhythm, to consolidate rule. But it is also true, as Mr. Empson remarks, that "the double plot is carrying a fearful strain here."[9] Shakespeare is

[8] "A Note on Comedy," *Determinations*, ed. by F. R. Leavis (London, 1934).
[9] *Pastoral*, p. 46.

putting an enormous pressure on the comedy to resolve the challenge posed by the ironic perceptions presented in his historical action.

The process at work, here and earlier in the play, can be made clearer, I hope, by reference now to the carrying off of bad luck by the scapegoat of saturnalian ritual. We do not need to assume that Shakespeare had any such ritual patterns consciously in mind; whatever his conscious intention, it seems to me that these analogues illuminate patterns which his poetic drama presents concretely and dramatically. After such figures as the Mardi Gras or Carnival have presided over a revel, they are frequently turned on by their followers, tried in some sort of court, convicted of sins notorious in the village during the last year, and burned or buried in effigy to signify a new start. In other ceremonies described in *The Golden Bough*, mockery kings appear as recognizable substitutes for real kings, stand trial in their stead, and carry away the evils of their realms into exile or death. One such scapegoat figure, as remote historically as could be from Shakespeare, is the Tibetan King of the Years, who enjoyed ten days' misrule during the annual holiday of Buddhist monks at Lhasa. At the climax of his ceremony, after doing what he liked while collecting bad luck by shaking a black yak's tail over the people, he mounted the temple steps and ridiculed the representative of the Grand Llama, proclaiming heresies like "What we perceive through the five senses is no illusion. All you teach is untrue." A few minutes later, discredited by a cast of loaded dice, he was chased off to exile and possible death in the mountains.[10] One cannot help thinking of Falstaff's catechism on honor, spoken just before another valuation of honor is expressed in the elevated blank verse of a hero confronting death: "Can honour . . . take away the grief of a wound? No. . . . What is honour? a word. What is that word, honour? Air." Hal's final expulsion of Falstaff appears in the light of these analogies to carry out an impersonal pattern, not merely political but ritual in character. After the guilty reign of Bolingbroke, the prince is making a fresh start as the new king. At a level beneath the moral notions of a personal reform, we can see a nonlogical process of purification by sacrifice—the sacrifice of Falstaff. The career of the

[10] See James G. Frazer, *The Scapegoat* (London, 1914), pp. 218-223 and passim.

old king, a successful usurper whose conduct of affairs has been sceptical and opportunistic, has cast doubt on the validity of the whole conception of a divinely-ordained and chivalrous kingship to which Shakespeare and his society were committed. And before Bolingbroke, Richard II had given occasion for doubts about the rituals of kingship in an opposite way, by trying to use them magically. Shakespeare had shown Richard assuming that the symbols of majesty should be absolutes, that the names of legitimate power should be transcendently effective regardless of social forces. Now both these attitudes have been projected also in Falstaff; he carries to comically delightful and degraded extremes both a magical use of moral sanctions and the complementary opportunistic manipulation and scepticism. So the ritual analogy suggests that by turning on Falstaff as a scapegoat, as the villagers turned on their Mardi Gras, the prince can free himself from the sins, the "bad luck," of Richard's reign and of his father's reign, to become a king in whom chivalry and a sense of divine ordination are restored.

But this process of carrying off bad luck, if it is to be made *dramatically* cogent, as a symbolic action accomplished in and by dramatic form, cannot take place magically in Shakespeare's play. When it happens magically in the play, we have, I think, a failure to transform ritual into comedy. In dealing with fully successful comedy, the magical analogy is only a useful way of organizing our awareness of a complex symbolic action. The expulsion of evil works as dramatic form only in so far as it is realized in a movement from participation to rejection which happens, moment by moment, in our response to Falstaff's clowning misrule. We watch Falstaff adopt one posture after another, in the effort to give himself meaning at no cost; and moment by moment we see that the meaning is specious. So our participation is repeatedly diverted to laughter. The laughter, disbursing energy originally mobilized to respond to a valid meaning, signalizes our mastery by understanding of the tendency which has been misapplied or carried to an extreme.

Consider, for example, the use of magical notions of royal power in the most famous of all Falstaff's burlesques:

> By the Lord, I knew ye as well as he that made ye. . . . Was it for me to kill the heir apparent? Should I turn upon the true

prince? Why, thou knowest I am as valiant as Hercules; but beware instinct. The lion will not touch the true prince. Instinct is a great matter. I was now a coward on instinct. I shall think the better of myself, and thee, during my life—I for a valiant lion, and thou for a true prince. But, by the Lord, lads, I am glad you have the money. Hostess, clap to the doors: watch to-night, pray to-morrow.

(II.iv.295-306)

Here Falstaff has recourse to the brave conception that legitimate kingship has a magical potency. This is the sort of absolutist appeal to sanctions which Richard II keeps falling back on in his desperate "conjuration" (*R.II* III.ii.23) by hyperbole:

> So when this thief, this traitor, Bolingbroke, . . .
> Shall see us rising in our throne, the East,
> His treasons will sit blushing in his face,
> Not able to endure the sight of day . . .
> The breath of worldly men cannot depose
> The deputy elected by the Lord.
> For every man that Bolingbroke hath press'd
> To lift shrewd steel against our golden crown,
> God for his Richard hath in heavenly pay
> A glorious angel.
>
> (*R.II* III.ii.47-61)

In Richard's case, a tragic irony enforces the fact that heavenly angels are of no avail if one's coffers are empty of golden angels and the Welsh army have dispersed. In Falstaff's case, the irony is comically obvious, the "lies are like the father that begets them; gross as a mountain, open, palpable" (II.iv.249-250). Hal stands for the judgment side of our response, while Falstaff embodies the enthusiastic, irrepressible conviction of fantasy's omnipotence. The Prince keeps returning to Falstaff's bogus "instinct"; "Now, sirs . . . You are lions too, you ran away upon instinct, you will not touch the true prince; no—fie!" (II.iv.29-34) After enjoying the experience of seeing through such notions of magical majesty, he is never apt to make the mistake of assuming that, just because he is king, lions like Northumberland will not touch him. King Richard's bad luck came precisely from such an assumption—unexamined, of course, as fatal assumptions always are. Freud's account of bad luck, in *The Psychopathology of Everyday Life*, sees it as the expression of unconscious motives which resist the conscious goals of the personality. This view helps to explain how the acting out of disruptive motives in saturnalia or in comedy can serve to master potential aberration by revaluing it in relation to the whole of experience. So Falstaff, in acting out this absolutist aberration, is taking away what might have been Hal's bad luck, taking it away not in a magical way, but by extending the sphere of conscious control. The comedy is a civilized equivalent of the primitive rite. A similar mastery of potential aberration is promoted by the experience of seeing through Falstaff's burlesque of the sort of headlong chivalry presented seriously in Hotspur.

In order to put the symbolic action of the comedy in larger perspective, it will be worth while to consider further, for a moment, the relation of language to stage action and dramatic situation in *Richard II*. That play is a pioneering exploration of the semantics of royalty, shot through with talk about the potency and impotence of language. In the first part, we see a Richard who is possessor of an apparently magical omnipotence: for example, when he commutes Bolingbroke's banishment from ten to six years, Bolingbroke exclaims:

> How long a time lies in one little word!
> Four lagging winters and four wanton springs
> End in a word: such is the breath of kings.
> (*R.II* I.iii.213-215)

Richard assumes he has such magic breath inevitably, regardless of "the breath of worldly men." When he shouts things like "Is not the king's name twenty thousand names? / Arm, arm, my name!" he carries the absolutist assumption to the giddiest verge of absurdity. When we analyze the magical substitution of words for things in such lines, looking at them from outside the rhythm of feeling in which they occur, it seems scarcely plausible that a drama should be built around the impulse to adopt such an assumption. It seems especially implausible in our own age, when we are so conscious, on an abstract level, of the dependence of verbal efficacy on the social group. The analytical situation involves a misleading perspective, however; for, whatever your assumptions about semantics, when you have to *act*, to *be* somebody or become somebody, there is a moment when you have to have faith that the unknown world beyond will respond to the names you commit yourself to as right names.[11] The Elizabethan mind, moreover, generally assumed that one played one's part in a divinely ordained pageant where each man *was* his name and the role his name implied. The expression of this faith, and of the outrage of it, is particularly drastic in the Elizabethan drama, which can be regarded, from this vantage, as an art form developed to express the shock and exhilaration of the discovery that life is not pageantry. As Professor Tillyard has pointed out, *Richard II* is the most ceremonial of all Shakespeare's plays, and the ceremony all comes to nothing.[12] In Richard's deposition scene, one way in which anguish at his fall is expressed is by a focus on his loss of names: he responds to Northumberland's "My Lord—" by flinging out

> No lord of thine, thou haught insulting man,
> Nor no man's lord. I have no name, no title—
> No, not that name was given me at the font—
> But 'tis usurp'd. Alack the heavy day,
> That I have worn so many winters out
> And know not now what name to call myself!
> O that I were a mockery king of snow,
> Standing before the sun of Bolingbroke
> To melt myself away in water-drops!
> (*R.II* IV.i.253-262)

His next move is to call for the looking glass in which he stares at his face to look for the meaning the face has lost. To lose one's meaning, one's social role, is to be reduced to mere body.

Here again the tragedy can be used to illuminate the comedy. Since the Elizabethan drama was a double medium of words and of physical gestures, it frequently expressed the pathos of the loss of meaning by emphasizing moments when word and gesture, name and body, no longer go together, just as it presented the excitement of a gain of meaning by showing a body seizing on

[11] I am indebted to my colleagues Professor Theodore Baird and Professor G. Armour Craig for this way of seeing the relation of names to developing situations.

[12] See *Shakespeare's History Plays* (New York, 1946), pp. 245ff.

names when a hero creates his identity. In the deposition scene, Richard says "mark me how I will undo myself" (IV.i.203). Then he gives away by physical gestures the symbolic meanings which have constituted that self. When at last he has no name, the anguish is that the face, the body, remain when the meaning is gone. There is also something in Richard's lines which, beneath the surface of his self-pity, relishes such undoing, a self-love which looks towards fulfillment in that final reduction of all to the body which is death. This narcissistic need for the physical is the other side of the attitude that the magic of the crown should altogether transcend the physical—and the human:

> Cover your heads, and mock not flesh and blood
> With solemn reverence. Throw away respect,
> Tradition, form, and ceremonious duty;
> For you have but mistook me all this while.
> I live with bread like you, feel want, taste grief,
> Need friends. Subjected thus,
> How can you say to me I am a king?
> (*R.II* III.ii.171-177)

In expressing the disappointment of Richard's magical expectations, as well as their sweeping magnificence, the lines make manifest the aberration which is mastered in the play by tragic form.

The same sort of impulse is expressed and mastered by comic form in the Henry IV comedy. When Richard wishes he were a mockery king of snow, to melt before the sun of Bolingbroke, the image expresses on one side the wish to escape from the body with which he is left when his meaning has gone—to weep himself away in water drops. But the lines also look wistfully towards games of mock royalty where, since the whole thing is based on snow, the collapse of meaning need not hurt. Falstaff is such a mockery king. To be sure, he is flesh and blood, of a kind: he is tallow, anyway. He "sweats to death / And lards the lean earth as he walks along." Of course he is not just a mockery, not just his role, not just bombast. Shakespeare, as always, makes the symbolic role the product of a life which includes contradictions of it, such as the morning-after regrets when Falstaff thinks of the inside of a church and notices that his skin hangs about him like an old lady's loose gown. Falstaff is human enough so that "Were't not for laughing, . . . [we] should pity him." But we do laugh, because when Falstaff's meanings collapse, little but make-believe has been lost:

> *Prince.* Thy state is taken for a join'd-stool, thy golden sceptre for a leaden dagger, and thy precious rich crown for a pitiful bald crown. (II.iv.418-420)

Falstaff's effort to make his body and furnishings mean sovereignty is doomed from the start; he must work with a leaden dagger, the equivalent of a Vice's dagger of lath. But Falstaff does have golden words, and an inexhaustible vitality in using them. He can name himself nobly, reordering the world by words so as to do himself credit:

> No, my good lord. Banish Peto, banish Bardolph, banish Poins; but for sweet Jack Falstaff, kind Jack Falstaff, true Jack Falstaff, valiant Jack Falstaff, and therefore more valiant being, as he is, old Jack Falstaff, banish not him thy Harry's company, banish not him thy Harry's company. Banish plump Jack, and banish all the world! (II.iv.519-527)

I quote such familiar lines to recall their effect of incantation: they embody an effort at a kind of magical naming. Each repetition of "sweet Jack Falstaff, kind Jack Falstaff" aggrandizes an identity which the serial clauses caress and cherish. At the very end, in "plump Jack," the disreputable belly is glorified.

In valid heroic and majestic action, the bodies of the personages are constantly being elevated by becoming the vehicles of social meanings; in the comedy, such elevation becomes burlesque, and in the repeated failures to achieve a fusion of body and symbol, abstract meanings keep falling back into the physical. "A plague of sighing and grief! it blows a man up like a bladder" (II.iv.365-366). The repetition of such joking about Falstaff's belly makes it meaningful in a very special way, as a symbol of the process of inflation and collapse of meaning. So it represents the power of the individual life to continue despite the collapse of social roles. This continuing on beyond definitions is after all what we call "the body" in one main meaning of the term: Falstaff's belly is thus the essence of body—an essence which can be defined only dynamically, by failures of meaning. The effect of indestructible vitality is reinforced by the association of Falstaff's figure with the gay eating and drinking of Shrove Tuesday and Carnival.[13] Whereas, in the tragedy, the reduction is to a body which can only die, here reduction is to a body which typifies our power to eat and drink our way through a shambles of intellectual and moral contradictions.

So we cannot resist sharing Falstaff's genial self-love when he commends his vision of plump Jack to the Prince, just as we share the ingenuous self-love of a little child. But the dramatist is ever on the alert to enforce the ironies that dog the tendency of fantasy to equate the self with "all the world." So a most monstrous watch comes beating at the doors which have been clapped to against care; everyday breaks in on holiday.

The Trial of Carnival in PART TWO

In *Part One*, Falstaff reigns, within his sphere, as Carnival; *Part Two* is very largely taken up with his trial. To put Carnival on trial, run him out of town, and burn or bury him is in folk custom a way of limiting, by ritual, the attitudes and impulses set loose by ritual. Such a trial, though conducted with gay hoots and jeers, serves to swing the mind round to a new vantage, where it sees misrule no longer as a benign release for the individual, but as a source of destructive consequences for society.[14] This sort of reckoning is what *Part Two* brings to Falstaff.

But Falstaff proves extremely difficult to bring to book—more difficult than an ordinary mummery king—because his burlesque and mockery are developed to a point where the mood of a moment crystallizes as a settled attitude of scepticism. As we have observed before, in a static, monolithic society, a Lord of Misrule can be put back in his place after the revel with relative ease. The festive

[13] See above, pp. 67-73, for the relation of Falstaff to Nashe's pageant figure of Bacchus, to Shrove Tuesday and other mummery roles where the praise of food, drink, and folly was a traditional holiday exercise.

[14] The ritual of Carnival in Italy and its relation to Italian comedy has recently been exhibited in Professor Paolo Toschi's *Le origini del teatro italiano* (Torino, 1955) with a fullness and clarity made possible by the rich popular Italian heritage.

burlesque of solemn sanctities does not seriously threaten social values in a monolithic culture, because the license depends utterly upon what it mocks: liberty is unable to envisage any alternative to the accepted order except the standing of it on its head. But Shakespeare's culture was not monolithic: though its moralists assumed a single order, scepticism was beginning to have ground to stand on and look about—especially in and around London. So a Lord of Misrule figure, brought up, so to speak, from the country to the city, or from the traditional past into the changing present, could become on the Bankside the mouthpiece not merely for the dependent holiday scepticism which is endemic in a traditional society, but also for a dangerously self-sufficient everyday scepticism. When such a figure is set in an environment of sober-blooded great men behaving as opportunistically as he, the effect is to raise radical questions about social sanctities. At the end of *Part Two*, the expulsion of Falstaff is presented by the dramatist as getting rid of this threat; Shakespeare has recourse to a primitive procedure to meet a modern challenge. We shall find reason to question whether this use of ritual entirely succeeds.

But the main body of *Part Two*, what I am seeing as the trial, as against the expulsion, is wonderfully effective drama. The first step in trying Carnival, the first step in ceasing to be his subjects, would be to stop calling him "My Lord" and call him instead by his right name, Misrule. Now this is just the step which Falstaff himself takes for us at the outset of *Part Two*; when we first see him, he is setting himself up as an institution, congratulating himself on his powers *as* buffoon and wit. He glories in his role with what Dover Wilson has aptly called "comic hubris."[15] In the saturnalian scenes of *Part One*, we saw that it is impossible to say just who he is; but in *Part Two*, Falstaff sets himself up at the outset as Falstaff:

> I am not only witty in myself, but the cause that wit is in other men. . . .
>
> A pox of this gout! or, a gout of this pox! for one or the other plays the rogue with my great toe. 'Tis no matter if I do halt. I have the wars for my colour, and my pension shall seem the

[15] *The Fortunes of Falstaff* (New York, 1944), Ch. V, "Falstaff High on Fortune's Wheel," p. 94.

> more reasonable. A good wit will make use of anything. I will turn diseases to commodity. (I.ii.11-12, 273-278)

In the early portion of *Part One* he never spoke in asides, but now he constantly confides his schemes and his sense of himself to the audience. We do not have to see through him, but watch instead from inside his façades as he imposes them on others. Instead of warm amplifications centered on himself, his talk now consists chiefly of bland impudence or dry, denigrating comments on the way of the world. Much of the comedy is an almost Jonsonian spectacle where we relish a witty knave gulling fools.

It is this self-conscious Falstaff, confident of setting up his holiday license on an everyday basis, who at once encounters, of all awkward people, the Lord Chief Justice. From there on, during the first two acts, he is constantly put in the position of answering for his way of life; in effect he is repeatedly called to trial and keeps eluding it only by a "more than impudent sauciness" (II.i.123) and the privilege of his official employment in the wars. Mistress Quickly's attempt to arrest him is wonderfully ineffectual; but he notably fails to thrust the Lord Chief Justice from a level consideration. Hal and Poins then disguise themselves, not this time for the sake of the incomprehensible lies that Falstaff will tell, but in order to try him, to see him "bestow himself . . . in his true colours" (II.ii.186). So during the first two acts we are again and again put in the position of judging him, although we continue to laugh with him. A vantage is thus established from which we watch him in action in Gloucestershire, where the Justice he has to deal with is so shallow that Falstaff's progress is a triumph. The comedy is still delightful; Falstaff is still the greatest of wits, but we are constantly shown fun that involves fraud. Falstaff himself tells us about his game, with proud relish. Towards the end of the play, Hal's reconciliation with his father and then with the Lord Chief Justice reemphasizes the detached vantage of judgment. So no leading remarks are necessary to assure our noting and marking when we hear Falstaff shouting, "Let us take any man's horses; the laws of England are at my commandment. Blessed are they that have been my friends, and woe unto my lord chief justice!" (V.iii.140-144) The next moment we watch Doll and the Hostess being hauled off by Beadles because "the man is dead that you and Pistol beat among you" (V.iv.18).

Many of the basic structures in this action no doubt were shaped by morality-play encounters between Virtues and Vices,[16] encounters which from my vantage here can be seen as cognate to the festive and scapegoat pattern. The trial of Falstaff is so effective *as drama* because no one conducts it—it happens. Falstaff, being a dramatic character, not a mummery, does not know when he has had his day. And he does not even recognize the authority who will finally sentence him: he mistakes Hal for a bastard son of the king's (II.iv.307). The result of the trial is to make us see perfectly the necessity for the rejection of Falstaff as a man, as a favorite for a king, as the leader of an interest at court.

But I do not think that the dramatist is equally successful in justifying the rejection of Falstaff as a mode of awareness. The problem is not in justifying rejection morally but in making the process cogent *dramatically*, as in *Part One* we reject magical majesty or intransigent chivalry. The bad luck which in *Part Two* Falstaff goes about collecting, by shaking the black yak's tail of his wit over people's heads, is the impulse to assume that nothing is sacred. In a play concerned with ruthless political maneuver, much of it conducted by impersonal state functionaries, Falstaff turns up as a functionary too, with his own version of maneuver and impersonality: "If the young dace be a bait for the old pike, I see no reason in the law of nature but I may snap at him" (III.ii.356-359). Now this attitude is a most appropriate response to the behavior of the high factions beneath whose struggles Falstaff plies his retail trade. In the Gaultree parleys, Lord John rebukes the Archbishop for his use of the counterfeited zeal of God—and then himself uses a counterfeited zeal of gentlemanly friendship to trick the rebels into disbanding their forces. The difference between his behavior and Falstaff's is of course that Lancaster has reasons of state on his side, a sanction supported, if not by legitimacy, at least by the desperate need for social order. This is a real difference, but a bare and harsh one. After all, Falstaff's little commonwealth of man has its pragmatic needs too: as he explains blandly to the Justice, he needs great infamy, because

[16] *Ibid.*, pp. 17-22.

"he that buckles him in my belt cannot live in less" (I.iii.159-160).

The trouble with trying to get rid of this attitude merely by getting rid of Falstaff is that the attitude is too pervasive in the whole society of the play, whether public or private. It is too obviously *not* just a saturnalian mood, the extravagance of a moment: it is presented instead as in grain, as the way of the world. Shakespeare might have let the play end with this attitude dominant, a harsh recognition that life is a nasty business where the big fishes eat the little fishes, with the single redeeming consideration that political order is better than anarchy, so that there is a pragmatic virtue in loyalty to the power of the state. But instead the dramatist undertakes, in the last part of the play, to expel this view of the world and to dramatize the creation of legitimacy and sanctified social power. Although the final scenes are fascinating, with all sorts of illuminations, it seems to me that at this level they partly fail.

We have seen that Shakespeare typically uses ritual patterns of behavior and thought precisely in the course of making clear, by tragic or comic irony, that rituals have no *magical* efficacy. The reason for his failure at the close of *Part Two* is that at this point he himself uses ritual, not ironically transformed into drama, but magically. To do this involves a restriction instead of an extension of awareness. An extension of control and awareness is consummated in the epiphany of Hal's majesty while he is standing over Hotspur and Falstaff at the end of *Part One*. But *Part Two* ends with drastic restriction of awareness which goes with the embracing of magical modes of thought, not humorously but sentimentally.

It is true that the latter half of *Part Two* very effectively builds up to its finale by recurrent expression of a laboring need to be rid of a growth or humor. King Henry talks of the body of his kingdom as foul with rank diseases (III.i.39), and recalls Richard's prophecy that "foul sin gathering head / Shall break into corruption" (III.i.76-77). There are a number of other images of expulsion, such as the striking case where the rebels speak of the need to "purge th' obstructions which begin to stop / Our very veins of life" (IV.i.65-66). Henry himself is sick in the last half of the play, and there are repeated suggestions that his sickness is the consequence both of his sinful usurpation and of the struggle to defend it. Since his usurpation was almost a public duty, and his defense of order clearly for England's sake as well as his own advantage, he becomes in these last scenes almost a sacrificial figure, a king who sins for the sake of society, suffers for society in suffering for his sin, and carries his sin off into death. Hal speaks of the crown having "fed upon the body of my father" (IV.v.160). Henry, in his last long speech, summarizes this pattern in saying:

God knows, my son,
By what bypaths and indirect crook'd ways
I met this crown; and I myself know well
How troublesome it sat upon my head.
To thee it shall descend with better quiet,
Better opinion, better confirmation;
For all the soil of the achievement goes
With me into the earth.

(IV.v.184-191)

The same image of burying sin occurs in some curious lines with which Hal reassures his brothers:

My father is gone wild into his grave;
For in his tomb lie my affections . . .

(V.ii.123-124)

This conceit not only suggests an expulsion of evil, but hints at the patricidal motive which is referred to explicitly elsewhere in these final scenes and is the complement of the father-son atonement.

Now this sacrificial imagery, where used by and about the old king, is effectively dramatic, because it does not ask the audience to abandon any part of the awareness of a human, social situation which the play as a whole has expressed. But the case is altered when Hal turns on "that father ruffian" Falstaff. The new king's whip-lash lines stress Falstaff's age and glance at his death:

I know thee not, old man. Fall to thy prayers.
How ill white hairs become a fool and jester!
I have long dreamt of such a kind of man,
So surfeit-swell'd, so old, and so profane;
But being awak'd, I do despise my dream.
Make less thy body, hence, and more thy grace;

Leave gormandising. Know the grave doth gape
For thee thrice wider than for other men.
(V.v.51-58)

The priggish tone, to which so many have objected, can be explained at one level as appropriate to the solemn occasion of a coronation. But it goes with a drastic narrowing of awareness. There are of course occasions in life when people close off parts of their minds—a coronation is a case in point: Shakespeare, it can be argued, is simply putting such an occasion into his play. But even his genius could not get around the fact that to block off awareness of irony is contradictory to the very nature of drama, which has as one of its functions the extension of such awareness. Hal's lines, redefining his holiday with Falstaff as a dream, and then despising the dream, seek to invalidate that holiday pole of life, instead of including it, as his lines on his old acquaintance did at the end of *Part One*. (Elsewhere in Shakespeare, to dismiss dreams categorically is foolhardy.) And those lines about the thrice-wide grave: are they a threat or a joke? We cannot tell, because the sort of consciousness that would confirm a joke is being damped out: "Reply not to me with a fool-born jest" (V.v.59). If ironies about Hal were expressed by the context, we could take the scene as the representation of his becoming a prig. But there is simply a blur in the tone, a blur which results, I think, from a retreat into magic by the *dramatist*, as distinct from his characters. Magically, the line about burying the belly is exactly the appropriate threat. It goes with the other images of burying sin and wildness and conveys the idea that the grave can swallow what Falstaff's belly stands for. To assume that one can cope with a pervasive attitude of mind by dealing physically with its most prominent symbol—what is this but magic-mongering? It is the same sort of juggling which we get in Henry IV's sentimental lines taking literally the name of the Jerusalem chamber in the palace:

Laud be to God! Even there my life must end.
It hath been prophesied to me many years,
I should not die but in Jerusalem . . .
(IV.v.236-238)

One can imagine making a mockery of Henry's pious ejaculation by catcalling a version of his final lines at the close of *Richard II* (V.vi.49-50):

> Is this that voyage to the Holy Land
> To wash the blood from off your guilty hand?

An inhibition of irony goes here with Henry's making the symbol do for the thing, just as it does with Hal's expulsion of Falstaff. A return to an official view of the sanctity of state is achieved by sentimental use of magical relations.

We can now suggest a few tentative conclusions of a general sort about the relation of comedy to ritual. It appears that comedy uses ritual in the process of redefining ritual as the expression of particular personalities in particular circumstances. The heritage of ritual gives universality and depth. The persons of the drama make the customary gestures developed in ritual observance, and, in doing so, they project in a wholehearted way attitudes which are not normally articulated at large. At the same time, the dramatization of such gestures involves being aware of their relation to the whole of experience in a way which is not necessary for the celebrants of a ritual proper. In the actual observance of customary misrule, the control of the disruptive motives which the festivity expresses is achieved by the group's recognition of the place of the whole business within the larger rhythm of their continuing social life. No one need decide, therefore, whether the identifications involved in the ceremony are magically valid or merely expressive. But in the drama, perspective and control depend on presenting, along with the ritual gestures, an expression of a social situation out of which they grow. So the drama must control magic by re-understanding it as imagination: dramatic irony must constantly dog the wish that the mock king be real, that the self be all the world or set all the world at naught. When, through a failure of irony, the dramatist presents ritual as magically valid, the result is sentimental, since drama lacks the kind of control which in ritual comes from the auditors' being participants. Sentimental "drama," that which succeeds in being neither comedy nor tragedy, can be regarded from this vantage as theater used as a substitute for ritual, without the commitment to participation and discipline proper to ritual nor the commitment to the fullest understanding proper to comedy or tragedy.

Historically, Shakespeare's drama can be seen as part of the process by which our culture has moved from absolutist modes of thought towards a historical and psychological view of man. But though the Renaissance moment made the tension between a magical and an empirical view of man particularly acute, this pull is of course always present: it is the tension between the heart and the world. By incarnating ritual as plot and character, the dramatist finds an embodiment for the heart's drastic gestures while recognizing how the world keeps comically and tragically giving them the lie.

Chapter 9

THE ALLIANCE OF SERIOUSNESS AND LEVITY IN *AS YOU LIKE IT*

In a true piece of Wit all things must be
Yet all things there agree.
—Cowley, quoted by T. S. Eliot in "Andrew Marvell"

Then is there mirth in heaven
When earthly things made even
Atone together.
—*As You Like It*

SHAKESPEARE's next venture in comedy after *The Merchant of Venice* was probably in the Henry IV plays, which were probably written in 1597-98. Thus the Falstaff comedy comes right in the middle of the period, from about 1594 to 1600 or 1601, when Shakespeare produced festive comedy. *Much Ado About Nothing*, *As You Like It*, and *Twelfth Night* were written at the close of the period, *Twelfth Night* perhaps after *Hamlet*. *The Merry Wives of Windsor*, where Shakespeare's creative powers were less fully engaged, was produced sometime between 1598 and 1602, and it is not impossible that *All's Well That Ends Well* and even perhaps *Measure for Measure* were produced around the turn of the century, despite that difference in tone that has led to their being grouped with *Hamlet* and *Troilus and Cressida*.[1] I shall deal only with *As You Like It* and *Twelfth Night*; they are the two last festive plays, masterpieces that include and extend almost all the resources of the form whose development we have been following. What I would have to say about *Much Ado About Nothing* can largely be inferred from the discussion of the other festive plays. To consider the

[1] For the chronology, see E. K. Chambers, *William Shakespeare* (Oxford, 1930), I, 248-249 and 270-271.

various other sorts of comedy which Shakespeare produced around the inception of the period when his main concern became tragedy would require another, different frame of reference.

As You Like It is very similar in the way it moves to *A Midsummer Night's Dream* and *Love's Labour's Lost*, despite the fact that its plot is taken over almost entirely from Lodge's *Rosalynde*. As I have suggested in the introductory chapter, the reality we feel about the experience of love in the play, reality which is not in the pleasant little prose romance, comes from presenting what was sentimental extremity as impulsive extravagance and so leaving judgment free to mock what the heart embraces.[2] The Forest of Arden, like the Wood outside Athens, is a region defined by an attitude of liberty from ordinary limitations, a festive place where the folly of romance can have its day. The first half of *As You Like It*, beginning with tyrant brother and tyrant Duke and moving out into the forest, is chiefly concerned with establishing this sense of freedom; the traditional contrast of court and country is developed in a way that is shaped by the contrast between everyday and holiday, as that antithesis has become part of Shakespeare's art and sensibility. Once we are securely in the golden world where the good Duke and "a many merry men . . . fleet the time carelessly," the pastoral motif as such drops into the background; Rosalind finds Orlando's verses in the second scene of Act III, and the rest of the play deals with love. This second movement is like a musical theme with imitative variations, developing much more tightly the sort of construction which played off Costard's and Armado's amorous affairs against those of the nobles in Navarre, and which set Bottom's imagination in juxtaposition with other shaping fantasies. The love affairs of Silvius and Phebe, Touchstone and Audrey, Orlando and Rosalind succeed one another in the easy-going sequence of scenes, while the dramatist deftly plays each off against the others.

The Liberty of Arden

The thing that asks for explanation about the Forest of Arden

[2] I hope that a reader who is concerned only with *As You Like It* will nevertheless read the generalized account of festive comedy in Ch. 1, for that is assumed as a background for the discussion here.

is how this version of pastoral can feel so free when the Duke and his company are so high-minded. Partly the feeling of freedom comes from release from the tension established in the first act at the jealous court:

> Now go we in content
> To liberty, and not to banishment.
> (I.iii.139-140)

Several brief court scenes serve to keep this contrast alive. So does Orlando's entrance, sword in hand, to interrupt the Duke's gracious banquet by his threatening demand for food. Such behavior on his part is quite out of character (in Lodge he is most courteous); but his brandishing entrance gives Shakespeare occasion to resolve the attitude of struggle once again, this time by a lyric invocation of "what 'tis to pity and be pitied" (II.vii.117).

But the liberty we enjoy in Arden, though it includes relief from anxiety in brotherliness confirmed "at good men's feasts," is somehow easier than brotherliness usually is. The easiness comes from a witty redefinition of the human situation which makes conflict seem for the moment superfluous. Early in the play, when Celia and Rosalind are talking of ways of being merry by devising sports, Celia's proposal is "Let us sit and mock the good housewife Fortune from her wheel" (I.ii.34-35). The two go on with a "chase" of wit that goes "from Fortune's office to Nature's" (I.ii.43), whirling the two goddesses through many variations; distinctions between them were running in Shakespeare's mind. In Act II, the witty poetry which establishes the greenwood mood of freedom repeatedly mocks Fortune from her wheel by an act of mind which goes from Fortune to Nature:

> A fool, a fool! I met a fool i' th' forest, . . .
> Who laid him down and bask'd him in the sun
> And rail'd on Lady Fortune in good terms, . . .
> "Good morrow, fool," quoth I. "No, sir," quoth he,
> "Call me not fool till heaven hath sent me fortune."
> And then he drew a dial from his poke,
> And looking on it with lack-lustre eye,
> Says very wisely, 'It is ten o'clock.
> Thus we may see.' quoth he, 'how the world wags.

'Tis but an hour ago since it was nine,
And after one more hour 'twill be eleven;
And so, from hour to hour, we ripe and ripe,
And then, from hour to hour, we rot and rot;
And thereby hangs a tale.'
(II.vii.12-28)

Why does Jaques, in his stylish way, say that his lungs "began to crow like chanticleer" to hear the fool "thus moral on the time," when the moral concludes in "rot and rot"? Why do we, who are not "melancholy," feel such large and free delight? Because the fool "finds," with wonderfully bland wit, that nothing whatever happens under the aegis of Fortune. ("Fortune reigns in gifts of the world," said Rosalind at I.ii.44.) The almost tautological inevitability of nine, ten, eleven, says that all we do is ripe and ripe and rot and rot. And so there is no reason not to bask in the sun and "lose and neglect the creeping hours of time" (II.vii.112). As I observed in the introductory chapter, Touchstone's "deep contemplative" moral makes the same statement as the spring song towards the close of the play: "How that a life was but a flower." When they draw the moral, the lover and his lass are only thinking of the "spring time" as they take "the present time" when "love is crowned with the prime." (The refrain mocks them a little for their obliviousness, by its tinkling "the only pretty ring time.") But Touchstone's festive gesture is *not* oblivious.

The extraordinary thing about the poised liberty of the second act is that the reduction of life to the natural and seasonal and physical works all the more convincingly as a festive release by including a recognition that the physical can be unpleasant. The good Duke, in his opening speech, can "translate the stubbornness of fortune" into a benefit: he does it by the witty shift which makes the "icy fang / And churlish chiding of the winter wind" into "counsellors / That feelingly persuade me what I am" (II.i.6-11). The two songs make the same gesture of welcoming physical pain in place of moral pain:

Come hither, come hither, come hither!
Here shall he see
No enemy
But winter and rough weather.
(II.v.5-8)

They are patterned on holiday drinking songs, as we have seen already in considering the Christmas refrain, "Heigh-ho, sing heigh-ho, unto the green holly,"[3] and they convey the free solidarity of a group who, since they relax in physical pleasures together, need not fear the fact that "Most friendship is feigning, most loving mere folly."

Jaques speech on the seven ages of man, which comes at the end of Act II, just before "Blow, Blow, thou winter wind," is another version of the liberating talk about time; it expands Touchstone's "And thereby hangs a tale." The simplification, "All the world's a stage," has such imaginative reach that we are as much astonished as amused, as with Touchstone's summary ripe and rot. But simplification it is, nevertheless; quotations (and recitations) often represent it as though it were dramatist Shakespeare's "philosophy," his last word, or one of them, about what life really comes to. To take it this way is sentimental, puts a part in place of the whole. For it only is *one* aspect of the truth that the roles we play in life are settled by the cycle of growth and decline. To face this part of the truth, to insist on it, brings the kind of relief that goes with accepting folly—indeed this speech is praise of folly, superbly generalized, praise of the folly of living in time (or is it festive abuse? the poise is such that relish and mockery are indistinguishable). Sentimental readings ignore the wit that keeps reducing social roles to caricatures and suggesting that meanings really are only physical relations beyond the control of mind or spirit:

> Then a soldier, . . .
> Seeking the bubble reputation
> Even in the cannon's mouth. And then the justice,
> In fair round belly with good capon lin'd . . .
> (III.vii.149-154)

Looking back at time and society in this way, we have a detachment and sense of mastery similar to that established by Titania and Oberon's outside view of "the human mortals" and their weather.

Counterstatements

That Touchstone and Jaques should at moments turn and

[3] See above, pp. 113-116.

mock pastoral contentment is consistent with the way it is presented; their mockery makes explicit the partiality, the displacement of normal emphasis, which is implicit in the witty advocacy of it.

If it do come to pass
That any man turn ass,
Leaving his wealth and ease
A stubborn will to please . . .
(II.v.52-55)

The folly of going to Arden has something about it of Christian humility, brotherliness and unworldliness ("Consider the lilies of the field . . ."), but one can also turn it upside down by "a Greek invocation to call fools into a circle" and find it stubbornness. Touchstone brings out another kind of latent irony about pastoral joys when he plays the role of a discontented exile from the court:

Corin. And how like you this shepherd's life, Master Touchstone?

Touchstone. Truly, shepherd, in respect of itself, it is a good life; but in respect that it is a shepherd's life, it is naught. In respect that it is solitary, I like it very well; but in respect that it is private, it is a very vile life. Now in respect it is in the fields, it pleaseth me well; but in respect it is not in the court, it is tedious. As it is a spare life, look you, it fits my humour well; but as there is no more plenty in it, it goes much against my stomach.
(III.ii.12-22)

Under the apparent nonsense of his self-contradictions, Touchstone mocks the contradictory nature of the desires ideally resolved by pastoral life, to be at once at court and in the fields, to enjoy both the fat advantages of rank and the spare advantages of the mean and sure estate. The humor goes to the heart of the pastoral convention and shows how very clearly Shakespeare understood it.

The fact that he created both Jaques and Touchstone out of whole cloth, adding them to the story as it appears in Lodge's *Rosalynde*, is an index to what he did in dramatizing the prose romance. Lodge, though he has a light touch, treats the idyllic material at face value. He never makes fun of its assumptions, but stays safely within the convention, because he has no securely grounded attitude towards it, not being sure of its relation to reality. Shakespeare scarcely changes the story at all, but where in Lodge it is presented in the flat, he brings alive the dimension of its relation to life as a whole. The control of this dimension makes his version solid as well as delicate.

Although both Jaques and Touchstone are connected with the action well enough at the level of plot, their real position is generally mediate between the audience and something in the play, the same position Nashe assigns to the court fool, Will Summers, in *Summer's Last Will and Testament.*[4] Once Jaques stands almost outside the play, when he responds to Orlando's romantic greeting: "Good day and happiness, dear Rosalind!" with "Nay then, God b'wi'you, and you talk in blank verse!" (IV.i.31). Jaques' factitious melancholy, which critics have made too much of as a "psychology," serves primarily to set him at odds both with society and with Arden and so motivate contemplative mockery. Touchstone is put outside by his special status as a fool. As a fool, incapable, at least for professional purposes, of doing anything right, he is beyond the pale of normal achievements. In anything he tries to do he is comically disabled, as, for example, in falling in love. All he achieves is a burlesque of love. So he has none of the illusions of those who try to be ideal, and is in a position to make a business of being dryly objective. "Call me not fool till heaven hath sent me fortune." Heaven sends him Audrey instead, "an ill-favour'd thing, sir, but mine own" (V.iv.60)—not a mistress to generate illusions. In *As You Like It* the court fool for the first time takes over the work of comic commentary and burlesque from the clown of the earlier plays; in Jaques' praise of Touchstone and the corrective virtues of fooling, Shakespeare can be heard crowing with delight at his discovery. The figure of the jester, with his recognized social role and rich traditional meaning, enabled the dramatist to embody in a character and his relations with other characters the comedy's purpose of maintaining objectivity.

The satirist presents life as it is and ridicules it because it is not ideal, as we would like it to be and as it should be. Shakespeare goes the other way about: he represents or evokes ideal life, and then makes fun of it because it does not square with life as it

[4] See above, Ch. 4, pp. 61-67.

ordinarily is. If we look for social satire in *As You Like It*, all we find are a few set pieces about such stock figures as the traveller and the duelist. And these figures seem to be described rather to enjoy their extravagance than to rebuke their folly. Jaques, in response to a topical interest at the time when the play appeared, talks a good deal about satire, and proposes to "cleanse the foul body of th' infected world" (II.vii.60) with the fool's medicine of ridicule. But neither Jaques, the amateur fool, nor Touchstone, the professional, ever really gets around to doing the satirist's work of ridiculing life as it is, "deeds, and language, such as men do use."[5] After all, they are in Arden, not in Jonson's London: the infected body of the world is far away, out of range. What they make fun of instead is what they can find in Arden—pastoral innocence and romantic love, life as it might be, lived "in a holiday humour." Similar comic presentation of what is not ideal in man is characteristic of medieval fool humor, where the humorist, by his gift of long ears to the long-robed dignitaries, makes the point that, despite their pageant perfection, they are human too, that "stultorum numerus infinitus est." Such humor is very different from modern satire, for its basic affirmation is not man's possible perfection but his certain imperfection. It was a function of the pervasively formal and ideal cast of medieval culture, where what should be was more present to the mind than what is: the humorists' natural recourse was to burlesque the pageant of perfection, presenting it as a procession of fools, in crowns, mitres, caps, and gowns. Shakespeare's point of view was not medieval. But his clown and fool comedy is a response, a counter-movement, to artistic idealization, as medieval burlesque was a response to the ingrained idealism of the culture.

"all nature in love mortal in folly"

I have quoted already in the Introduction a riddling comment of Touchstone which moves from acknowledging mortality to accepting the folly of love:

> We that are true lovers run into strange capers; but as all is mortal in nature, so is all nature in love mortal in folly.
>
> (II.iv.53-56)

[5] Ben Jonson, *Every Man in his Humour*, Prologue, l.21.

The lovers who in the second half of the play present "nature in love" each exhibit a kind of folly. In each there is a different version of the incongruity between reality and the illusions (in poetry, the hyperboles) which love generates and by which it is expressed. The comic variations are centered around the seriously-felt love of Rosalind and Orlando. The final effect is to enhance the reality of this love by making it independent of illusions, whose incongruity with life is recognized and laughed off. We can see this at closer range by examining each affair in turn.

All-suffering Silvius and his tyrannical little Phebe are a bit of Lodge's version taken over, outwardly intact, and set in a wholly new perspective. A "courting eglogue" between them, in the mode of Lodge, is exhibited almost as a formal spectacle, with Corin for presenter and Rosalind and Celia for audience. It is announced as

> a pageant truly play'd
> Between the pale complexion of true love
> And the red glow of scorn and proud disdain.
> (III.iv.55-57)

What we then watch is played "truly"—according to the best current convention: Silvius, employing a familiar gambit, asks for pity; Phebe refuses to believe in love's invisible wound, with exactly the literal-mindedness about hyperbole which the sonneteers imputed to their mistresses. In Lodge's version, the unqualified Petrarchan sentiments of the pair are presented as valid and admirable. Shakespeare lets us feel the charm of the form; but then he has Rosalind break up their pretty pageant. She reminds them that they are nature's creatures, and that love's purposes are contradicted by too absolute a cultivation of romantic liking or loathing: "I must tell you friendly in your ear, / Sell when you can! you are not for all markets" (III.v.59-60). Her exaggerated downrightness humorously underscores the exaggerations of conventional sentiment. And Shakespeare's treatment breaks down Phebe's stereotyped attitudes to a human reality: he lightly suggests an adolescent perversity underlying her resistance to love. The imagery she uses in disputing with Silvius is masterfully squeamish, at once preoccupied with touch and shrinking from it:

'Tis pretty, sure, and very probable
That eyes, which are the frail'st and softest things,
Who shut their coward gates on atomies,
Should be call'd tyrants, butchers, murtherers!
. . . lean but upon a rush,
The cicatrice and capable impressure
Thy palm some moment keeps; but now mine eyes,
Which I have darted at thee, hurt thee not, . . .
(III.v.11-25)

Rosalind, before whom this resistance melts, appears in her boy's disguise "like a ripe sister," and the qualities Phebe picks out to praise are feminine. She has, in effect, a girlish crush on the femininity which shows through Rosalind's disguise; the aberrant affection is happily got over when Rosalind reveals her identity and makes it manifest that Phebe has been loving a woman. "Nature to her bias drew in that" is the comment in *Twelfth Night* when Olivia is fortunately extricated from a similar mistaken affection.

Touchstone's affair with Audrey complements the spectacle of exaggerated sentiment by showing love reduced to its lowest common denominator, without any sentiment at all. The fool is detached, objective and resigned when the true-blue lover should be

All made of passion, and all made of wishes,
All adoration, duty, and observance.
(V.ii.101-102)

He explains to Jaques his reluctant reasons for getting married:

Jaques. Will you be married, motley?

Touchstone. As the ox hath his bow, sir, the horse his curb, and the falcon her bells, so man hath his desires; and as pigeons bill, so wedlock would be nibbling. (III.iii.79-83)

This reverses the relation between desire and its object, as experienced by the other lovers. They are first overwhelmed by the beauty of their mistresses, then impelled by that beauty to desire them. With Touchstone, matters go the other way about: he discovers that man has his troublesome desires, as the horse his curb; then he decides to cope with the situation by marrying Audrey:

Come, sweet Audrey.
We must be married, or we must live in bawdry.
(III.iii.98-99)

Like all the motives which Touchstone acknowledges, this priority of desire to attraction is degrading and humiliating. One of the hall-marks of chivalric and Petrarchan idealism is, of course, the high valuation of the lover's mistress, the assumption that his desire springs entirely from her beauty. This attitude of the poets has contributed to that progressively-increasing respect for women so fruitful in modern culture. But to assume that only one girl will do is, after all, an extreme, an ideal attitude: the other half of the truth, which lies in wait to mock sublimity, is instinct—the need of a woman, even if she be an Audrey, because "as pigeons bill, so wedlock would be nibbling." As Touchstone put it on another occasion:

If the cat will after kind,
So be sure will Rosalinde.
(III.ii.109-110)

The result of including in Touchstone a representative of what in love is unromantic is not, however, to undercut the play's romance: on the contrary, the fool's cynicism, or one-sided realism, forestalls the cynicism with which the audience might greet a play where his sort of realism had been ignored. We have a sympathy for his downright point of view, not only in connection with love but also in his acknowledgment of the vain and self-gratifying desires excluded by pastoral humility; he embodies the part of ourselves which resists the play's reigning idealism. But he does not do so in a fashion to set himself up in opposition to the play. Romantic commentators construed him as "Hamlet in motely," a devastating critic. They forgot, characteristically, that he is ridiculous: he makes his attitudes preposterous when he values rank and comfort above humility, or follows biology rather than beauty. In laughing at him, we reject the tendency in ourselves which he for the moment represents. The net effect of the fool's part is thus to consolidate the hold of the serious themes by exorcising opposition. The final Shakespearean touch is to make the fool aware that in humiliating himself he is performing a public service. He goes through his part with an irony founded on the fact (and it is a fact) that he is only making manifest the folly which others, including the audience, hide from themselves.

Romantic participation in love and humorous detachment from its follies, the two polar attitudes which are balanced against each other in the action as a whole, meet and are reconciled in Rosalind's personality. Because she remains always aware of love's illusions while she herself is swept along by its deepest currents, she possesses as an attribute of character the power of combining wholehearted feeling and undistorted judgment which gives the play its value. She plays the mocking reveller's role which Berowne played in *Love's Labour's Lost*, with the advantage of disguise. Shakespeare exploits her disguise to permit her to furnish the humorous commentary on her own ardent love affair, thus keeping comic and serious actions going at the same time. In her pretended role of saucy shepherd youth, she can mock at romance and burlesque its gestures while playing the game of putting Orlando through his paces as a suitor, to "cure" him of love. But for the audience, her disguise is transparent, and through it they see the very ardor which she mocks. When, for example, she stages a gayly overdone take-off of the conventional impatience of the lover, her own real impatience comes through the burlesque; yet the fact that she makes fun of exaggerations of the feeling conveys an awareness that it has limits, that there is a difference between romantic hyperbole and human nature:

> *Orlando.* For these two hours, Rosalind, I will leave thee.
> *Rosalind.* Alas, dear love, I cannot lack thee two hours!
> *Orlando.* I must attend the Duke at dinner. By two o'clock I will be with thee again.
> *Rosalind.* Ay, go your ways, go your ways! I knew what you would prove. My friends told me as much, and I thought no less. That flattering tongue of yours won me. 'Tis but one cast away, and so, come death! Two o'clock is your hour?
>
> (IV.i.181-190)

One effect of this indirect, humorous method of conveying feeling is that Rosalind is not committed to the conventional language and attitudes of love, loaded as these inevitably are with sentimentality. Silvius and Phebe are her foils in this: they take their conventional language and their conventional feelings perfectly seriously, with nothing in reserve. As a result they seem naïve and rather trivial. They are no more than what they say, until Rosalind comes forward to realize their personalities for the audience by suggesting what they humanly are beneath what they romantically think themselves. By contrast, the heroine in expressing her own love conveys by her humorous tone a valuation of her sentiments, and so realizes her own personality for herself, without being indebted to another for the favor. She uses the convention where Phebe, being unaware of its exaggerations, abuses it, and Silvius, equally naïve about hyperbole, lets it abuse him. This control of tone is one of the great contributions of Shakespeare's comedy to his dramatic art as a whole. The discipline of comedy in controlling the humorous potentialities of a remark enables the dramatist to express the relation of a speaker to his lines, including the relation of naïveté. The focus of attention is not on the outward action of saying something but on the shifting, uncrystallized life which motivates what is said.

The particular feeling of headlong delight in Rosalind's encounters with Orlando goes with the prose of these scenes, a medium which can put imaginative effects of a very high order to the service of humor and wit. The comic prose of this period is first developed to its full range in Falstaff's part, and steals the show for Benedict and Beatrice in *Much Ado About Nothing.* It combines the extravagant linguistic reach of the early clowns' prose with the sophisticated wit which in the earlier plays was usually cast, less flexibly, in verse. Highly patterned, it is built up of balanced and serial clauses, with everything linked together by alliteration and kicked along by puns. Yet it avoids a stilted, Euphuistic effect because regular patterns are set going only to be broken to underscore humor by asymmetry. The speaker can rock back and forth on antitheses, or climb "a pair of stairs" (V.ii.42) to a climax, then slow down meaningly, or stop dead, and so punctuate a pithy reduction, bizarre exaggeration or broad allusion. T. S. Eliot has observed that we often forget that it was Shakespeare who wrote the greatest prose in the language. Some of it is in *As You Like It.* His control permits him to convey the constant shifting of attitude and point of view which expresses Rosalind's excitement and her poise. Such writing, like the brushwork and line of great painters, is in one sense everything. But the whole design supports each stroke, as each stroke supports the whole design.

The expression of Rosalind's attitude towards being in love, in the great scene of disguised wooing, fulfills the whole movement of the play. The climax comes when Rosalind is able, in the midst of her golden moment, to look beyond it and mock its illusions, including the master illusion that love is an ultimate and final experience, a matter of life and death. Ideally, love should be final, and Orlando is romantically convinced that his is so, that he would die if Rosalind refused him. But Rosalind humorously corrects him, from behind her page's disguise:

> . . . Am I not your Rosalind?
>
> *Orlando.* I take some joy to say you are, because I would be talking of her.
>
> *Rosalind.* Well, in her person, I say I will not have you.
>
> *Orlando.* Then, in mine own person, I die.
>
> *Rosalind.* No, faith, die by attorney. The poor world is almost six thousand years old, and in all this time there was not any man died in his own person, videlicet, in a love cause. Troilus had his brains dash'd out with a Grecian club; yet he did what he could to die before, and he is one of the patterns of love. Leander, he would have liv'd many a fair year though Hero had turn'd nun, if it had not been for a hot midsummer night; for (good youth) he went but forth to wash him in the Hellespont, and being taken with the cramp, was drown'd; and the foolish chroniclers of that age found it was 'Hero of Sestos.' But these are all lies. Men have died from time to time, and worms have eaten them, but not for love.
>
> *Orlando.* I would not have my right Rosalind of this mind, for I protest her frown might kill me.
>
> *Rosalind.* By this hand, it will not kill a fly! (IV.i.90-108)

A note almost of sadness comes through Rosalind's mockery towards the end. It is not sorrow that men die from time to time, but that they do not die for love, that love is not so final as romance would have it. For a moment we experience as pathos the tension between feeling and judgment which is behind all the laughter. The same pathos of objectivity is expressed by Chaucer in the sad smile of Pandarus as he contemplates the illusions of Troilus' love. But in *As You Like It* the mood is dominant only in the moment when the last resistance of feeling to judgment is being surmounted: the illusions thrown up by feeling are mastered by laughter and so love is reconciled with judgment. This resolution is complete by the close of the wooing scene. As Rosalind rides the crest of a wave of happy fulfillment (for Orlando's behavior to the pretended Rosalind has made it perfectly plain that he loves the real one) we find her describing with delight, almost in triumph, not the virtues of marriage, but its fallibility:

> Say 'a day' without the 'ever.' No, no, Orlando! Men are April when they woo, December when they wed. Maids are May when they are maids, but the sky changes when they are wives.
> (IV.i.146-150)

Ordinarily, these would be strange sentiments to proclaim with joy at such a time. But as Rosalind says them, they clinch the achievement of the humor's purpose. (The wry, retarding change from the expected cadence at "but the sky changes" is one of those brush strokes that fulfill the large design.) Love has been made independent of illusions without becoming any the less intense; it is therefore inoculated against life's unromantic contradictions. To emphasize by humor the limitations of the experience has become a way of asserting its reality. The scenes which follow move rapidly and deftly to complete the consummation of the love affairs on the level of plot. The treatment becomes more and more frankly artificial, to end with a masque. But the lack of realism in presentation does not matter, because a much more important realism in our attitude towards the substance of romance has been achieved already by the action of the comedy.

In writing of Marvell and the metaphysical poets, T. S. Eliot spoke of an "alliance of levity and seriousness (by which the seriousness is intensified)." What he has said about the contribution of wit to this poetry is strikingly applicable to the function of Shakespeare's comedy in *As You Like It*: that wit conveys "a recognition, implicit in the expression of every experience, of other kinds of experience which are possible."[6] The likeness does not consist simply in the fact that the wit of certain of Shakespeare's characters at times is like the wit of the metaphysicals. The crucial similarity is in the way the humor functions in the play as a whole to implement a wider awareness, maintaining proportion where less disciplined and coherent art falsifies by presenting a part as though it were the whole. The dramatic form is very different from the lyric: Shakespeare does not have or need the sustained, inclusive poise of metaphysical poetry when, at its rare best, it fulfills Cowley's ideal:

> In a true piece of Wit all things must be
> Yet all things there agree.

The dramatist tends to show us one thing at a time, and to realize that one thing, in its moment, to the full; his characters go to extremes, comical as well as serious; and no character, not even a Rosalind, is in a position to see all around the play and so be completely poised, for if this were so the play would cease to be dramatic. Shakespeare, moreover, has an Elizabethan delight in extremes for their own sake, beyond the requirements of his form and sometimes damaging to it, an expansiveness which was subordinated later by the seventeenth century's conscious need for coherence. But his extremes, where his art is at its best, are balanced in the whole work. He uses his broad-stroked, wide-swung comedy for the same end that the seventeenth-century poets achieved by their wire-drawn wit. In Silvius and Phebe he exhibits the ridiculous (and perverse) possibilities of that exaggerated romanticism which the metaphysicals so often mocked in their serious love poems. In Touchstone he includes a representative of just those aspects of love which are not romantic, hypostatizing as a character what in direct lyric expression would be an irony:

> Love's not so pure and abstract as they use
> To say who have no mistress but their muse.

By Rosalind's mockery a sense of love's limitations is kept alive at the very moments when we most feel its power:

[6] *Selected Essays, 1917-1932* (New York, 1932), pp. 255 and 262.

But at my back I always hear
Time's winged chariot hurrying near.

The fundamental common characteristic is that the humor is not directed at "some outside sentimentality or stupidity," but is an agency for achieving proportion of judgment and feeling about a seriously felt experience.

As You Like It seems to me the most perfect expression Shakespeare or anyone else achieved of a poise which was possible because a traditional way of living connected different kinds of experience to each other. The play articulates fully the feeling for the rhythms of life which we have seen supporting Nashe's strong but imperfect art in his seasonal pageant. Talboys Dimoke and his friends had a similar sense of times and places when they let holiday lead them to making merry with the Earl of Lincoln; by contrast, the Puritan and/or time-serving partisans of Lincoln could not or would not recognize that holiday gave a license and also set a limit. An inclusive poise such as Shakespeare exhibits in Rosalind was not, doubtless, easy to achieve in any age; no culture was ever so "organic" that it would do men's living for them. What Yeats called Unity of Being became more and more difficult as the Renaissance progressed; indeed, the increasing difficulty of poise must have been a cause of the period's increasing power to express conflict and order it in art. We have seen this from our special standpoint in the fact that the everyday-holiday antithesis was most fully expressed in art when the keeping of holidays was declining.

The humorous recognition, in *As You Like It* and other products of this tradition, of the limits of nature's moment, reflects not only the growing consciousness necessary to enjoy holiday attitudes with poise, but also the fact that in English Christian culture saturnalia was never fully enfranchised. Saturnalian customs existed along with the courtly tradition of romantic love and an ambient disillusion about nature stemming from Christianity. In dramatizing love's intensity as the release of a festive moment, Shakespeare keeps that part of the romantic tradition which makes love an experience of the whole personality, even though he ridicules the wishful absolutes of doctrinaire romantic love. He does not found his comedy on the sort of saturnalian simplification which equates love with sensual gratification. He includes spokesmen for this sort of release in reduction; but they are never given an unqualified predominance, though they contribute to the atmosphere of liberty within which the aristocratic lovers find love. It is the latter who hold the balance near the center. And what gives the predominance to figures like Berowne, Benedict and Beatrice, or Rosalind, is that they enter nature's whirl consciously, with humor that recognizes it as only part of life and places their own extravagance by moving back and forth between holiday and everyday perspectives. Aristophanes provides a revealing contrast here. His comedies present experience entirely polarized by saturnalia; there is little *within* the play to qualify that perspective. Instead, an irony attaches to the whole performance which went with the accepted place of comedy in the Dionysia. Because no such clear-cut role for saturnalia or saturnalian comedy existed within Shakespeare's culture, the play itself had to place that pole of life in relation to life as a whole. Shakespeare had the art to make this necessity into an opportunity for a fuller expression, a more inclusive consciousness.

Chapter 10

TESTING COURTESY AND HUMANITY IN *TWELFTH NIGHT*

. . . nature to her bias drew in that.

THE title of *Twelfth Night* may well have come from the first occasion when it was performed, whether or not Dr. Leslie Hotson is right in arguing that its first night was the court celebration of the last of the twelve days of Christmas on January 6, 1600-1601.[1]

[1] In *The First Night of "Twelfth Night"* (New York, 1954), Dr. Hotson has recovered, once again, documents that are astonishingly *à propos.* The most exciting is a long letter home written by a real nobleman named Orsino, who was Elizabeth's honored guest when she witnessed a play "in the Hall, which was richly hanged and degrees placed round about it." Don Virginio Orsino's account to his Duchess of the way he was honored gives a vivid picture of the Twelfth Day occasion at court, which Mr. Hotson skillfully supplements with other evidence, much of it also new, so as to give us the most complete and graphic description we have of the circumstances of a dramatic performance at a court holiday. The Duke's candid letter reports that "there was acted a mingled comedy, with pieces of music and dances" (*una commedia mescolata, con musiche e balli*). But then it adds "and this too I am keeping to tell by word of mouth." What maddening bad luck! Here, and everywhere else, the clinching proof eludes Dr. Hotson, despite his skill and persistence. He himself cannot resist regarding it as a fact that *Twelfth Night* was the play in question on January 6, 1600-1601. But a sceptic can begin by asking where, in *Twelfth Night*, are those *balli* which Don Virginio witnessed—the play is notable, among Shakespeare's gay comedies, for its *lack* of dances. One could go on to ask whether it would not be more likely that the name Orsino would be used sometime *after* the great man's visit, when the elegant ring of it would still sound in people's ears but no offense be done. A devil's advocate could go on and on, so rich, and so conjectural, is Dr. Hotson's book.

But it makes a real contribution, even if one is not convinced that the play on that night must have been *Twelfth Night*, and even if one rejects many of its sweeping conclusions about such matters as staging. Dr. Hotson is a "literalist of the historical imagination," to use Marianne Moore's phrase. He has produced something equivalent to an "imaginary garden with real toads in" it—real circumstances and actions of Elizabethan life. He makes us aware of what the high day at court was like. And he describes and exemplifies many features of Twelfth Night custom in a fresh way, and so defines for us the *sort* of thing that Shakespeare refers to by his title. He also provides, from his remarkable knowledge of the period, a wealth of useful incidental glosses to hard places in the play.

But useful as his book can be, whether literally right or not, it is very misleading

The title tells us that the play is like holiday misrule—though not just like it, for it adds "or what you will." The law student John Manningham, who saw it at the Middle Temple's feast on February 2, 1602, wrote in his diary that it was "much like the Comedy of Errores, or Menechmi in Plautus, but most like and neere to that in Italian called *Inganni.*" We have the now-familiar combination of festive, literary and theatrical traditions. In addition to Plautine situation and Italian comedy, Shakespeare drew on a prose romance (derived indirectly from Italian comedy), Rich's *Apolonius and Silla.* He used no written source for the part Manningham specially praised: "A good practice in it to make the Steward beleeve his Lady widdowe was in love with him. . . ."[2]

Shakespeare can be inclusive in his use of traditions because his powers of selection and composition can arrange each element so that only those facets of it show which will serve his expressive purpose. He leaves out the dungeon in which Rich's jealous Orsino shuts up Viola, as well as Sebastian's departure leaving Olivia with child; but he does not hesitate to keep such events as the shipwreck, or Sebastian's amazing marriage to a stranger, or Orsino's threat to kill Viola. It is not the credibility of the event that is decisive, but what can be expressed through it. Thus the shipwreck is made the occasion for Viola to exhibit an undaunted, aristocratic mastery of adversity—she settles what she shall do next almost as though picking out a costume for a masquerade:

> I'll serve this duke,
> Thou shalt present me as an eunuch to him;
> It may be worth thy pains. For I can sing,
> And speak to him in several sorts of music . . .
> (I.ii.55-58)

in one respect. For he writes as though the festive quality of *Twelfth Night* were wholly derived, on a one-to-one sort of basis, from its being commissioned for a court revel. He neglects the fact that, whatever its first night, the play was designed to work, also, on the public stage, so that it had to project the spirit of holiday into forms that would be effective everyday. He also ignores the fact that by the time Shakespeare came to write *Twelfth Night*, festive comedy was an established specialty with him.

[2] E. K. Chambers, *William Shakespeare*, II, 327-328.

What matters is not the event, but what the language says as gesture, the aristocratic, free-and-easy way she settles what she will do and what the captain will do to help her. The pathetical complications which are often dwelt on in the romance are not allowed to develop far in the play; instead Viola's spritely language conveys the fun she is having in playing a man's part, with a hidden womanly perspective about it. One cannot quite say that she is playing in a masquerade, because disguising *just* for the fun of it is a different thing. But the same sort of festive pleasure in transvestism is expressed.

It is amazing how little happens in *Twelfth Night*, how much of the time people are merely talking, especially in the first half, before the farcical complications are sprung. Shakespeare is so skillful by now in rendering attitudes by the gestures of easy conversation that when it suits him he can almost do without events. In the first two acts of *Twelfth Night* he holds our interest with a bare minimum of tension while unfolding a pattern of contrasting attitudes and tones in his several persons. Yet Shakespeare's whole handling of romantic story, farce, and practical joke makes a composition which moves in the manner of his earlier festive comedies, through release to clarification.[3]

"A most extracting frenzy"

Olivia's phrase in the last act, when she remembers Malvolio and his "madness," can summarize the way the play moves:

> A most extracting frenzy of mine own
> From my remembrance clearly banish'd his.
> (V.i.288-289)

People are caught up by delusions or misapprehensions which take them out of themselves, bringing out what they would keep hidden or did not know was there. *Madness* is a key word. The outright gull Malvolio is already "a rare turkey-cock" from "contemplation" (II.v.35) before Maria goes to work on him with her forged letter. "I do not now fool myself, to let imagination jade

[3] I hope that a reader who is concerned only with *Twelfth Night* will nevertheless take the time to read the generalized account of festive comedy in Ch. 1, for that introduction is assumed in the discussion here.

me" (II.v.179), he exclaims when he has read it, having been put "in such a dream that, when the image of it leaves him, he must run mad" (II.v.210-211). He is too self-absorbed actually to run mad, but when he comes at Olivia, smiling and cross-gartered, she can make nothing else of it: "Why, this is very mid-summer madness" (III.iv.61). And so the merrymakers have the chance to put him in a dark room and do everything they can to face him out of his five wits.

What they bring about as a "pastime" (III.iv.151), to "gull him into a nayword, and make him a common recreation" (II.iii.145-146), happens unplanned to others by disguise and mistaken identity. Sir Toby, indeed, "speaks nothing but madman" (I.v.115) without any particular occasion. "My masters, are you mad?" (II.iii.93) Malvolio asks as he comes in to try to stop the midnight singing. Malvolio is sure that he speaks for the countess when he tells Toby that "though she harbors you as her kinsman, she's nothing allied to your disorders" (II.iii.103). But in fact this sober judgment shows that he is not "any more than a steward" (II.iii.122). For his lady, dignified though her bearing is, suddenly finds herself doing "I know not what" (I.v.327) under the spell of Viola in her page's disguise: "how now? / Even so quickly may one catch the plague?" (I.v.313-314) "Poor lady," exclaims Viola, "she were better love a dream!" (II.ii.27) In their first interview, she had told the countess, in urging the count's suit, that "what is yours to bestow is not yours to reserve" (I.v.200-201). By the end of their encounter, Olivia says the same thing in giving way to her passion: "Fate, show thy force! Ourselves we do not owe" (I.v.329). And soon her avowals of love come pouring out, overcoming the effort at control which shows she is a lady:

> O, what a deal of scorn looks beautiful
> In the contempt and anger of his lip!
> A murd'rous guilt shows not itself more soon
> Than love that would seem hid: love's night is noon.
> Cesario, by the roses of the spring,
> By maidhood, honour, truth, and everything,
> I love thee so . . .
>
> (III.i.157-163)

A little later, when she hears about Malvolio and his smile, she summarizes the parallel with "I am as mad as he, / If sad and merry madness equal be" (III.iv.15-16).

The farcical challenge and "fight" between Viola and Sir Andrew are another species of frantic action caused by delusion. "More matter for a May morning" (III.iv.156) Fabian calls it as they move from pretending to exorcise Malvolio's devil to pretending to act as solicitous seconds for Sir Andrew. When Antonio enters the fray in manly earnest, there is still another sort of comic error, based not on a psychological distortion but simply on mistaken identity. This Plautine sort of confusion leads Sebastian to exclaim, "Are all the people mad?" (IV.i.29) Just after we have seen "Malvolio the lunatic" (IV.ii.26) baffled in the dark room ("But tell me true, are you not mad indeed? or do you but counterfeit?" IV.ii.121-123), we see Sebastian struggling to understand his wonderful encounter with Olivia:

> This is the air; that is the glorious sun;
> This pearl she gave me, I do feel't and see't;
> And though 'tis wonder that enwraps me thus,
> Yet 'tis not madness.
> (IV.iii.1-4)

The open-air clarity of this little scene anticipates the approaching moment when delusions and misapprehensions are resolved by the finding of objects appropriate to passions. Shakespeare, with fine stagecraft, spins the misapprehensions out to the last moment. He puts Orsino, in his turn, through an extracting frenzy, the Duke's frustration converting at last to violent impulses toward Olivia and Cesario, before he discovers in the page the woman's love he could not win from the countess.

That it should all depend on there being an indistinguishable twin brother always troubles me when I think about it, though never when I watch the play. Can it be that we enjoy the play so much simply because it is a wish-fulfillment presented so skillfully that we do not notice that our hearts are duping our heads? Certainly part of our pleasure comes from pleasing make-believe. But I think that what chance determines about particular destinies is justified, as was the case with *The Merchant of Venice*, by the play's realizing dynamically general distinctions and tendencies in life.

"You are betroth'd both to a maid and man"

The most fundamental distinction the play brings home to us is the difference between men and women. To say this may seem to labor the obvious; for what love story does not emphasize this difference? But the disguising of a girl as a boy in *Twelfth Night* is exploited so as to renew in a special way our sense of the difference. Just as a saturnalian reversal of social roles need not threaten the social structure, but can serve instead to consolidate it, so a temporary, playful reversal of sexual roles can renew the meaning of the normal relation. One can add that with sexual as with other relations, it is when the normal is secure that playful aberration is benign. This basic security explains why there is so little that is queazy in all Shakespeare's handling of boy actors playing women, and playing women pretending to be men. This is particularly remarkable in *Twelfth Night*, for Olivia's infatuation with Cesario-Viola is another, more fully developed case of the sort of crush Phebe had on Rosalind. Viola is described as distinctly feminine in her disguise, more so than Rosalind:

> . . . they shall yet belie thy happy years
> That say thou art a man. Diana's lip
> Is not more smooth and rubious; thy small pipe
> Is as the maiden's organ, shrill and sound,
> And all is semblative a woman's part.
>
> (I.iv.30-34)

When on her embassy Viola asks to see Olivia's face and exclaims about it, she shows a woman's way of relishing another woman's beauty—and sensing another's vanity: " 'Tis beauty truly blent. . . ." "I see you what you are—you are too proud" (I.v.257, 269). Olivia's infatuation with feminine qualities in a youth takes her, doing "I know not what," from one stage of life out into another, from shutting out suitors in mourning for her brother's memory, to ardor for a man, Sebastian, and the clear certainty that calls out to "husband" in the confusion of the last scene.

We might wonder whether this spoiled and dominating young heiress may not have been attracted by what she could hope to dominate in Cesario's youth—but it was not the habit of Shakespeare's age to look for such implications. And besides, Sebastian is not likely to be dominated; we have seen him respond to Andrew when the ninny knight thought he was securely striking Cesario:

> *Andrew.* Now, sir, have I met you again? There's for you!
> *Sebastian.* Why, there's for thee, and there, and there!
> (IV.i.26-27)

To see this manly reflex is delightful—almost a relief—for we have been watching poor Viola absurdly perplexed behind her disguise as Sir Toby urges her to play the man: "Dismount thy tuck, be yare in thy preparation. . . . Therefor on, or strip your sword naked; for meddle you must, that's certain" (III.iv.244-245, 274-276). She is driven to the point where she exclaims in an aside: "Pray God defend me! A little thing would make me tell them how much I lack of a man" (III.iv.331-333). What she lacks, Sebastian has. His entrance in the final scene is preceded by comical testimony of his prowess, Sir Andrew with a broken head and Sir Toby halting. The particular implausibility that there should be an identical man to take Viola's place with Olivia is submerged in the general, beneficent realization that there is such a thing as a man. Sebastian's comment when the confusion of identities is resolved points to the general force which has shaped particular developments:

> So comes it, lady, you have been mistook.
> But nature to her bias drew in that.
> (V.i.266-267)

Over against the Olivia-Cesario relation, there are Orsino-Cesario and Antonio-Sebastian. Antonio's impassioned friendship for Sebastian is one of those ardent attachments between young people of the same sex which Shakespeare frequently presents, with his positive emphasis, as exhibiting the loving and lovable qualities later expressed in love for the other sex.[4] Orsino's fascination with Cesario is more complex. In the opening scene, his restless sensibility can find no object: "naught enters there, . . . / But falls into abatement . . . / Even in a minute" (I.i.11-14). Olivia might be

[4] The latest treatment of this motif, in *The Two Noble Kinsmen* (especially Act I, Scene iii), is as generously beautiful as the exquisite handling of it which we have examined in *A Midsummer Night's Dream* (above, pp. 129-130).

an adequate object; she at least is the Diana the sight of whom has, he thinks, turned him to an Acteon torn by the hounds of desires. When we next see him, and Cesario has been only three days in his court, his entering question is "Who saw Cesario, ho?" (I.iv.10) and already he has unclasped to the youth "the book even of [his] secret soul" (I.iv.14). He has found an object. The delight he takes in Cesario's fresh youth and graceful responsiveness in conversation and in service, is one part of the spectrum of love for a woman, or better, it is a range of feeling that is common to love for a youth and love for a woman. For the audience, the woman who is present there, behind Cesario's disguise, is brought to mind repeatedly by the talk of love and of the differences of men and women in love. "My father had a daughter loved a man . . ." (II.iv.110)

> She never told her love,
> But let concealment, like a worm i' th' bud,
> Feed on her damask cheek. (II.iv.113-115)

This supremely feminine damsel, who "sat like patience on a monument," is not Viola. She is a sort of polarity within Viola, realized all the more fully because the other, active side of Viola does not pine in thought at all, but instead changes the subject: ". . . and yet I know not. / Sir, shall we to this lady?—Ay, that's the theme" (II.iv.124-125). The effect of moving back and forth from woman to sprightly page is to convey how much the sexes differ yet how much they have in common, how everyone who is fully alive has qualities of both. Some such general recognition is obliquely suggested in Sebastian's amused summary of what happened to Olivia:

> You would have been contracted to a maid;
> Nor are you therein, by my life, deceiv'd:
> You are betroth'd both to a maid and man.
> (V.i.267-270)

The countess marries the man in this composite, and the count marries the maid. He too has done he knows not what while nature drew him to her bias, for he has fallen in love with the maid without knowing it.

Liberty Testing Courtesy

We have seen how each of the festive comedies tends to focus on a particular kind of folly that is released along with love—witty masquerade in *Love's Labour's Lost*, delusive fantasy in *A Midsummer Night's Dream*, romance in *As You Like It*, and, in *The Merchant of Venice*, prodigality balanced against usury. *Twelfth Night* deals with the sort of folly which the title points to, the folly of misrule. But the holiday reference limits its subject too narrowly: the play exhibits the liberties which gentlemen take with decorum in the pursuit of pleasure and love, including the liberty of holiday, but not only that. Such liberty is balanced against time-serving. As Bassanio's folly of prodigality leads in the end to gracious fulfillment, so does Viola's folly of disguise. There is just a suggestion of the risks when she exclaims, not very solemnly,

> Disguise, I see thou art a wickedness
> Wherein the pregnant enemy does much.
> (II.ii.28-29)

As in *The Merchant of Venice* the story of a prodigal is the occasion for an exploration of the use and abuse of wealth, so here we get an exhibition of the use and abuse of social liberty.

What enables Viola to bring off her role in disguise is her perfect courtesy, in the large, humanistic meaning of that term as the Renaissance used it, the *corteziania* of Castiglione. Her mastery of courtesy goes with her being the daughter of "that Sebastian of Messalina whom I know you have heard of": gentility shows through her disguise as does the fact that she is a woman. The impact on Olivia of Cesario's quality as a gentleman is what is emphasized as the countess, recalling their conversation, discovers that she is falling in love:

> 'What is thy parentage?'
> 'Above my fortunes, yet my state is well.
> I am a gentleman.' I'll be sworn thou art.
> Thy tongue, thy face, thy limbs, actions, and spirit
> Do give thee fivefold blazon. Not too fast! soft, soft!
> Unless the master were the man.
> (I.v.308-313)

We think of manners as a mere prerequisite of living decently, like cleanliness. For the Renaissance, they could be almost the end of life, as the literature of courtesy testifies. *Twelfth Night* carries further an interest in the fashioning of a courtier which, as Miss Bradbrook points out,[5] appears in several of the early comedies, especially *The Two Gentlemen of Verona*, and which in different keys Shakespeare was pursuing, about the same time as he wrote *Twelfth Night*, in *Hamlet* and *Measure for Measure*. People in *Twelfth Night* talk of courtesy and manners constantly. But the most important expression of courtesy of course is in object lessons. It is their lack of breeding and manners which makes the comic butts ridiculous, along with their lack of the basic, free humanity which, be it virile or feminine, is at the center of courtesy and flowers through it.

Mr. Van Doren, in a fine essay, observes that *Twelfth Night* has a structure like *The Merchant of Venice*. "Once again Shakespeare has built a world out of music and melancholy, and once again this world is threatened by an alien voice. The opposition of Malvolio to Orsino and his class parallels the opposition of Shylock to Antonio and his friends. The parallel is not precise, and the contrast is more subtly contrived; Shakespeare holds the balance in a more delicate hand. . . ."[6] One way in which this more delicate balance appears is that the contest of revellers with intruder does not lead to neglecting ironies about those who are on the side of pleasure. We are all against Malvolio, certainly, in the great moment when the whole opposition comes into focus with Toby's "Dost thou think, because thou art virtuous, there shall be no more cakes and ale?" (II.iii.123-125) The festive spirit shows up the kill-joy vanity of Malvolio's decorum. The steward shows his limits when he calls misrule "this uncivil rule." But one of the revellers is Sir Andrew, who reminds us that there is no necessary salvation in being a fellow who delights "in masques and revels sometimes altogether" (I.iii.121). There was no such ninny pleasure-seeker in *The Merchant of Venice*; his role continues Shallow's, the would-be-reveller who is comically inadequate. To put such a leg as his into "a flame-coloured stock" only shows how meager it is. This thin

[5] *Shakespeare and Elizabethan Poetry*, Ch. IX.
[6] *Shakespeare*, p. 161.

creature's motive is self-improvement: he is a version of the stock type of prodigal who is gulled in trying to learn how to be gallant. As in Restoration comedy the fop confirms the values of the rake, Auguecheek serves as foil to Sir Toby. But he also marks one limit as to what revelry can do for a man: "I would I had bestowed that time in the tongues that I have in fencing, dancing and bear-baiting" (I.iii.97-99).

Sir Toby is gentlemanly liberty incarnate, a specialist in it. He lives at his ease, enjoying heritage, the something-for-nothing which this play celebrates, as *The Merchant of Venice* celebrates wealth—what he has without having to deserve it is his kinsman's place in Olivia's household:

> *Maria.* What a caterwauling do you keep here! If my lady have not call'd up her steward Malvolio and bid him turn you out of doors, never trust me.
>
> *Sir Toby.* My lady's a Catayan, we are politicians, Malvolio's a Peg-a-Ramsay, and [sings] "Three merry men be we." Am I not consanguineous? Am I not of her blood? Tilly-vally, lady.
>
> (II.iii.76-83)

Sir Toby has by consanguinity what Falstaff has to presume on and keep by his wits: "Shall I not take mine ease in mine inn but I shall have my pocket pick'd?" (*1 H.IV* III.iii.92-94) So Sir Toby is witty without being as alert as Sir John; he does not need to be:

> *Olivia.* Cousin, cousin, how have you come so early by this lethargy?
>
> *Toby.* Lechery? I defy lechery. There's one at the gate.
>
> *Olivia.* Ay, marry, what is he?
>
> *Toby.* Let him be the devil an he will. I care not!
>
> Give me faith, say I. Well, it's all one.
>
> (I.v.131-137)

Stage drunkenness, here expressed by wit that lurches catch-as-catch-can, conveys the security of "good life" in such households as Olivia's, the old-fashioned sort that had not given up "house-keeping." Because Toby has "faith"—the faith that goes with belonging—he does not need to worry when Maria teases him about confining himself "within the modest limits of order." "Confine? I'll confine myself no finer than I am" (I.iii.8-11). In his talk as in his clothes, he has the ease of a gentleman whose place in the world is secure, so that, while he can find words like *consanguineous* at will, he can also say "Sneck up!" to Malvolio's accusation that he shows "no respect of persons, places nor time" (II.iii.99). Sir Toby is the sort of kinsman who would take the lead at such Christmas feasts as Sir Edward Dymoke patronized in Lincolnshire —a Talboys Dymoke.[7] His talk is salted with holiday morals: "I am sure care's an enemy of life" (I.iii.2-3). "Not to be abed before midnight is to be up betimes" (II.iii.1-2). He is like Falstaff in maintaining saturnalian paradox and in playing impromptu the role of lord of misrule. But in his whole relation to the world he is fundamentally different from Prince Hal's great buffoon. Falstaff makes a career of misrule; Sir Toby uses misrule to show up a careerist.

There is little direct invocation by poetry of the values of heritage and housekeeping, such as we get of the beneficence of wealth in *The Merchant of Venice*. But the graciousness of community is conveyed indirectly by the value put on music and song, as Mr. Van Doren observes. The Duke's famous opening lines start the play with music. His hypersensitive estheticism savors strains that have a dying fall and mixes the senses in appreciation: "like the sweet sound / That breathes upon a bank of violets" (I.i.5-6). Toby and his friends are more at ease about "O mistress mine," but equally devoted to music in their way. (Toby makes fun of such strained appreciation as the Duke's when he concludes their praises of the clown's voice with "To hear by the nose, it is dulcet in contagion" II.iii.57-58.) Back at court, in the next scene, the significance of music in relation to community is suggested in the Duke's lines about the "old and antique song":

> Mark it, Cesario; it is old and plain.
> The spinsters and the knitters in the sun,
> And the free maids that weave their thread with bones,
> Do use to chant it. It is silly sooth,
> And dallies with the innocence of love
> Like the old age.
>
> (II.iv.44-49)

[7] The whole encounter between Talboys Dymoke's revellers and the Earl of Lincoln is remarkably like that between Sir Toby's group and Malvolio. See above, Ch. 3, pp. 37-51. The parallels are all the more impressive because no influence or "source" relationship is involved; there must have been many such encounters.

The wonderful line about the free maids, which throws such firm stress on "free' by the delayed accent, and then slows up in strong, regular monosyllables, crystallizes the play's central feeling for freedom in heritage and community. It is consciously nostalgic; the old age is seen from the vantage of "these most brisk and giddy-paced times" (II.iv.6).

Throughout the play a contrast is maintained between the taut, restless, elegant court, where people speak a nervous verse, and the free-wheeling household of Olivia, where, except for the intense moments in Olivia's amorous interviews with Cesario, people live in an easy-going prose. The contrast is another version of pastoral. The household is more than any one person in it. People keep interrupting each other, changing their minds, letting their talk run out into foolishness—and through it all Shakespeare expresses the day-by-day going on of a shared life:

> *Maria.* Nay, either tell me where thou hast been, or I will not open my lips so wide as a bristle may enter in way of thy excuse.
>
> (I.v.1-3)

> *Fabian.* . . . You know he brought me out o' favour with my lady about a bear-baiting here.
>
> *Toby.* To anger him we'll have the bear again . . .
>
> (II.v.8-11)

> *Fabian.* Why, we shall make him mad indeed.
>
> *Maria.* The house will be the quieter.
>
> (III.iv.146-147)

Maria's character is a function of the life of "the house"; she moves within it with perfectly selfless tact. "She's a beagle true-bred," says Sir Toby: her part in the housekeeping and its pleasures is a homely but valued kind of "courtiership."

All of the merrymakers show a fine sense of the relations of people, including robust Fabian, and Sir Toby, when he has need. The fool, especially, has this courtly awareness. We see in the first scene that he has to have it to live: he goes far enough in the direction of plain speaking to engage Olivia's unwilling attention, then brings off his thesis that *she* is the fool so neatly that he is forgiven. What Viola praises in the fool's function is just what we should expect in a play about courtesy and liberty:

> This fellow is wise enough to play the fool,
> And to do that well craves a kind of wit.
> He must observe their mood on whom he jests.
> The quality of persons and the time . . .
>
> (III.i.67-70)

It is remarkable how little Feste says that is counterstatement in Touchstone's manner: there is no need for ironic counterstatement, because here the ironies are embodied in the comic butts. Instead what Feste chiefly does is sing and beg—courtly occupations—and radiate in his songs and banter a feeling of liberty based on accepting disillusion. "What's to come is still unsure . . . Youth's a stuff will not endure" (II.iii.50, 53). In *The Merchant of Venice*, it was the gentlefolk who commented "How every fool can play upon the word!" but now it is the fool himself who says, with mock solemnity: "To see this age! A sentence is but a chev'ril glove to a good wit!" (III.i.12-13). He rarely makes the expected move, but conveys by his style how well he knows what moves are expected:

> so that, conclusions to be as kisses, if your four negatives make your two affirmatives, why then, the worse for my friends and the better for my foes.
>
> *Duke.* Why, this is excellent.
>
> *Feste.* By my troth, sir, no; though it pleases you to be one of my friends.
>
> (V.i.24-29)

His feeling for people and their relations comes out most fully when he plays "Sir Topas the curate, who comes to visit Malvolio the lunatic" (IV.ii.25-26). This is the pastime of "dissembling" in a minister's gown that led to so much trouble for Sir Edward Dymoke's bailiff, John Craddock the elder.[8]

Viola, who as "nuntio" moves from tense court to relaxed household, has much in common with Feste in the way she talks, or better, uses talk; but she also commands effortlessly, when there is occasion, Shakespeare's mature poetic power:

[8] See above, pp. 46-48.

It gives a very echo to the seat
Where love is throned.
(II.iv.21-22)

"Thou dost speak masterly," the Duke exclaims—as we must too. Part of her mastery is that she lets herself go only rarely, choosing occasions that are worthy. Most of the time she keeps her language reined in, often mocking it as she uses it, in Feste's fashion. Perhaps it is because he finds himself beaten at his own game that he turns on her ungraciously, as on no one else:

> *Viola.* I warrant thou art a merry fellow and car'st for nothing.
> *Clown.* Not so, sir; I do care for something; but in my conscience, sir, I do not care for you. If that be to care for nothing, sir, I would it would make you invisible. (III.i.32-35)

Once when she is mocking the elaborate language of compliment, greeting Olivia with "the heavens rain odors on you," Sir Andrew overhears and is much impressed: "That youth's a rare courtier. 'Rain odors'—well" (III.i.97-98). He plans to get her fancy words by heart. Of course, as a rare courtier, she precisely does *not* commit herself to such high-flown, Osric-style expressions. Her constant shifting of tone in response to the situation goes with her manipulation of her role in disguise, so that instead of simply listening to her speak, we watch her conduct her speech, and through it feel her secure sense of proportion and her easy, alert consciousness: "To one of your receiving," says Olivia, "enough is shown" (III.i.131-132).

Olivia says that "it was never merry world / Since lowly feigning was called compliment" (III.i.109-110). As Sir Toby is the spokesman and guardian of that merry world, Malvolio is its antagonist. He shows his relation to festivity at once by the way he responds to Feste, and Olivia points the moral: he is "sick of self love" and tastes "with a distempered appetite." He is not "generous, guiltless, and of free disposition." Of course, nothing is more helpful, to get revelry to boil up, than somebody trying to keep the lid on—whatever his personal qualities. But the "stubborn and uncourteous parts" in Malvolio's character, to which Fabian refers in justifying the "device," are precisely those qualities which liberty shows up. Malvolio wants "to confine himself finer than he is," to paraphrase Toby in reverse: he practices behavior to his own shadow. His language is full of pompous polysyllables, of elaborate syntax deploying synonyms:

> Do ye make an alehouse of my lady's house, that ye squeak out your coziers' catches without any mitigation or remorse of voice? Is there no respect of place, persons, nor time in you?
> (II.iii.96-99)

In "loving" his mistress, as Cesario her master, he is a kind of foil, bringing out her genuine, free impulse by the contrast he furnishes. He does not desire Olivia's person; *that* desire, even in a steward, would be sympathetically regarded, though not of course encouraged, by a Twelfth-Night mood. What he wants is "to be count Malvolio," with "a demure travel of regard—telling them I know my place, as I would they should do theirs" (II.v.59-61). His secret wish is to violate decorum himself, then relish to the full its power over others. No wonder he has not a free disposition when he has such imaginations to keep under! When the sport betrays him into a revelation of them, part of the vengeance taken is to make him try to be festive, in yellow stockings, and crossgartered, and smiling "his face into more lines than is in the new map with the augmentation of the Indies" (III.ii.91-93). Maria's letter *tells* him to go brave, be gallant, take liberties! And when we see him "acting this in an obedient hope," (as he puts it later) he is anything but free: "This does make some obstruction of the blood, this cross-gartering . . ." (III.iv.21-23).

In his "impossible passages of grossness," he is the profane intruder trying to steal part of the initiates' feast by disguising himself as one of them—only to be caught and tormented for his profanation. As with Shylock, there is potential pathos in his bafflement, especially when Shakespeare uses to the limit the conjuring of devils out of a sane man, a device which he had employed hilariously in *The Comedy of Errors*. There is no way to settle just how much of Malvolio's pathos should be allowed to come through when he is down and out in the dark hole. Most people now agree that Charles Lamb's sympathy for the steward's enterprise and commiseration for his sorrows is a romantic and bourgeois distortion. But he is certainly pathetic, if one thinks about it, because he is so utterly cut off from everyone else by his anxious self-love. He lacks the freedom which makes Viola so perceptive, and is correspondingly oblivious:

> *Olivia.* What kind o' man is he?
> *Malvolio.* Why, of mankind.
> (I.v.159-160)

He is too busy carrying out his mistress' instructions about privacy to notice that she is bored with it, as later he is too busy doing her errand with the ring to notice that it is a love-token. He is imprisoned in his own virtues, so that there is sense as well as nonsense in the fool's "I say there is no darkness but ignorance, in which thou art more puzzled than the Egyptians in their fog" (IV.ii.46-49). The dark house is, without any straining, a symbol: when Malvolio protests about Pythagoras, "I think nobly of the soul and no way approve his opinion," the clown's response is "Remain thou still in darkness." The pack of them are wanton and unreasonable in tormenting him; but his reasonableness will never let him out into "the air; . . . the glorious sun" (IV.iii.1) which they enjoy together. To play the dark-house scene for pathos, instead of making fun out of the pathos, or at any rate out of most of the pathos, is to ignore the dry comic light which shows up Malvolio's virtuousness as a self-limiting automatism.

Malvolio has been called a satirical portrait of the Puritan spirit, and there is some truth in the notion. But he is not hostile to holiday because he is a Puritan; he is like a Puritan because he is hostile to holiday. Shakespeare even mocks, in passing, the thoughtless, fashionable antipathy to Puritans current among gallants. Sir Andrew responds to Maria's "sometimes he is a kind of Puritan," with "if I thought that, I'd beat him like a dog" (II.iii.151-153). "The devil a Puritan he is, or anything constantly," Maria observes candidly, "but a time-pleaser" (II.iii.159-160). Shakespeare's two greatest comic butts, Malvolio and Shylock, express basic human attitudes which were at work in the commercial revolution, the new values whose development R. H. Tawney described in *Religion and the Rise of Capitalism.* But both figures are conceived at a level of esthetic abstraction which makes it inappropriate to identify them with specific social groups in the mingled actualities of history: Shylock, embodying ruthless money power, is no more to be equated with actual bankers than Malvolio, who has something of the Puritan ethic, is to be thought of as a portrait of actual Puritans. Yet, seen in the perspective of literary and social history, there is a curious appropriateness in Malvolio's presence, as a kind of foreign body to be expelled by laughter, in Shakespeare's last free-and-easy festive comedy. He is a man of business, and, it is passingly suggested, a hard one; he is or would like to be a rising man, and to rise he *uses* sobriety and morality. One could moralize the spectacle by observing that, in the long run, in the 1640's, Malvolio *was* revenged on the whole pack of them.

But Shakespeare's comedy remains, long after 1640, to move audiences through release to clarification, making distinctions between false care and true freedom and realizing anew, for successive generations, powers in human nature and society which make good the risks of courtesy and liberty. And this without blinking the fact that "the rain it raineth every day."

Outside the Garden Gate

Twelfth Night is usually placed just before *Hamlet* and the problem plays to make neat groupings according to mood, but it may well have been written after some of these works. In thinking about its relation to the other work of the period from 1600 to 1602 or 1603, it is important to recognize the independent artistic logic by which each play has its own unity. There are features of *Twelfth Night* that connect it with all the productions of this period. There is the side of Orsino's sensibility, for example, which suggests Troilus' hypersensitivity:

> Enough, no more!
> 'Tis not so sweet now as it was before.
> (I.i.7-8)

> How will she love when the rich golden shaft
> Hath kill'd the flock of all affections else
> That live in her; when liver, brain, and heart,
> Those sovereign thrones, are all supplied and fill'd,

Her sweet perfections, with one self king!
Away before me to sweet beds of flow'rs!
(I.i.35-40)

Troilus carries this sort of verse and feeling farther:

What will it be
When that the wat'ry palates taste indeed
Love's thrice-repured nectar? Death, I fear me;
Sounding destruction; or some joy too fine,
Too subtile-potent, tun'd too sharp in sweetness
For the capacity of my ruder powers.
(*Troi.* III.ii.21-26)

Troilus' lines are a much more physical and more anxious development of the exquisite, uncentered sort of amorousness expressed by Orsino. But in *Twelfth Night* there is no occasion to explore the harsh anti-climax to which such intensity is vulnerable, for instead of meeting a trivial Cressida in the midst of war and lechery, Orsino meets poised Viola in a world of revelry. The comparison with *Troilus and Cressida* makes one notice how little direct sexual reference there is in *Twelfth Night*—much less than in most of the festive comedies. It may be that free-hearted mirth, at this stage of Shakespeare's development, required more shamefastness than it had earlier, because to dwell on the physical was to encounter the "monstruosity in love" which troubled Troilus: "that the desire is boundless and the act a slave to limit" (*Troi.* III.ii.89-90).

It is quite possible that *Measure for Measure* and *All's Well That Ends Well* did not seem to Shakespeare and his audiences so different from *Twelfth Night* as they seem to us. Both of them use comic butts not unlike Andrew and Malvolio: Lucio and Parolles are, each his way, pretenders to community who are shown up ludicrously by their own compulsions, and so expelled. Our difficulty with these plays, what makes them problem plays, is that they do not feel festive; they are not merry in a deep enough way. Part of our response may well be the result of changes in standards and sentiments about sexual behavior, and of alterations in theatrical convention. But the fact remains that in both plays, release often leads, not simply to folly, but to the vicious or contemptible;

and the manipulations of happy accidents which make all well in the end are not made acceptable by the achievement of distinctions about values or by a convincing expression of general beneficent forces in life. Shakespeare's imagination tends to dwell on situations and motives where the energies of life lead to degradation or destruction:

> Our natures do pursue
> Like rats that ravin down their proper bane,
> A thirsty evil, and when we drink, we die.
> (*Meas.* I.ii.132-134)

> There's not a soldier of us all that, in the thanksgiving before meat, do relish the petition well that prays for peace.
> (*Meas.* I.ii.14-17)

> Pompey, you are partly a bawd, Pompey, howsoever you colour it in being a tapster, are you not? . . .
> *Pompey.* Truly, sir, I am a poor fellow that would live.
> (*Meas.* II.i.230-235)

This sort of paradox is not brought home to us in *Twelfth Night.* In the problem comedies, vicious or perverse release leads to developments of absorbing interest, if not always to a satisfying movement of feeling in relation to awareness. But that is beyond our compass here.

We can notice here that the fool in *Twelfth Night* has been over the garden wall into some such world as the Vienna of *Measure for Measure.* He never tells where he has been, gives no details. But he has an air of knowing more of life than anyone else—too much, in fact; and he makes general observations like

> Anything that's mended is but patch'd; virtue that transgresses is but patch'd with sin, and sin that amends is but patch'd with virtue. If that this simple syllogism will serve, so; if it will not, what remedy?
> (I.v.52-56)

His part does not darken the bright colors of the play; but it gives them a dark outline, suggesting that the whole bright revel emerges from shadow. In the wonderful final song which he is left alone on stage to sing, the mind turns to contemplate the limitations of revelry: "By swaggering could I never thrive. . . ." The morning after, the weather when the sky changes, come into the song:

With tosspots still had drunken heads
For the rain it raineth every day.
(V.i.412-413)

It goes outside the garden gate:

But when I come to man's estate,
With hey, ho, the wind and the rain,
'Gainst knaves and thieves men shut their gate,
For the rain it raineth every day.
(V.i.402-405)

Yet the poise of mirth, achieved by accepting disillusion, although it is now precarious, is not lost:

A great while ago the world begun,
With hey, ho, the wind and the rain;
But that's all one, our play is done,
And we'll strive to please you everyday.
(V.i.414-417)

There is a certain calculated let-down in coming back to the play in this fashion; but it is the play which is keeping out the wind and the rain.

The festive comic form which Shakespeare had worked out was a way of selecting and organizing experience which had it own logic, its own autonomy: there is no necessary reason to think that he did not play on that instrument in *Twelfth Night* after making even such different music as *Hamlet.* Indeed, across the difference in forms, the comedy has much in common with the tragedy: interest in courtesy and free-hearted manners; consciousness of language and play with it as though a sentence were but a chev'ril glove; the use of nonsequitur and nonsense. Malvolio absurdly dreams of such a usurpation of heritage, "having come from a day bed, where I have left Olivia sleeping," as Claudius actually accomplishes. The tragedy moves into regions where the distinction between madness and sanity begins to break down, to be recovered only through violence; the fooling with madness in the comedy is an enjoyment of the control which knows what is mad and what is not. The relation between the two plays, though not so close, is not unlike that which we have noticed between *Romeo and Juliet* and *A Midsummer Night's Dream.*

But there is a great deal in *Hamlet* which the festive comic form cannot handle. The form can only deal with follies where nature to her bias draws; the unnatural can appear only in outsiders, intruders who are mocked and expelled. But in *Hamlet*, it is insiders who are unnatural. There is a great deal of wonderful fooling in the tragedy: Hamlet's playing the all-licensed fool in Claudius' court and making tormented fun out of his shocking realization of the horror of life. For sheer power of wit and reach of comic vision, there are moments in *Hamlet* beyond anything in the comedies we have considered. But to control the expression of the motives he is presenting, Shakespeare requires a different movement, within which comic release is only one phase. After *Twelfth Night*, comedy is always used in this subordinate way: saturnalian moments, comic counterstatements, continue to be important resources of his art, but their meaning is determined by their place in a larger movement. So it is with the heroic revels in *Antony and Cleopatra*, or with the renewal of life, after tragedy, at the festival in *The Winter's Tale.*

Index

The Library of Congress has cataloged this book as follows:

Barber, Cesar Lombardi. Shakespeare's festive comedy; a study of dramatic form and its relation to social custom. Princeton, Princeton University Press, 1959. x, 266 p. 25 cm. Bibliographical footnotes. 1. Shakespeare, William—Comedies. 2. English drama (Comedy)—Hist. & crit. 3. England—Soc. life & cust. PR2981.B3 (822.33) 59-5588. Library of Congress